英语社论语篇主观性的实现与劝说功能

Realizations and Persuasive Functions of Subjectivity in English Editorials

张现荣　著

山东大学出版社

图书在版编目(CIP)数据

英语社论语篇主观性的实现与劝说功能/张现荣著.
—济南:山东大学出版社,2018.5
ISBN 978-7-5607-6075-9

Ⅰ. ①英… Ⅱ. ①张… Ⅲ. ①英语-报刊-社论-研究 Ⅳ. ①G210

中国版本图书馆 CIP 数据核字(2018)第 114941 号

责任编辑:张申华
封面设计:张 荔

出版发行:山东大学出版社
社 址 山东省济南市山大南路 20 号
邮 编 250100
电 话 市场部(0531)88364466
经 销:山东省新华书店
印 刷:济南新科印务有限公司
规 格:720 毫米×1000 毫米 1/16
14.5 印张 268 千字
版 次:2018 年 5 月第 1 版
印 次:2018 年 5 月第 1 次印刷
定 价:30.00 元

Preface

At the beginning of the 20th century, subjectivity was introduced into linguistics and has been studied as a linguistic phenomenon. The studies of subjectivity have been mainly confined to the field of cognitive linguistics; they explore the process of subjectivized items from the perspective of grammaticalization and focus on the diachronic development and cognitive construal of those subjectivized items. However, little research has been done to explore the subjectivity within the realm of SFL, and studies have also been rarely spotted on the functions of subjectivity in the process of producing discourse production. The realizations and the interpersonal functions of subjectivity in discourse have been a much neglected area so far.

The choice of editorials as the research data is due to the following two factors. Firstly, editorials are well formed written texts. Exploring the persuasive functions of subjectivity in editorials can contribute to revealing the interpersonal functions of subjectivity in written discourse. Secondly, editorials have a large audience. In modern times, newspaper editorials have become an inseparable part in everyday life and an important way of acquiring information about the world. Besides, lots of English learners use editorials as reading materials. Owing to the important roles of editorials, the present study takes editorials as its data to study the realizations and persuasive functions of subjectivity in editorials. The data are collected from the official website of *The New York Times*, concerning the hard news of terrorist attacks of September 11, 2001. A corpus is compiled, containing 87 English editorials labeled as SAEC. The corpus tool brat is introduced and a statistical software brat-aid is designed to make annotations and statistics.

The theoretical framework of this study is tentatively constructed within the field of SFL, which is based on a comprehensive review of the cognitive research on subjectivisation and Finegan's established framework on subjectivisation studies. Following the point that discourse production is the dynamic process of performing social actions, the study explores the realizations of subjectivity by turning to the linguistic resources of modal assessment. To be more specific, the realizations of subjectivity are studied in three arenas of the system of MODALITY, the system of JUDGEMENT and the system of ENGAGEMENT, and the interpersonal functions of subjectivity in discourse are noticed. Also, by focusing on the ways of realizations of subjectivity in the process of making editorials, the study goes further on the way that argumentativity and persuasiveness are constructed in modal assessment with the aim to fulfill the persuasive function.

The research has reported some significant findings as follows. Argumentativity is constructed from these four aspects: modal orientation, modal value, subjective judgement and subjective expectation. Both the implicitly subjective and objective orientations are taken to construct argumentative negotiation so as to negotiate with readers and have them persuaded. Argumentative strength is scaled by modal value. The medium value is used to make subjective assessments on possibility, usuality and inclinations, which shows that these assessments are evaluated pertinently to the textual information. The high value is strikingly used in the modality of obligation, implying the writer's unflinching desirability that the reader is obliged to undertake the suggested proposals. Argumentative strength is expressed on the base of evaluation according to social esteem and social sanction, whereby the writer expresses condemnation on the terrorist attacks, inspects misconducts around terrorist attacks, and highlights the capacity in dealing with the negative effects caused by these attacks. The direction of argumentative strength works as the discourse strategy to express the subjective expectation to prop up the stance. Mostly, it is expressed by acknowledging and endorsing supporting opinions as the expectancy. However, the counter-expectancy is implied by distancing opposite opinions to weaken the strength. Persuasiveness is built up by using the strategies of modalization, affective judgement and perspectivation. Modalization occurs much more frequently than modulization, which shows that recommendations are given after making full argument and analysis of relevant information. Moreover, propositional comments and speech functional comments scatter in discourse, guiding the reader's construal of the stance. Qualificative propositional comments, especially prediction, presumption, or desirability, are mostly used, by which the persuasive power of the proposition referring correctly to the context with logical ratiocination is transmitted. Speech functional comments are chosen to indicate validity of propositions evaluated from the writer's perspective, which function as linguistic signs to lead the reader to follow the procedure of rationalization. Perpectivation is taken to engage in the speeches or citations made by the authoritative powers, by which persuasiveness is intensified by the supporting opinions sourced to the third party.

This research tries to offer a relatively comprehensive and integrated analytical framework within SFL for studying the realizations and the interpersonal functions of subjectivity in editorials. The software brat is newly introduced to the field of linguistic study with brat-aid invented and annotation file revised, which sheds light on the research of subjectivity in SFL. To sum up, based on the theory of subjectivisation and interpersonal functions, the exploration of the persuasive function of subjectivity in terms of argumentativity and persuasiveness of editorials is of great theoretical and practical significance.

List of Tables

List of Figures

List of Abbreviations

SFL: Systemic Functional Linguistics

SAEC: Sept. 11 Attack Editorials Corpus

NYT: *The New York Times*

NLP: Natural Language Processing

URIs: Uniform Resource Identifiers

ModPos: Modality Possibility

Modadjunct: Modal Adjunct

ModUsu: Modality Usuality

ModObl: Modality Obligation

ModInc: Modality Inclination

Contents

Introduction

0.1 Research Background

For a good part of the 20th century, the study of subjectivity in language was not a research topic of major concern. While the significance of subjectivity in language was identified as early as in Bréal's (1900) writings, it is only the last three or four decades that have seen a reversion of interest, mainly in the field of the cognitive-functional linguistics. As Lyons (1982: 103) has noted, "Modern Anglo-American linguistics has been dominated by the intellectualist prejudice that language is, essentially, if not solely, an instrument for the expression of propositional thoughts". The humanistic feature of language constrains language users' choices in the linguistic system, and also people's understanding of linguistic expressions. (Miao, 2009: 68)

Of particular importance in this respect is Benveniste, who (1971) made differentiation between the "grammatical subject" (sujet d'énoncé) of an utterance and the "speaking subject" (sujet d'énonciation) of the utterance and noted that subjectivity is such an essential property of language that it could not still function "as language if it was organized differently" (Benveniste, 1958: 261). The importance of subjectivity was further intensified by Lyons (1977, 1982), and was given increasing attention in the cognitive-functional field. Two main research strains have developed referring to the ideas of Traugott and Langacker. In Traugott's approach, subjectivity is constructed in a semantic process whereby a linguistic element, say, morpheme, word, phrase or construction etc. develops new senses that involve speaker-reference or speaker-perspective. For Langacker, an expression's meaning always contains both subjectively and objectively construed elements, and over time, individual conceptual elements comprised in this expression come to be construed with a greater degree of subjectivity or objectivity—"a semantic shift... result in a global meaning becoming more subjective" (Langacker, 2006: 18).

However, language is used in the course of communication for the speaker to express attitudes and beliefs. Subjectivity is, by nature, a universal phenomenon in language and a fundamental property of linguistic communication. As Benveniste (1971: 226) addressed:

> It is in the instance of discourse in which "I" designates the speaker that the speaker proclaims himself as the "subject". And so it is literally true that the basis of subjectivity is in the exercise of language... Language is so organized that it permits each speaker to appropriate to himself an entire language by designating himself as "I".

The notion of subjectivity explored here focuses on the expression of speaking self and displaying the representation of a speaker's perspective or point of view in the process of constructing discourse. Broadly speaking, subjectivity explored here deals with the self-consciousness of expressing the speaker's feelings, evaluation, attitudes etc. with the motivation-oriented choices of linguistic devices. In this sense, the study of subjectivity focuses on linguistic forms and their functions associated with the context, which forms the fundamental connection between subjectivity in language and subjectivity in discourse. Languages possess linguistic devices to sign the speaker's subjective perspective that presupposes its application in discourse, i. e. in socially situated language use, which consists of a speaker, addressee (s), a setting, purpose(s) and topic (s). It offers remarkably different points of view concerning the research of subjectivity, ranging from semantics, to pragmatics and rhetorical, discourse and interactional analysis.

Subjectivity can be studied from different theoretical and methodological perspectives as a linguistic phenomenon. As Benveniste (1971: 225) put, language is marked so deeply by the expression of subjectivity that one might ask if it could still function and be called language if it were constructed otherwise. Benveniste introduced the term of linguistic subjectivity, and brought it into the linguist's attention. The significance of subjectivity was further stressed by Lyons (1977, 1982), and was then given increasing attention in cognitive-functional field, such as the cognitive-construing framework concerning asymmetrical viewing arrangements between the subject and the target of conception (Langacker, 1990, 1999a, 1999b, 2002, 2006), and the phenomenon of subjectivisation in grammaticalization process (Athanasiadou, 2006; Traugott, 1985, 1999, 2003, 2006; Traugott & Dasher, 2002; de Smet & Verstraete, 2006). Recent studies concern what and how the subjective marker functions in discourse, which cover the following aspects: hedging (e.g. Hyland, 1998; Markkanen & Schroder, 1990), positioning (e.g. Bamberg, 1997; Davis & Harre, 1990), evidentiality (e.g. Aikhenvald, 2004; Chafe & Nichols, 1986), stance (e.g. Biber & Finegan, 1988, 1989; Englebretson, 2007; Jaffe, 2009), affect (e.g. Bednarek, 2008; Besnier, 1990, 1993; Ochs & Schieffelin, 1989), appraisal (Martin & White, 2005). Matching to different approaches, some methods called comprehensive analytical models are employed, such as appraisal analysis. (Martin & White, 2005) Nowadays, subjectivity is studied from different angles with different theoretical frameworks towards various linguistic aspects.

0.2 Research Rationale

As Benveniste (1971: 224) pointed out, "Subjectivity... is only the emergence in the being of fundamental property of language". In natural language, subjectivity refers to a speaker's expressing opinions, evaluations, and speculations in language, which will leave the speaker's imprint in a discourse or a conversation. (Banfield, 1982; Wiebe, 1994; Wiebe et al., 2004) Subjectivity is realized through subjectivisation, which consists primarily of tense, aspect and modality etc. occurring in forms of single lexical, complex expressions, syntactic devices, and/or strategies. (Finegan, 1995; Wiebe et al., 2004)

Previous studies mainly focus on the way that subjectivity is construed by subjectivisation with subjectivized meanings planted in the grammaticalizing process. However, subjectivity is not merely limited to a single linguistic form whether it is a lexical word or a syntactic construction. As a fundamental property of language, subjectivity must be understood by taking language as a systemic whole. According to Benveniste (1971), subjectivity can be elucidated from three different perspectives. Firstly, language establishes the foundation of subjectivity because, as a matter of fact, language is responsible for subjectivity in that subjectivity is realized by language resources. Language is organized so well that it permits each speaker to appropriate to himself the entire linguistic resource by designating himself as "ego". Then, language is like a meaning potential reservoir in that linguistic resources indicate "person", "temporality", "spatiality", etc., enabling the speaker to establish the concept of subject in reality. Secondly, the term "subjectivity" refers to "the capacity of the speaker to posit himself as subject" (Benveniste, 1971: 224). As a psychic unit, the speaker has the capacity of transcending the limitation of the actual experience assembled in the real world and of manifesting the permanence of the consciousness as well. Language has provided linguistic resources with the personal pronouns which are the centric basis to construct the concept of subjectivity in language. This self-consciousness of choosing process will imprint in discourse the moment the utterance takes place. Thirdly, although language potentially contains linguistic forms that are appropriate for expressing subjectivity, it is discourse that provokes the emergence of subjectivity. The speaker consistently expresses his evaluations, opinions, and attitudes in the process of communicating with others.

All these three aspects of subjectivity work simultaneously and systematically in communication. Communication is a goal-driven consultative process including such steps as planning, design and implementation of strategic interventions, which are used to monitor the changes in participants' attitudes and behaviors that are laid down by the communicating intention. To reveal the intention advanced in discourse is a means to explore what and how the speaker intends to perform by means of choosing linguistic resources (Edwards, 2006, 2008; Haugh, 2008a, 2008b). Then, the study of subjectivity focuses on linguistic items with subjectivized meanings at all levels, which makes the realization of subjectivity extend beyond the traditional grammatical categories of tense, aspect, and modality, etc. (Baumgarten, Bois & House, 2012: 6), involving all kinds of linguistic resources ranging from phonology to discourse level (Hunston & Thompson, 1999; Ochs & Schieffelin, 1989).

The New York Times is chosen as research data due to three reasons. Firstly, discourse analysis of media texts becomes a consolidated research strand. (van Dijk, 1988a, 1988b; Ungerer, 2000) In contrast, newspaper editorials have been a neglected area, especially compared with the abundant research on other newspaper text types such as news writing. Although newspaper editorials have been referred to as an important public "Cinderella" genre (Ansari & Babaii, 2005), researches pertaining to these kind of opinion articles are relatively rare. Secondly, the linguistic features of editorials attract the researcher's attention. An editorial is "generally regarded as the newspaper's analysis, discussion, opinion or verdict on the issues of the day" (Bhatia, 1993: 170), and offers the use of fresh, topical and up-to-date language, which is internationally acceptable but maintains a local flavor. The editorial is mainly to motivate and persuade the readers to consider ideas or to give opinions on the issue of the day, which is realized in the process of producing editorials by choosing proper lexico-grammatical resources. That builds up the most significant aspect of the editorials: the editorial writers can choose proper linguistic resources to create favorable or unfavorable bias in their arguments. (Bhatia, 1993) Also, these editorial discourses are the constructions of journalists and editors of the elites, whose opinions are hidden subtly in expressions and often revealed in mild forms (van Dijk, 1995b, 1995c, 1995d). Thirdly, the achievements in the field of discourse analysis of editorials encourage us to go a little further. Referring to Halliday's interpersonal function of language (Halliday, 2002: 200), Bonyadi (2011) analyzed linguistic realization of modality in the selected editorials in both *The New York Times* and *Tehran Times*. Therefore, the theoretical framework, researching methodology and analysis approaches not only set up the model to make discourse analysis on the editorials in the realm of SFL, but also shed lights on us in working out our researching plan with SFL and appraisal system as the working model.

Based on a comprehensive review of the cognitive research on subjectivisation and Finegan's established framework on subjectivisation study, the theoretical framework of this study is tentatively constructed within the field of SFL. Following the point that discourse production is the dynamic process of performing social actions, the study explores the realizations of subjectivity by turning to the linguistic resources of modal assessment. To be more specific, the realizations of subjectivity is studied in three arenas of the system of MODALITY, the system of JUDGEMENT and the system of ENGAGEMENT, and the interpersonal function of subjectivity in discourses is noticed. Also, focusing on the ways how subjectivity is realized in the process of making editorials, the study goes further on the way that argumentativity and persuasiveness are constructed in modal assessment with the aim to fulfill the persuasive function.

0.3 Research Objectives and Research Questions

This study is to develop a corpus-based subjectivity analytical and annotation system, with the aim to make functional descriptions of realizations of subjectivity and then find out how these realizations of subjectivity co-work in editorials to successfully perform the persuasive function. The main focus is to explore how subjectivity is realized by the lexico-grammatical system, i. e. choosing subjective elements such as subjectivized words, phrases, syntactic devices and negotiating with other information sourced to other voices. The relation between the source and information in the process of producing editorial discourses needs to be discussed. Specifically, the research objectives designed in the present study are:

(1) To build up a theoretical framework within the realm of SFL, aiming to carry out discourse analysis of subjectivity in editorials.

(2) To prove the concept of subjectivity given here reasonably and workably in the discourse analysis associating with the persuasive function of editorials, effectively.

(3) To investigate various realizations of subjectivity in editorials, and exploit motivations of expressing the persuasive function in subjectification.

With such research objectives kept in mind, research questions are put forth as follows:

(1) How does the writer realize subjectivity in linguistic resources of modal assessment in editorials?

(2) How does the editorial writer realize the persuasive function through building up argumentativity in terms of subjectivity?

(3) How does the editorial writer realize the persuasive function by means of constructing persuasiveness by subjectification strategies?

All in all, the focus of the present study is on the discourse semantic system of subjectivity which is realized by lexico-grammatical resources of modal assessment: how they help the editorial author to fulfill the persuasive function in the process of producing editorials.

0.4 Organization of This Book

This book consists of eight parts. The first or the present one is the Introduction, which makes a brief introduction about this study, setting out the research background, rationale about the whole study, research objectives, and research questions.

Chapter 1 outlines a literature review of previous studies of subjectivity in different fields of linguistics, especially in cognitive linguistics, pragmatics and discursive semantics. Meanwhile, the achievements and research gaps are exhibited in terms of research methodology, objects of study and research levels. Based on the former studies, the present study aims to study subjectivity in the process of producing editorials at the discourse level within SFL.

Chapter 2 provides the ratiocinating process in which the theoretical framework in the realm of SFL is built up by referring to the theoretical principles of SFL. This framework is made not only referring to the three arenas of studying subjectivity and subjectivisation proposed by Finegan, but also absorbing research findings obtained in the fields of cognitive linguistics and pragmatics. According to this theoretical model, realizations of modal assessment make up language potential that the writer can choose to express subjectivity in the process of producing the discourse. Then, not only are expressions of modal assessment regarded as the linguistic resources readily chosen to realize subjectivity, but the operations in virtue of linguistic devices are also thought of as the ways that reflect the capacity of the writer to consciously express subjectivity.

Chapter 3 introduces the methodology in detail adopted in the present study. As this study is a corpus-based analysis, this chapter begins with how the corpus is complied and processed. The corpus tool "brat" is introduced concerning how to work out annotating procedures in annotation files and how to make annotations with examples displayed. This chapter ends with the detailed description of installing brat and of designing brat-aid which helps to do data statistics.

Chapter 4 focuses on the realizations of subjectivity in modal assessment and their distribution patterns in this database. The network system of MODALITY is regarded as the main area involving modal operators, propositional comments and speech functional comments. We also pay attention to how subjectivity is realized in the expressions of JUDGEMENT and by leading in the information sourced to other voices strategically by virtue of the system of ENGAGEMENT. We make statistic analysis of the data obtained through the concordance tool brat-aid. Description of distribution patterns is done with some corresponding examples.

Chapter 5 deals with different ways that the writer takes advantages of modal assessment to build up argumentativity. In editorials, argumentativity is the state of being argumentative and constructed in the process of developing an argument. The writer chooses the linguistic resources of modal assessment in different ways so as to indicate how he negotiates with the readers so as to have them convinced, how he graduates the strength of subjectivity and how he expresses the expectation in the process of making modal evaluations. Argumentativity is constructed from the authorial perspective and defined from four aspects, namely modal orientation, modal value, subjective judgement and subjective expectation. It functions to regulate the interpersonal relationship so as to agglomerate argumentative strength and control argumentative direction in editorials for the persuasive purpose.

Chapter 6 provides us with a new angle to study how linguistic subjectivisations of editorials function as a source of their persuasiveness. Persuasiveness is, as the core character of editorials, constituted through persuasive technologies in order to change the reader's attitudes and behaviors. Based on Finegan's study of subjectivity and subjectivisation, we study the persuasive function of editorials by constructing persuasiveness from three aspects: subjective modalization, affective judgement and perspectivation.

Chapter 7 summarizes the major findings of this research. Some limitations of the present study are also revealed. In the end, some suggestions are offered for future researches.

Chapter 1
Literature Review

In a broad sense, subjectivity has been traditionally contrasted with "objectivity". As the locus of scientific investigation, "objectivity" is always put to the centre of the positivist tradition in the West while subjectivity has been thought as the way related to the expression of personal opinions, beliefs, and attitudes that are supposed to be too ephemeral and idiosyncratic to deserve much attention. However, as the research tendency tracks back to the social sciences and the humanities again, subjectivity becomes a ubiquitous notion figured strikingly once more, and it has also obtained a prominent place in linguistic reasoning as the human beings attempt to recognize the world by the everyday-using language from the cognitive and functional perspective.

1.1 Previous Studies of Subjectivity

Subjectivity is originally used as a central philosophical concept, which is introduced into linguistics and studied as linguistic phenomenon by linguist Bréal (1900) at the beginning of the 20th century. From then on, the studies of subjectivity have achieved great progresses in the field of linguistics.

1.1.1 Introduction to the Concept of Subjectivity

Lyons (1982: 103) argues that "modern Anglo-American linguistics... has been dominated by the intellectualist prejudice that language is, essentially, if not solely, an instrument for the expression of propositional thought", where "propositional thought" is to be related to the objective description of reality. Compared to this propositional prejudice, continental European linguists such as Bréal (1900), Bühler (1990), and Jakobson (1957) have focused on subjectivity. But perhaps the clearest expression of the opposition is Benveniste's (1958: 225) distinction between the syntactic subject (its original French term "sujet d'enoncé") and the speaking subject (the French counterpart "sujet d'énociation"), with his understanding of subjectivity as one of the most pervasive functions of language.

The concept of subjectivity is explored with respect to the attributes of language and the capacities of the speaker. According to Benveniste (1958: 224), it is defined as the attributes of language: man can constitute himself as a subject in and through language, because language alone establishes the concept of "ego" in reality as the speaking subject who can say "ego" by using language. That is where we see the foundation of "subjectivity", which is determined by the linguistic status of "person". And, the concept of subjectivity refers to the capacity of the speaker to posit himself as the "subject", which is defined not by the feeling that everyone experiences of being himself, but as the psychic unity that makes the permanence of the consciousness and transcends the totality of the actual experiences it assembles. Therefore, subjectivity is emphasized as a fundamental property of language and a kind of capacity that humans speak themselves out in language. In this way, consciousness of self is built up into the discourse by means of the speaker's choosing language resources. In other words, language is possible only because each speaker sets himself up as a "subject" by referring to "himself" as "I" in the discourse. The subject "I" posits another person completely exterior to "me", which becomes my echo to whom "I" say "you" and who says "you" to "me". This polarity of the first and second persons is the fundamental condition in language, of which the process of communication shared is only a mere pragmatic consequence. Moreover, it is a polarity as it offers a type of opposition whose equivalent is encountered nowhere else outside of language, i. e. "ego" always has a position of transcendence with regard to "you". Although the discursive "ego" and "you" constitute an interior and exterior opposition, they are complementary on the one hand, and reversible on the other. Nevertheless, according to Benveniste, the third person merely functions as the form of the pronominal paradigm without denoting a person because it refers to an object located outside direct address. It then exists and is characterized only by its opposition to the speaker "I" who situates it as "non-person" as uttering it. Therefore, the third person, say, "he" takes its value from the fact that it is necessarily part of a discourse uttered by "I". Obviously, the condition of man in language is unique.

As a matter of fact, language is responsible for the concept of subjectivity in all its parts. As Benveniste (1958: 225) says, "Language is so deeply marked by the expression of subjectivity that one might ask if it could still function and be called language if it were constructed otherwise". Clearly, language is so organized that it will permit every speaker to appropriate to himself an entire language by designating himself as "I". Benveniste (1958) notes that the first person is a rich source of subjectivity in language in that it provides the reference point in this bringing out of subjectivity in language. He also identifies deictic terms and tense as subjective in that they make spatial and temporal reference to the speaker. These deictic terms are the indicators of deixis, the demonstratives, adverbs, and adjectives, such as "this", "here", "now," and their numerous correlatives, "that", "yesterday", "last year", "tomorrow", etc. Also, he discusses meaning distinctions presented in utterances (by which) contain the same cognitive verbs but contrast in their subjects. When "I" occurs as the formal subject with verbs such as "feel", "suppose", "believe", and "presume", etc., it typically expresses the speaker's attitude concerning the following piece of discourse in the current context, for this kind of verbs are all logical operations which, when put in the domain of the first person, describe me as reasoning and reflecting. All the verbs cited above are followed by connective "that" and a proposition, with the proposition beyond the personal-verb government being the real utterance. It follows that the subjective context (expressing presumption, inference, doubt) is suited to characterize the attitude of the speaker with respect to the statement that he is making. However, when these verbs occur with third person subject, they merely function to convey something descriptive or informative. Therefore, in a discussion of linguistic subjectivity, Benveniste characterizes subjectivity as the ability of speakers to regard themselves as the ego subjects, and he mentions various ways in which common grammatical categories contribute to the expressive capacity of the speakers.

Like Benveniste, Lyons establishes the concept of subjectivity through focusing on tense and deixis which characterize the subjective phenomena, because they make reference to the discourse context, and consequently, to the speaker as well. Lyons disputes the notion of subjectivity against its intellectualist and objectivist prejudice attributed to the empirical tradition, for British empiricism and Cartesian rationalism both share such intellectualist and objectivist prejudice that language acts essentially as an instrument for the expression of propositional thoughts. This research tradition is ill-influenced, which gives no attention at all to the non-propositional component of language or plays down its importance. Subjectivity in the empiricism tradition was associated with a certain kind of unscientific and untestable mentalism. As to the plight situation where subjectivity is given an irrelevantly pejorative interpretation, Lyons discusses this term in contrast to Cartesian or post-Cartesian dualism, which concerns the philosophical distinction between "subject" and "object". Lyons steps out of this sharply dualistic, Cartesian or post-Cartesian opposition of the subject and object of cognition. He claims that there is a distinction in language between subjective utterances by which the speaker expresses himself and objective utterances that merely express communicable propositions, and that the distinction between these types is gradual but not absolute. He (1982: 337) defines subjectivity as sets of properties of being either a subject of consciousness of cognition, feeling and perception, or a subject of action of an agent, which denotes the property of human beings what Descartes himself calls a "thinking entity" and identifies with the self ego. In this way, Lyons disputes the notion that linguistic self-expression may be equated with the assertion of a set of propositions.

In discussion, Lyons raises up the conception of locutionary subjectivity. It is essentially named as the subjectivity of utterances, which is the locutionary agent's, including the speaker's, the writer's, or the speaker's expression of himself in the act of utterance. Generally, locutionary subjectivity is thought simply as self-expression in the use of language (Lyons, 1982: 337). Lyons emphasizes how the speaker forms the self in the actual use of language by adopting some linguistic mechanism, namely, reference, tense, aspect and mood. Reference is such a relation that holds between the speaker and the issue what they are talking about on particular occasions, which are meaningfully context-dependent and intrinsically anchored by deixis and indexicality. And tense is relevant to the temporal deictic reference which is grammaticalized as tense inflections and/or lexicalized in a range of adverbs. The grammatical categories of mood and tense are interdependent in all natural languages. Mood results from the grammaticalization of modality. Subjective modality is usually used by the speaker to express his own beliefs and attitudes or his own wills and authorities, which are lexicalized or semi-lexicalized by means of modal operators (e. g. , may, must), modal adjectives (e. g. , possible, certain), modal adverbs (e. g. , possibly, certainly) and modal particles (e. g. , perhaps) in English.

Lyons' study of the locutionary subjectivity has a far-reaching influence. This way of defining subjectivity in accordance with the speaker's intention widely enlightens other researchers to carry out their own studies in this field. Linguistic forms, such as deixis, commentary adverbs, epistemic modality, are adopted as the overt forms conveying the speaker's subjective meaning and reflecting his self consciousness of expressing certain beliefs, attitudes and emotions. All these prove that language has developed a certain system of self-expressing mechanisms that manifest efficiently the speaker's own beliefs, attitudes and emotions in the socially appropriate context. That is, the self ego which the speaker is to express is the product of the social and interpersonal roles that he has acted in the past, and it manifests itself in the way that the speaker is playing in the context of utterance and that can be retraced in a socially identifiable way.

The concept of subjectivity that Benveniste (1971) and Lyons (1977, 1982) have constructed acts as the beginning step to bring the study of subjectivity into the field of linguistics. They attempt to find out from the pragmatic perspective what linguistic constructions, lexicons or grammatical forms, have the semantic features referring to the speaker, and then depend on the ego-centric point of the speaker. Although these static studies on the subjectivity have taken both the user of language and the constraints of the uttering context on the choices of linguistic forms into account, they focus mainly on the same linguistic form which varies historically in terms of the semantic value influenced by the uttering context, but ignore the dynamic choices that the speaker makes in the context.

All in all, Benveniste and Lyons take the bird's-eye-view on subjectivity from the linguistic angle based on the practical uses of language with the premise of regarding language as the unified system. (Benveniste, 1971, 1958; Lyons, 1982) The most typical features in this stage are that subjectivity characterizes the self-expressing potential of language, and that typical linguistic forms are chosen to define the subjective characteristics. The research model developed in this period characterizes the static description of the subjective linguistic forms.

1.1.2 Cognitive Approaches

Two significant tokens in the linguistic history imply that the study of linguistic subjectivity and subjectification has entered into the maturity stage. The first refers to the successful holding of the international seminar centering on the topic of the study of linguistic subjectivity and subjectivisation, and subsequently the publication of the collected papers. The other is that there comes into being the identical demarcation of terms of subjectivity and subjectivisation in the linguistic field. The researchers in this stage mainly attempt to build on the dynamic mode based on the micro-construe of subjectivity, focusing on linguistic realizations of subjectivity and the grammatical process of some linguistic forms as subjectification.

In 1992, the international seminar with topics of subjectivity and subjectivisation convened in University of Cambridge, which concerns realizations of subjectivity and relevant processes of linguistic evolution. And in 1995, the collected papers were published as *Subjectivity and Subjectivisation: Linguistic Perspectives* (Stein & Wright, 1995). This book reflects the trend of growing attentions in linguistics and relevant disciplines required by the centrality of the speaker in language. And at the same time, an international team of contributors carry out a series of studies on grammatical, diachronic, and literary aspects of subjectivity and subjectivisation, from a variety of perspectives including historical linguistics, formal semantics, and discourse analysis. From then on, the identical demarcation of the terms, namely subjectivity and subjectivisation, has generally been accepted in the linguistic academic circle.

> The subjectivity explored here concerns expression of self and the representation of a speaker's (or, more generally, a locutionary agent's) perspective or point of view in discourse—what has been called a speaker's imprint. In turn, subjectivisation refers to the structure and strategies that languages involve in the linguistic realization of subjectivity or to the relevant processes of linguistic evolution. (Finegan, 1995: 1)

And Finegan (1995:4) develops his studies into three main areas: a locutionary agent's perspective as shaping linguistic expression; a locutionary agent's expression of affect towards the propositions contained in utterances; and, a locutionary agent's expression of the modality or epistemic status of the propositions contained in utterances.

The main research strains in cognitive linguistics that have developed in the course of studying subjectivity are those referring to the approaches of Langacker and his followers. Langacker, in his seminal 1985 paper "Observations and Speculations on Subjectivity", has already set up the foundations of his approach to subjectivity which he has further refined and revised over the past thirty years. He argues that subjectivity should be studied from viewing arrangement, but rather pertaining to the semantic content of a linguistic expression (Langacker, 1985). The notions of the subjective construe and the objective construe are built up in accordance with the asymmetry relation between the observer in a perceptual situation and the entity that is observed (Langacker, 1985: 120), whereby the maximal subjectivity is characteristic of "the viewer's role as such" off the stage and the maximal objectivity characterizes "the onstage focus of attention" (Langacker, 2008:77) on the object of perception. In other words, an entity is maximally subjective when it remains off the stage and implicit, inhering in the very process of conception without being as its target, and it is construed with maximal objectivity when being put on the stage as an explicit focus of attention.

For Langacker (2006:18), an expression is neither subjective nor objective, that is, "a semantic shift does not... result in a global meaning becoming more subjective". According to this view, the meaning of an expression always comprises both subjectively and objectively construed elements, and it is some individual conceptual elements within an expression's meaning that may come to be construed with a great degree of subjectivity or objectivity as time goes on. Langacker regards linguistic realizations of subjectivity as a primarily synchronic phenomenon, but he also stresses that subjectivisation is the result of attenuation of the objectively construed subject, thus implying its diachronic character. Attenuation in the subject control is a pervasive, multifaceted phenomenon that plays a major role in the course of grammaticalization, imposing important influences on synchronic analysis and descriptions of subjectivity. Agreeing with Verhagen (1995) and Harder (1996), Langacker (1999b) has suggested that the subjective component exists there all along, being immanent in the objective conception and simply left behind as the latter attenuates away. In Langacker's (1990, 2002, 2006) approach, the term subjectivity doesn't pertain to the semantic process of the linguistic item; rather, it should be studied from the viewing perspective used to construe a given conceptual content. The perceptual asymmetry plays the most important role in the course of construing the meaning of subjectivity with the observing viewpoint of the speaker and the hearer being profiled.

1.1.3 Pragmatic Approaches

Generally, Langacker studies subjectivity in terms of construal relations while Traugott seems to develop her understanding of subjectivity through reinforcing its pragmatic side. Traugott (1989, 1995a, 1995b, 1999, 2003, 2006, 2010) and Traugott & Dasher (2002) have studied linguistic realizations of subjectivity, and the principal thoughts and research findings are put forth in a series of works.

Traugott thinks that subjectivity actually results from the diachronic process. From this point, subjectivity is treated as the process whereby "meanings tend to become increasingly situated in the speaker's subjective beliefs and attitudes towards the proposition" (Traugott, 1989: 31). Regarding subjectivity as a pragmatic-semantic process, Traugott illustrates how certain expressions initially articulating concrete, lexical, and objective meanings have come through frequently repeated use in certain linguistic context, to serve abstract, pragmatic, interpersonal, speaker-based functions. If the meaning of a lexical item or linguistic structure is originally grounded in the reference of socio-physical world, it is possible that over time and by frequent uses the speaker will develop some abstract meanings that are grounded in the speaker's world, in reasoning, belief, or meta-textual attitudes to the discourse. In other words, subjectivity is "the sema-siological development of meanings associated with a form so that it comes to mark subjectivity explicitly" (Traugott, 1999: 179). According to Traugott, subjectivity is a semantic process, by which a linguistic element such as morphemes, words, phrases or structures etc. develops new senses which involve epistemic meanings primarily focused on the speaker's belief and knowledge state.

In this process, grammaticalization plays an important role whereby linguistic items or constructions come to be reanalyzed as having syntactical and morphological functions. As Traugott (2010: 35) points out, grammaticalization in some sense works as semanticization, which requires the new subjective meanings to be conventionally coded by the forms with new form-meaning pairs as results. And this process crucially reanalyses the process of subjectivity encoded pragmatic meanings that arise in the speaker-based meanings. From this point, subjectivity refers to the tendency that lexical material "tends to become increasingly based in the speaker's or writer's subjective belief states or attitudes towards what is being said and how it is being said" (Traugott, 2003: 125). In Traugott's approach, subjectivity is a semantic process relevant to grammaticalization or semanticization, which requires the newly-occurred subjectivized meaning to be conventionally encoded by some certain linguistic form, with the new form-meaning pairs emerged as the result of the grammatical evolution, accompanied mostly by phonological changes. The realizations of subjectivity in linguistic forms discussed are as follows: deixis, adverbs, linguistic expressions marking tense and aspect, auxiliaries, quasi-auxiliaries; and some syntactic forms such as phrase structures and sentential patterns etc. (Traugott & Dasher, 2002)

de Smet & Verstraete (2006: 384) put forth the conception of "pragmatic subjectivity", which refers to the aspect of subjectivity inherent in language uses and independent of the semantics of some certain expression. Therefore, the notion of subjectivity is thought as inherent in language uses and independent of the semantics of a particular expression, which is inherent "in the use of any expression" and thus called "pragmatic subjectivity". Accordingly, subjectivity is coded by means of form-meaning pairs out of everyday speeches, and realized by linguistic forms and strategies. In this sense, language can be said to be strongly marked by subjectivity since any selection out of linguistic repertoire must have been passed through the speaker. The subjectively-urged motivation in expressing oneself mainly focuses on the part of the speaker's role in the utterance that bears the responsibility for choosing that specific perspective which strikes out the choice of specific linguistic item or structures to construe a particular entity or situation. The speaker, as the conceptualizing subject, accounts for an expression's specificity of lexicalization, its information structure. Thus, the relative prominence of its participants which relates to speaker-oriented, or even speaker-imposed can be understood to be subjective.

Verstraete (2006: 10) makes further explanation about the concept of pragmatic subjectivity as: the choice of specific lexical items or construction types that refer to a particular entity or situation always imposes a specific perspective on that entity or situation, and it is part of the speaker's role in the utterance that he is the one who bears responsibility for choosing that specific perspective. Compared with this pragmatic subjectivity, de Smet & Verstraete distinguish two types of subjectivity with the speaker-relatedness being part of this expression's inherent meaning, and ideational and interpersonal subjectivity indicating the speaker-positioning and the speaker-interlocutor interaction. Importantly, this division is not just semantic; moreover the concept of the ideational and interpersonal expressions shows divergent syntactic behavior pragmatically.

1.1.4 Discoursive Semantic Approaches

The discourse sense of subjectivity is not paramount in linguistic analysis partly because formal and structural linguistics traditionally insist on studying language by treating it as the expression of so-called objective propositions, instead of concerning the process of displaying the self in discourse. However, subjectivity in its humanistic sense is not new to linguistics any more, but it is up to nowadays witnessed as a renaissance of interest in this topic as a critical facet of language, i. e. language is not strictly the expression of propositional thoughts, neither as autonomous structures nor as representing logical propositions, but language is regarded as the communicating process of perceiving, feeling, and even speaking subjects.

The term of subjectivity explored at present has close relations with the notion of discourse, for subjectivity concerns the process of consciously expressing self and representing the speaker's point of view in discourse. Therefore, subjectivity is central to constructing discourse stance, which mainly focuses on the intersections of language resources and language choices while expressing the self. As Julia Kristeva (1989: 11) has put forth:

> Discourse implies first the participation of the subject in his language through his speech, as an individual. Using the anonymous structure of la langue, the subject forms and transforms himself in the discourse he communicates to the other. la langue, common to all, becomes in discourse the vehicle of a unique message. The message belongs to the particular structure of a given subject who

imprints a specific seal upon the required structure of la langue. Without being aware of it, the subject thus makes his mark on la langue.

Therefore, subjectivity concerns the way that the speaker speaks him/herself out by using the linguistic forms, in other words, the involvement of a locutionary agent in a discourse, and the effect of that involvement on the formal shape of discourse.

The study of subjectivity at the discourse level can trace back to the discussion under literary pragmatics, in which its pedigree is well established in the field of western scholarship. In western languages, in fact, subjectivity has received its most intense scrutiny in literary expression, among which free indirect style plays as a striking manifestation of the narrated subjectivity that has been studied since the turn of the century. However, far from being limited to literary texts, subjectivity is paid attention to in the field of linguistics and studied as an all-encompassing linguistic phenomenon. Particularly influential on the approaches taken in this study is the conception of subjectivity adumbrated by John Lyons. He characterizes subjectivity as "the way in which natural languages, in their structure and their normal manner of operation, provide for the locutionary agent's expression of himself and of attitudes and beliefs" (Lyons, 1982: 102), and then he implies the fact that the speaker intends to express self in an utterance that can't be reduced "to the assertion of a set of proposition" (Lyons, 1982: 104). As Benveniste (1971: 226) has observed, "A language without the expression of person can't be imagined", and the representation and expression of subjectivity are variegated in discourse cross languages. To mark subjectivity, some linguists explore morphology, which may be the marker most readily tracked; others mark subjectivity in a variety of more subtle forms, ranging from intonation to word order, and even to discursive structure.

As Finegan (1995: 3) has pointed out, language users can typically express their affect to what has been articulated. Affect is then regarded as an aspect of subjectivity. Ochs & Schieffelin (1989: 9) has observed in their article "Language Has a Heart" that language is responsive to the fundamental need of the speaker to convey and assess feelings, moods, dispositions and attitudes. This need is as critical and as human as that of describing events. Interlocutors need not only a predication that a speaker is making, but also the affective orientation the speaker is presenting with regard to that particular predication. As one perspective explored to express subjectivity, affect can be studied concerning what and how linguistic resources are chosen to express the speaker's affect in discourse. And more similarly, Irvine (1982: 32) has explored an affective dimension of communication that would make the most use of all levels of linguistic organizations as well as the organization of discourse. In other words, linguistic resources available to express affect include not only lexicons but also grammatical and discourse structures as well. As Ochs & Schieffelin (1989:7) have claimed, a cross-linguistic research proves that languages have dedicated phonological, morpho-syntactic and discourse devices to intensify and specify attitudes, moods, feelings and disposition, which provides the speaker with the affective frame for propositions to be encoded. The way in which affect has been studied will surely shed lights on our study of subjectivity. Affect deals traditionally with the emotive aspect of meaning, which acts as the means by which the speaker positively or negatively evaluates entities, happenings and affairs encoded in discourse. In the domain of affect, the study of subjectivity evokes the rethinking of the relation between the way that the speaker expresses him/herself and the purpose that the speaker intends to convey by choosing language resources.

Concerning the pragmatic subjectivity expressed in the context, de Smet & Verstraete distinguish two types of what they term as semantic subjectivity in which the speaker-relatedness is one part "of the expression's inherent meaning" (de Smet & Verstraete, 2006: 385), from "ideational" and "interpersonal" subjectivity. Both of them are consistent with language metafunctions discussed in SFL which claim that the expression carries out the ideational function, the interpersonal function and the contextual function at the same time (Halliday, 1994a, 2004). These subcategorizations of subjectivity referring to SFL reflect that researches pertaining to subjectivity have been diversified. The distinction may be roughly drawn between a school of studying subjectivity as an essential property of language (Athanasiadou, 2006; Stein & Wright, 1995; Yaguello, 1994) and subjectivity as a linguistic phenomenon of discourse (Englebretson, 2007; Jaffe, 2009; Hunston & Thompson, 2000).

As the understanding of the conception of subjectivity is highly concerned, the study of subjectivity then goes ahead to how to explore the subjectivity. Edward Finegan (1995: 4) has developed three main arenas focusing on the recent studies of subjectivity, namely "perspective as shaping expression", "affect to the propositions contained in the utterance" and "modality or epistemic status of the propositions confused in the utterance". Finegan's framework sheds lights on the study of mapping actually realizations in linguistic forms to the different aspects of subjectivity, which paves the way for the construe and construction of subjectivity at the discourse level by means of linguistic items.

Above all, items from different levels of language structure, from phonology to discourse (c. f. Hunston & Thompson, 1999; Ochs & Schieffelin, 1989), can be drawn on to express the speaker's subjectivity. This research from the discourse perspective will extend the knowledge about the repertoire of varieties of subjective markers beyond the traditional grammatical categories such as deixis, tense, aspect and modality. Therefore, besides the grammatical markers, subjectivity can also be expressed lexically by the use of evaluative lexis, vague expressions, and so on; and through strategically discourse structuring, say, repetition, interactive sequencing, code switching; and even by the discourse network, that is, the linguistic resources, in particular the epistemic use of modal verbs and modal adverbs as a means of expressing the speaker's (un)certainty about the truth of the proposition and personal pronouns as means of indicating social relations, speaker's orientation and speaker's conception of the self. All of them can work together in the discourse constructing the process to construe the speaker's subjectivity.

1.2 Previous Studies of Subjectivisation

Subjectivisation is defined as linguistic structures and strategies that languages evolve to develop the due lexicogrammatical resources to realize subjectivity, or the relevant processes of linguistic evolution themselves (Finegan, 1995: 1). Review of subjectivisation categorized in terms of lexical, sentential and discourse level is made as following.

Approaches to subjectivisation, both in the cognitive field of linguistics and in the domain related to grammaticalization, have been in fact of a semantic-pragmatic nature. This process has been mainly concerning a semantic-pragmatic change about the subjectivized meaning. In this sense, subjectivisation refers to the process of semantic change by which meanings become increasingly anchored in the speaker's subjective belief, state, attitude towards the proposition, and thus grammaticalized as explicit markers with a coded symbolic and highly-conventionalized meaning in the grammar of a language (Langacker, 1985, 1991, 1999, 2008; Traugott, 1995, 1999a, 1999b, 2010; Traugott & Dasher, 2002, 2010).

Langacker presents subjectivisation as a primarily synchronic phenomenon. He has exclaimed that subjectivisation comes from the attenuation of the objectively construed subject, for the subjective component exists there all the time, being immanent in the objective conception and simply left behind as the objective meaning faded away. (Langacker, 1999b) Moreover, attenuation in the control of the subject is a pervasive process involving multifaceted factors, which plays a major function in the course of grammaticalization with important influence on synchronic analysis and descriptions. Four parameters are discussed when it comes to the driving force evolving fully as subjectivisation. They are (a) a change in status, especially from specific to generic, and from actual to potential; (b) a change in focus, i. e. the extent to which particular elements highlight out of the background as the focus of attention; (c) a shift in domain, from a physical interaction to an experiential or social one, e. g. the evolution of modals; (d) a change in the locus of potency or activity, moving from a focused onstage trajectory to an offstage addressee. (Langacker, 1999a) *Subjectivisation: Various Paths to Subjectivity* (Athanasiadou, Canakis & Cornillie, 2006) is mainly devoted to Langacker's approach, which proves to be at work in predominantly synchronic analysis of modals, adjectives and syntax. Therefore, attenuation and diffusion in the locus of control play a very important role in many cases of grammaticalization, resulting eventually in the transparency of the objective meaning.

However, Elizabeth Traugott concerns the phenomenon of subjectivisation in grammaticalization processes, and defines subjectivisation as the sema-siological process whereby meanings, as time goes on, become increasingly depending on the speaker's perspective and attitudes towards what is spoken and how it is expressed, externalizing their perspectives and attitudes that are constrained by the communicative world profiled through the speech event, instead of the so-called real world. (Traugott, 1995; Traugott & Dasher, 2002) Traugott finds sound evidences for her explanation of subjectivisation in her diachronic study of English modals, connectives, epistemic speech act verbs, modal verbs, and evidentials. In her opinion, subjectivisation is a semanticization process whereby a linguistic element (a morpheme, word, phrase or construction) develops some new speaker-perspective senses coded conventionally by the forms, with new form-meaning pairs as a result.

Following Traugott's approach, various case studies of subjectivisation are developed, which are summarized by Traugott Dasher (2002) as follows:

a) auxiliaries and quasi-auxiliaries expressing deontic and/or epistemic modality, e. g. *may*, *can*, *must*, *will*, *ought to* (Hopper & Traugott, 2003; Traugott, 1989; Traugott & Dasher, 2002);

b) various discourse particles conveying the speaker's epistemic attitude, e. g. stance adverbs such as *actually*, *strictly*, *loosely*, *really* and *frankly* (Powell, 1992), and the epistemic phrases *I think* and *I guess* (Vandelanotte, 2004);

c) discourse markers such as *in fact*, *indeed*, *besides*, *well*, *actually* (Traugott & Dasher, 2002) etc. , imprinting explicitly speaker's attitudes towards discourse structure, i. e. towards the relationship between what precedes and what follows, or of the connectivity between propositions; additive versus counter argumentative too (Schwenter & Waltereit, 2010) volitive and non-volitive modals (Narrog, 2005), *('d) better* (Denison & Cort, 2010);

d) hortative, as *let's* in *Let's go*, expressing the speaker's (condescending) support;

e) scalar adverbs such as *even* reflecting the speaker's relative ranking of alternatives, and rather than expressing speaker preference (Traugott, 1995); scalar intensifying uses of *kind of/kinda* (Margerie, 2010) and *complete*, *total*, *whole* (Ghesquière, 2010), modal adverbs such as *obviously*, *possibly*, *probably*, *evidently*, *apparently* (Traugott, 1989), which express the speaker's epistemic attitude with respect to a state of affairs, and nouns and adjectives expressing the speaker's evaluation;

f) subordinating conjunctions as *while* expressing the speaker's attitude of surprise (Traugott, 1995; Traugott & König, 1991), and linguistic expressions marking spatial, temporal, and person deixis (Traugott, 2003; Traugott & Dasher, 2002);

g) illocutionary speech-act verbs (including performatives), such as "asseveratives" *observe*, *insist*, *state*, *claim*, and *hypothesize*, whose meaning is similar to that of epistemic modals, and the "directives", *say*, *request*, *command*, *insist*, functioning similarly to deontic modals (see also Traugott, 1989; Traugott & Dasher, 2002).

1.3 Research Gaps

As literature review has shown, the studies of subjectivity and subjectivisation have received increasing interests in linguistics, and have made rapid progresses in most parts of relevant researches. Meanwhile, some research gaps are also revealed in the course of the study.

At the beginning, it seems evident that most definitions pertaining to the concept of subjectivity and subjectivisation are single-faceted. This gap can be manifested through the following well-known definitions of subjectivity and subjectivisation.

a) Subjectification represents a common type of semantic change, which shifts from a relatively objective construal of some entity to a subjective one. (Langacker, 1991: 324; 2000: 297).

b) Subjectification refers to such semantic-pragmatic process that meanings tend to become increasingly associated with the speaker's subjective belief, especially metatextual attitude toward discourse flow, by which meanings shift toward great subjectivity. (Traugott, 1995a: 31)

c) Subjectification is the sema-siological process whereby the speaker comes over time to develop meanings that construe his perspectives and attitudes as confirmed to the communicative world of the speech event, rather than by the so-called real world. (Traugott & Dasher, 2002: 30)

d) Subjectivity is represented by the expression of self and the realization of a speaker's... viewpoint in the discourse. (Finegan, 1995: 1)

e) Subjectivity refers to the way in which natural languages enable the speaker to express himself and his own attitudes and beliefs, in linguistic structures and the normal manner of operations. (Lyons, 1982: 102)

All the definitions of subjectivity and subjectivisation are given in cognitive theories and in grammaticalization frameworks, which are of a semantic-pragmatic nature. From this point, the former studies of subjectivity and subjectivisation almost all focus on the process that the subjectivized meaning is conventionalized or fossilized inside as signs that can be drawn on to express the speaker's attitude. As Benveniste (1971: 224-225) points out clearly, subjectivity has two basic facets: subjectivity is the fundamental property of language, which can help the speaker express his opinions properly; and, subjectivity refers to "the capacity of the speaker to posit himself as subject", which then enables the speaker to make best uses of linguistic resources to serve communicative intentions. Both facets can fuse together in the course of producing discourse. Clearly, as shown in the former studies, the speaker's capacities to express his attitudes in linguistic forms and/or with the help of linguistic devices do not receive sufficient attention as deserved.

Moreover, as the focus of the research turns back to the social sciences and the humanities again, the concept of subjectivity attracts more and more attention. However, many studies of subjectivity and subjectivisation are mainly confined to the fields of cognitive linguistics and pragmatics. In contrast, the studies of subjectivity and subjectivisation aren't given equal treatments in other domains of linguistics, especially within the realm of SFL. Within SFL, the concepts of subjectivity and subjectivisation are mentioned briefly and treated in diverse facets. The process of expressing subjectivity is, by nature, just the ways that modal assessments are realized. Modal assessment functions interpersonal meanings that are exchanged in discourse, by which the speaker either gives his assessment to or demands the addressee's assessment on some certain entity. Therefore, the system of modal assessment covers a wide range of interpersonal evaluations, which may be realized ranging from a whole text to a lexical item, including those described under the heading of APPRAISAL SYSTEM. (Matthiessen, Teruya & Lam, 2010; Matthiessen, 2007) According to Halliday (1994) and Halliday & Matthiessen (2004), expressions of subjectivity are indirect ways whereby modal assessments are realized in discourse. On the one hand, realizations of modal assessment make up in fact the linguistic potential, by which the speaker can choose due linguistic resources to realize subjectivity. On the other hand, realizations of modal assessment can be dealt with in accordance with different variables, as the expression of modality depends on the system of types of orientation in modality. Then, the distinction between subjective and objective modality cutting across the distinction between the explicit and implicit variants builds up a cline with different delicacies. Martin & White (2005) treat this cline as scaled systems consisting of a topological perspective on value and orientation, which includes an extra-subjective and an extra-objective option as well as values for hyper- and hypo-grades. Then, the writer can operate delicately to realize subjectivity by taking proper orientation and assigning due value. Inheriting the distinction between subjective and objective orientations, Martin and White then define the meaning of subjectivity as: the authorial voice gives his personal proposition as contingently and subjectively derived via a process of deduction, with expressing his personal opinion overtly or covertly. Therefore, the two facets of subjectivity should be paid attention to in the process of the study.

Methodologically, the former researches of subjectivity mainly focus on the diachronic processes that the subjectivized item generates and is conventionalized as certain subjectivisation during regular uses in a given context, which is often studied with respect to the process of grammaticalization. Sometimes, the synchronic studies of subjective markers encoded by linguistic items are conducted in relation with discourse features. Such kinds of studies are carried out about one subjectivized item or a set of them within one language or across languages with the aim to compare processes of a set of subjectivized items cross-linguistically. As the subjectivized item is evolved by being frequently used in certain discourse context, the discourse factor clearly plays a very important role in the process of subjectivisation. Furthermore, as the speaker is actually expressing his attitudes in the course of producing discourse, the study of subjectivity should be carried out at the discourse level (Finegan, 1995: 1; Lyons, 1982: 102). In fact, the production of discourse is such systematic processes that the writer takes advantages of different kinds of linguistic resources to make his subjective opinion clearly and logically expressed in discourse. Although in the former studies the critical role of the discourse is mentioned, it is rarely or never given the attention it deserves.

Finally, almost all studies of subjectivity focus on the processes in which the subjectivized items are conventionalized as semantic elements, no matter whether the studies are carried out within one language or across languages. In other words, the objects of the studies of subjectivity are mainly lexis, groups, or phrases. Sometimes, they study how certain sentential patterns are subjectivized to obtain special meanings that can be used to express the speaker's attitudes in the evolution, e. g. the sentential patterns with "ba" (Shen, 2002; Xi, 2008; Zhang, 2007) or the sentential patterns with "bei" (Qi, 2013; Ye, 2014). As we all know, the proposition is fully expressed in discourse. In order to realize personal opinions, the speaker will use all kinds of linguistic resources in virtue of linguistically-operating devices in order to make them interact systematically and logically. On the contrary, most of the former studies focus on the process in which some isolated items are diachronically subjectivized and conventionalized gradually as subjectivization, which will never give a worm's-eye view of the process in which the speaker actually expresses his attitudes and makes his communicative intention fulfilled.

1.4 Summary

Facing all these research gaps exposed in the former studies of subjectivity, the present study will then figure out some proper ways to settle them. Accordingly, this study will concern subjectivity expressed in the course of producing discourse; that is, it mainly focuses on the way that the writer draws on linguistic resources to make his subjective stance clearly expressed and understood properly, orienting to enact the communicative intention successfully.

Therefore, the present study will build up the theoretical framework within SFL and explore realizations of subjectivity in the process of expressing the subjective stance in discourse. The concept of subjectivity is revised to meet this research purpose, which is propitious to the present study. In this way, all linguistic resources that can be adopted to express modal assessment can also be used in the present study.

Chapter 2
Theoretical Considerations

This study mainly concerns how the author expresses subjectivity with regard to modal assessment in the context of editorials by means of choosing due linguistic resources. Then, the study goes in accordance to Finegan's framework of studying subjectivity from three arenas of modality, affect and perspective, which are identical with the system of MODALITY, the system of ENGAGEMENT, and the system of APPRAISAL in SFL, respectively. All these three systems concern the way that the speaker's attitudes and feelings are expressed from three different but inseparable angles, whose realizations in lexico-grammatical resources are categorized into modal assessment (Halliday & Matthiessen, 2004: 608). That is, modal assessment is regarded as lexico-grammatical potential ready to be chosen to realize subjectivity in SFL. Then, the research objects can be defined as due linguistic forms of modal assessment, corresponding to these three systems mentioned above, respectively. Here, the basic principles of SFL and subjectivity relevant to this study are introduced in order to make the preliminary preparation for building up the research framework.

2.1 Theoretical Foundations

According to Fowler (1977: 76), language would not allow users to say something without conveying some certain attitude to that something. In other words, hardly can one find a piece of written discourse which is purely objective, neutral, or value-free. Subjectivity is correspondingly regarded as speaking something and being realized by modal assessment to deliver the user's subjective stance while "saying something".

SFL is a part of social semiotic approach to language study, including "systemic" and "functional" aspects. Here, "systemic" means to regard language as "a network of systems, or interrelated sets of options for making meaning" (Halliday, 1994: 40). A systemic approach allows us to focus on meaningful choices in language without thinking of the particular structure that realizes it. "Functional" refers to Halliday's view that a language is interpreted as a system of meanings, accompanied by forms through which the meaning can be realized.

2.1.1 Stratification and Realization in SFL

In SFL, language is viewed as a social semiotic system. A semiotic system is a social network system with added components of meanings. Meaning then can be thought of as just a kind of social value; but it is value in a significantly different sense, which is construed symbolically. From this point, semiotic systems are social systems where value has been further transformed into meaning. (Halliday & Matthiessen, 1999) Language as the whole is involved in all kinds of human activities and affects everything we do. It construes all of our experience, and it enacts all of our interpersonal processes. (Halliday, 1997) Lexico-grammar is about linguistic resources that realize discourse semantics at the stratum of wording. A functional grammar means that it is based on meaning to make an interpretation of linguistic forms and every distinction recognized in the grammar makes some contribution to the form of the wording as an integrated whole. The lexico-grammar is a natural symbolic system in that both the kinds of grammatical pattern that have evolved in language, and the specific manifestations of each kind, bear a natural relation to the meanings they have evolved to express. (Halliday, 1994)

SFL is a multiperspective model, designed to give the linguistic analysts complementary lenses for interpreting language in use. Stratification means that language is a hierarchical-ordered stratified semiotic system involving strata of coding at different levels of abstraction. (Halliday & Matthiessen, 2004; Martin, 1992; Matthiessen & Bateman, 1991) The strata in the organization of language are semantics, lexico-grammar, phonology (graphology) and phonetics; and context is interpreted as a stratum above language. (Martin, 1992) In SFL, discourse semantics is one stratum to emphasize the fact that it is concerned with meanings within discourses, among which the speaker's assessment is established, targeted and sourced. Strata are related with each other through inter-stratal realization. Semantics is "the way into language" (Matthiessen, Teruya & Lam, 2010: 189) from context—the set of strategies for construing, enacting and presenting non-language as meaning. The pair is situation and discourse across the boundary between context and semantics: a situation is realized in a discourse, and there are certainly lower ranking correspondences between sub-situations and sub-discourses. Semantics thus operates in the semiotic environment of the context.

Across the boundary between semantics and lexico-grammar, the pair is move-message-figure and clause, which "are mapped onto one another in the unmarked case in their realization as a clause" (Matthiessen, Teruya & Lam, 2010: 206). In addition, sequences of figures are realized by clause complexes, and elements that make up figures are realized by groups. These are the congruent patterns; the relationship between semantics and lexico-grammar may be scrambled by grammatical metaphors. Interpersonal metaphor is regarded as the linguistic devices functioning the interpersonal interaction. Ontogenetically, it is said to come before ideational metaphor and textual metaphor, as it is related to what Halliday (1993: 18) has called the "interpersonal first principle" in learning.

Within SFL, language is meaning potential that will be realized by the choice of lexico-grammatical forms through the discourse process. The term "choice" has two meanings: "option" and "selection". (Halliday, 1969) In other words, "choice = option" contrasts in a system of options, so does the act of choosing among the options of a system—"choice = selection". (Matthiessen, Teruya & Lam, 2010) When "choice" means "option" as a term in a system, the nature of the choice is determined not only by what the option realizes when expressing the intra-stratal relationships either "from above" or "from below", but also by what systemic values of the option are made "from roundabout", contrasting with other potential options. In the second sense of choice, namely as an act of selecting an option in a system, choice is part of the overall account of the process of traversing a system network making selections along the way. (Matthiessen & Bateman, 1991) Therefore, choice plays a very important role in the course of construing meaning.

SFL holds that the language system allows more choices than those that are actually made. SFL can be located in a typology of grammatical theories based on the systemic and functional orientation. This view gives more weight to the paradigmatic axis than to the syntagmatic one, which enormously enlarges the scope of thing we have to deal with. The function structures are specified by means of realization statements associated with terms in systems; each realization statement specifies a fragment of structure. Systemic theory conceives lexico-grammar as a resource, according to which the primary mode of organization is paradigmatic, and the innovation of the system network is treated as a form of representation. However, the syntagmatic organization is represented by function structures—configurations of functions, which are characterized by the progression of elements related to sequence. (Halliday, 2003; Hasan, Matthiessen & Webster, 2005, 2007) The paradigmatic axis and the syntagmatic axis are the realization of the inter-axial relationship at a given rank by means of choosing linguistic resources.

Many selections are automated without conscious awareness. Choice does not imply that the selection of an option is either intentional or conscious. It may or may not be. (Halliday, 1969; Matthiessen & Bateman, 1991) When choices are made according to subjective intentions, the writer will surely leave the tracking imprint consciously that is regarded as linguistic distinctiveness of deviance in terms of style. Deviance dealing with the distinctiveness of discourses resides in its departure from the normal features, which refers to "features in the text which appear to first impressions as unususal or striking in some way and then explore their ramification" (Widdowson, 1975: 210). Such distinctively linguistic features provide the speaker with linguistic prints to express subjectivity, fundamentally. Degrees of subjectivity or objectivity and a range of graded values are thus distinctively imprinted according to different context situations, being deviant as linguistic forms. (Martin & White, 2005: 17)

All in all, within SFL, modal assessment construes the region of uncertainty that lies exactly between positive and negative polarities taking place at the stratum of semantics. The realization of subjectivity is fundamentally a process of choosing some appropriate lexico-grammatical forms in accordance to the contextual situation. Besides, all forms of modal assessment will then construct the writer's evaluation through discourse.

2.1.2 Subjectivity and Consciousness

Subjectivity functions as a fundamental property of language, which can express the speaker's attitudes and feelings with the help of linguistic prints that are left when the speaker speaks himself out. While the speaker constitutes himself as a speaking subject, the intrinsic features of subjectivity are highlighted from two sides: subjectivity regards language as a meaning potential that can provide all kinds of linguistic resources for the speaker to establish the concept of ego in reality; and, it is the capacity of the speaker as the psychic unity that transcends the totality of the actual experiences and makes the permanence of the consciousness. (Benveniste, 1958: 224) Subjectivity, as the property of language, concerns the feasibility of linguistic representation to constitute attitudes and beliefs represented in linguistic resources (Finegan, 1995; Langacker, 1991, 2000; Traugott, 1995b; Traugott & Dasher, 2002); also, it focuses on the consciousness of the speaker as he posits himself to be the ego (Benveniste, 1958; Lyons, 1982). Representation and consciousness are nuclear features of subjectivity.

Consciousness is the quality of being aware of external objects within oneself, which essentially connects with the capacity that human beings have to represent objects and states of affairs in the world. Consciousness, by nature, contains inner, qualitative, subjective states and processes. (Searle, 1999: 53) It is reduced to information processing in the brain and is also realized in the brain, which is ontologically subjective. Therefore, all other things will gain value, importance, merit, or worth only when they are in connection with consciousness. The most important feature is that it works by connecting with intentionality when coping with the world. Intentionality refers to various forms by which the mind can be involved in and impose effect on objects and states of affairs in the world. (Searle, 1999: 85) By intentionality, the speaker's subjective states relate him to the rest of the world. Consciousness and intentionality construct an connection, i. e. consciousness copes with the world with the help of intentionality; and, intentionality is understood in terms of consciousness. Intentionality plays an important role when consciousness represents the world to the speaker.

2.1.3 Subjectivity and Intentionality

Intentionality is a core content of human being's consciousness, acting as consciousness' initial step and going through the whole process. (Xu & Liao, 2013: 1) The speaker's intentionality is expressed in the act of using language; and this process reflects such intentional stance that the speaker intends to choose language in accordance with his intentionality, by which a psychological value orientation is especially reflected. Searle (1983) makes a functional framework from his speech act theory, and introduces the notion of intentional causation for specifying the mode of representation of intentional objects. Based on the framework of the speech act theory, Searle (1969) suggests that the intentional act involves "conditions of satisfaction" and "direction of fit", which is formulized as "A = F(p)". As the speaker intends to choose to express certain intentional contents, these intentional contents will be influenced by the speaker's intentional attitude which represents the speaker's psychological states that can be valued in terms of psychological evaluation and psychological orientation. Correspondingly, intentional attitude reflects intentional force which can be further differentiated in delicacy with respect to the qualitative or orientation. Therefore, it can be reliable to regard subjectivity as a hierarchical term which can be evaluated on the base of scale or orientation.

The notion of intentional causation refers to the systematic way that coordinates the representing capacity of the mind and the causal relations to the world, distinguishing such features as self-referentiality and mind-to-world direction of causation. (Searle, 1999: 105-106) Accordingly, explanations of rational human behavior essentially resort to the apparatus of intentional causation. Intentionality is purposive behavior, which is thought of as the core realization of self-consciousness while the speaker uses language to construct meanings in order to enact social activities. Here, meaning, referring to the illocutionary act, is termed as meaning intention which is divided into representing intention and communicating intention. (Duan Kaicheng, 2004: 9) Representing intention concerns the representing function of language in the speaker's viewpoint, and communicating intention stresses the effect of the utterances on the addressee. As indicated in the above explanation, representing intention is identical with subjectivity, and communicating intention is identical with intersubjectivity, in the assumption that intersubjectivity is one successive part of subjectivity. Generally speaking, meaning intention is realized as information flow when producing discourse oriented to some given communication intention.

2.2 The Conceptual Construct of Subjectivity

The concept of subjectivity has become increasingly popular in the cognitive-functional literature of the last thirty years or so. Up to now, there has not been a unified discussion of the terminology related to subjectivity and the nature of this notion. Therefore, it is necessary for us to explore the conceptual construct of subjectivity by connecting it to the present study before proposing the working model for studying subjectivity.

2.2.1 The Genesis from the Authorial Subjectivity

As to the paradox of the literary work in terms of the dual mode of existence, i. e. a linguistic object on one hand, and a virtual subject expressing various experiences which transcends linguistic limits on the other hand, Peter Boa (1978) puts forth the conception of the authorial subjectivity based on Paul Valery's "Ego Poeta". In Valery's view, Ego Poeta can be primarily regarded as a voice in the poem which has individuality but not personality, for the creating subject is transforming him through the creation of the works, the relatively disorganized empirical self being transformed into exceptional, and highly organized ego, involved in the medium of language even without being fully realized. (Valery, 1973: 301)

As an approach, the authorial subjectivity aims to reveal the subjectivity of the work related to the particular functioning of the authorial intentionality constituted by the consciously aesthetic-linguistic forms of the work. (Boa, 1978: 52) Although the literary work can be defined in terms of its objective linguistic properties, all the language forms are not rigid or petrified into pure formalism—"to take account only of the linguistic object sealed off in a closed system of language is to reduce the literary work to a purely decorative role and also the process of literary creation to the status of a game, a kind of verbal chess with words for pieces" (Boa, 1978: 51), but they reflect a kind of aesthetic linguistic activity mirrored in the consciously aesthetic forms of the work. While the literary work is the product of language, it is essentially an expression of the subjective vision outside language. That is, the product of a state of mind and a manner of composition reflects the general and central tendencies of the creating subject. By nature, the authorial subjectivity is closely related, on one hand, to the creating subject and to the process of creating on the other. The creating subject does not mean some universal essence, prescription of rules that might be made prior to any individual creative acts, but on the contrary, the attempt to describe some certain recurrent features of this subject indicates that it has its own relative continuity of identity, forming the aesthetic counterpart which can be summed up simply as style. In the process of creating the work, this identity may be established out of a consideration of the different individual manifestations of the creating subject coming out as some certain voice, which, as Paul Valery (1973: 435-436) has argued, has individuality instead of personality. In Valery's view, the creating subject is not expressing himself, but transforming himself by means of language into an impersonal reflection of the universal human, consequently all personal subjectivity being annulled in the anonymity of language. (Valery, 1973: 126) However, the creating subject would always leave some traces, such as a voice, whose phonetic qualities, peculiarities of rhythm, tone etc. define its subjective individuality imprinted in the work.

As for the connotation of the process of creating implied in the authorial subjectivity, it focuses on the very capacity for discourse composing itself, instead of tracing back to particular experiences or events described in the work. Based on ego poeta described by Valery's intellectual outlook as a whole unit, the authorial subjectivity points to the complex intellectual strategy behind the composition of the work affecting the development of both its themes and its form. (Valery, 1973: 117) The theme of separation and division in the discourse processing may be gradually crystallized round impersonal mythical figures and situation, which to some extent reflects the subject's consciousness of having separation and division exert their powers of organizing discourse that correspondingly allow the semantic implications to emerge as discourse phases go along. From this aspect, the authorial subjectivity is an approach more obviously applicable to some highly self-conscious writers who constantly construe the original intentions and rework their initial material with some perfectionist temperament and love of precision. Therefore, this approach will be applicable and efficient to discourses with typical genre features, such as editorials, which are characteristic of the linguistic forms, the discourse constructions, and so on.

2.2.2 Intersubjectivity: Successive Part of Subjectivity

Intersubjectivity, in a general sense, reflects the impact of the speech situation that involves a communicative relationship between speaker and hearer. Benveniste regards this speaking subject's awareness and attention to another participant as the fundamental condition for linguistic communication. (Benveniste, 1971: 230; Traugott, 2003: 128) As an intentional and mental agent, the speaking subject constructs subjectivity consciously and intentionally to have his own thoughts and beliefs shared in the intersubjective coordination. This sense of subjectivity lies in the recognition that one may have thoughts and beliefs differing from those of other people (Tomasello, 1999: 14-15), which forms the basis of intersubjectivity (Verhagen, 2005: 28). According to their points of view, intersubjectivity is one successive part of subjectivity, which will be made further explanation from two aspects.

Firstly, it is in the instance of discourse, in which "I" designates the speaker as the exact figure who proclaims himself to be the ego subject (Benveniste, 1958: 730). As language is responsible for subjectivity in all its parts, the "basis of subjectivity is in the exercise of language" (Benveniste, 1958: 730), in which the permanence of the consciousness and the capacity of the speaker make himself to express his beliefs and feelings as a "psychic unity that transcends the totality of the actual experiences" (Benveniste, 1958: 729). However, "language does not allow us to say something without conveying an attitude to that something" (Fowler, 1997: 76). It allows the speaker to express his evaluations, speculations and opinions in the context of a text or conversation. (Banfield, 1982; Wiebe, et al., 2004) The motivation of expressing attitudes and feeling is to have them shared with a wider group of people including the hearer (Nuyts, 2005:14), which goes into the stage of intersubjectivity. That is, rationalized from the speaker's perspective, subjectivity is originally oriented to intersubjectivity, because the purpose of expressing the subjective opinions is to have them shared intersubjectively. This view of intersubjectivity is supported by Verhagen. Verhagen (2005: 39) argues that the actual use of some expressions leads to the successful cognitive coordination between the speaker and the hearer, "so the expression may get started on a path towards conventionalization of subjectivity".

Secondly, as subjectification includes such meanings that not only encode but also regulate attitudes and beliefs, it inevitably involves intersubjectivity to some extent. (Traugott, 2003: 129) This is the well-known general unidirectionality of this process that intersubjectivity evolves from subjectivity, which is schematized as: non-/less subjective > subjective > intersubjective. (Traugott & Dasher, 2002: 225) As the indiscrete property of natural language, subjectivity refers to linguistic markers which could be found at all levels of language structure, from phonology to discourse, as means of indicating speaker's social relations, orientation and conception of the self. Then, it is basically authorial interests manifested in terms of the point of view, "angle of vision", "angle of telling" that determines the essence of a story's style and that provide the story with its particular "feel" and "color". (Simpson, 1993: 5) This self-expression in language forms indicates aspects of the speaker outside language, with bias to some degree subjectively involved, which means opinions and perceptions and the spatio-temporal positions from which an experience is described. That is, meanings, once subjectified, may be used to encode meanings anchored on the hearer. (Traugott, 2010: 35)

Taking intersubjectivity as its successive part, subjectivity exists in a particular context oriented to the reader to whom the speaker posits himself through linguistic means as a person in discourse. Hence, subjectivity is regarded as a linguistic phenomenon working at the discourse level.

2.2.3 Finegan's Research Model of Subjectivity

Finegan concerns the realization of subjectivity through subjectivisation in the the processes of linguistic evolution. To be concrete, subjectivity concerns the representation of a speaker's perspective being imprinted linguistically in discourse, and subjectivisation refers to the structure and strategies that languages use in the linguistic realization of subjectivity or the relevant processes of linguistic evolution. (Finegan, 1995: 1) Finegan has divided his studies into three main areas: a locutionary agent's perspective as shaping linguistic expression; a locutionary agent's expression of affect towards the propositions contained in utterances; and, a locutionary agent's expression of the modality or epistemic status of the propositions contained in utterances. (Finegan, 1995: 4) And, subjectivisation demonstrates distinctive linguistic features in each of these three.

As for the perspective, it refers to the fact that the speaker often has to choose due linguistic forms to represent an event from different angles. This choice indicates the perspective that is adopted the moment the utterance occurs, because "language is so organized that it permits each speaker to appropriate to himself an entire language by designating himself as 'I'. The personal pronouns provide the first step in this bringing out of subjectivity in language. Other classes of pronouns that share the same status depend in their turn upon these pronouns" (Benveniste, 1971: 226). Other classes, such as the indicators of deixis, demonstratives, adverbs, and adjectives, can organize the spatial and temporal relationships around this "I" when it is treated as the referent point. Therefore, "speaker perspective can be marked in verbs in lexical and constructional choices as well as in deictic choices. And also it can be marked in verbs through choices of transitivity, voice, or aspect" (Clark, 1990: 1201). All of these linguistic forms are defined through the instances of discourse in which they occur, depending upon the speaking "I" in discourse.

Affect traditionally deals with the means by which the speaker makes his evaluation on the things or events. It relates closely to the evaluative nature of language, for "languages are responsive to the fundamental need of the speaker to convey and assess feelings, moods, dispositions and attitudes. This need is as critical and as human as that of describing events. Interlocutors need to know not only what predication a speaker is making, but also the affective orientation the speaker is presenting with regard to that particular predication" (Ochs & Schieffelin, 1989: 9). Language users can typically express affect toward their articulated propositions, by which the speakers can not only overtly encode what they present as their own attitudes, but also can indirectly activate the evaluative position that the listeners make to supply their own assessments. These attitudinal evaluations reveal the speaker's feelings and values, which are related to the speaker's authority construed by the text, and operate rhetorically to construct relations of alignment and rapport between the writer and the actual or potential respondent. Martin & White (2005) put up the system of APPRAISAL which focuses on comprehensive analytical modes of affects, which regard judgment and appreciation as institutionalized affects.

When it comes to modality, Finegan stresses (1995: 5) that "it is perhaps the most thoroughly explored aspect of subjectivity, especially as expressed in verbs and, more recently, adverbs". In linguistics, modality is considered as the workable mechanism to express the speaker's evaluation, which refers to "aspects of meaning that cause sentences to be about the non-factual, or about the alternative possibilities for how things could be" (Fasold & Connor-Linton, 2006: 153). In the semantic-grammatical category, modality is construed as "the relativization of the validity of sentence meanings to a set of possible worlds" (Kiefer, 1994: 2515). In other words, modality allows language users to express what is, what would be, what may be, and what should be. According to Halliday's meta-functions in which language is said to fulfill, modality operates within the interpersonal function of the language with a wide range of variants of the expression in terms of the system of types of modality and the system of orientation in modality. (Halliday, 1994a: 354-358) Modality, as the expression of the interpersonal function of language, can be used as a linguistic tool to direct and control the behavior of the people. As discourse "represents values embedded in ideology, attitudes or power relation outside of the text" (Sulkunen & Törrönen, 1997: 45), modality plays a very important role for the speaker to express attitudes toward the proposition or proposals.

2.2.4 Discoursive Construction of Subjectivity as Subjective Stance

A social perspective on stance is adopted as the base for constructing the concept of the subjective stance. The subjective stance is the process of expressing the speakers' subjective views and displaying the speakers' subjective identities, feelings and attitudes (Scheibman, 2001: 61-62; Thompson & Hopper, 2001: 53), in the course of intersubjectively unfolding stance-taking in discourse (Haddington, 2004).

Different approaches are used to explore stance from different perspectives, and different labels are used, such as "evaluation", "evidentiality", "hedging", "appraisal", "positioning" "attitude" and "stance" (Biber, 2004, 2006; Gales, 2010; Davies & Harré, 1990; Martin & White, 2005; Ochs & Schieffelin, 1989). Pentti Haddington (2004) holds the discourse-functional view towards stance, and gives the definition that "stance is used to refer to the speakers' subjective attitudes toward something". According to Haddington, stance refers to a speaker's or writer's attitude, displays of emotions and desires, expressions of beliefs and certainty toward given issues, people, or the speakers' co-participants. Some linguistic markers will help to figure out the stance that the writer upholds, just as Biber & Finegan (1988:

11) claims that "by stance, we mean the lexical and grammatical expression of attitudes, feelings, judgments, or commitment concerning the propositional content of a message".

From the social perspective, stance is defined as a public act by a social actor, achieved dynamically by covert communicative means, of simultaneously evaluating objects, positioning subjects (self and others), and aligning with other subjects, with respect to any salient dimension of the socio-cultural field (Du Bois, 2007: 163). As a discourse is an interactively developing process with the aim to enact social actions, both communicating parties contribute with their positioning to the proposition and proposals expressed in discourse. Hence, the stance is constructed on the base of affect dispositions, interpersonal attitudes or strategic intentions, which can be studied subjectively from the speaker's perspective or intersubjectively by taking both of the speaker and the hearer into account. (Chindamo et al., 2012: 3)

From the speaker's perspective, the stance is constructed in the process of choosing due linguistic resources to have his opinion encoded with respect to the communicative intention. Choices of language resources are by nature conscious actions, which not only express the writer's subjective views but also display his subjective feelings and attitudes. (Kärkkäinen, 2003) As Haddington (2004) has pointed out, stance could be regarded as the individual linguistic act that is treated essentially as expressions of the writers' internal and subjective attitudes. For linguistic forms are conventionalized as language develops, they can be analyzed decontextually from their larger discourse environments as linguistic markers to map out the stance that the writer intends to convey (Wu, 2004: 3). This suggests that the subjective stance can be studied by treating some linguistic forms as the tokens that can be subjectivied to encode and regulate attitudes and beliefs.

2.2.5 A Working Definition of Subjectivity

As we extend our research not only on the way that the speaker expresses his attitudes and beliefs in lexico-grammatical resources, but also on the motivation upon which the speaker makes good use of linguistic resources to establish either a favorable or unfavorable bias throughout discourse to manipulate his readers' opinions, thus, the term of subjectivity is defined as follows:

> Subjectivity involves the text-showing signs of modal assessment that are

chosen to express the speaking subject's attitudes and feelings in the process of producing discourse with the aim to transmit the subjective stance so as to fulfill the interpersonal function.

This definition shows that the study of subjectivity is carried out in the realm of SFL. It involves aspects of subjectivity: (1) subjectivity is realized by linguistic realizations of modal assessment that cover all linguistic resources in the system of modality, the system of engagement, and the system of judgement; (2) subjectivity is constructed by the speaker's consciousness of choosing linguistic resources of modal assessment in the discoursive process; (3) subjectivity represents the intentionality of using language oriented to the communicative purpose. These aspects of subjectivity function simultaneously when the speaker presents judgment of probabilities or the obligation, linguistically categorized in Halliday's term (1994a: 89) as modalization to propositions and modulization to proposals respectively.

2.3 Research Objects

Subjectivity is realized by modal assessments, all of which are found to be used in editorials. Usually, the editorial writers, express their attitudes towards the events by using certain modal operators and modal adverbs. They use comment adjuncts to indicate the degree of evidentiality. Also, they employ some highly evaluative adverbs and adjectives to express their desirabilities or disappointments of affairs in editorials. Moreover, evaluative adjectives constructed as phrases are used to express the writer's attitudes and values. (Bonyadi, 2011: 6) Furthermore, some generic patterns are used as textual strategies to take advantages of opinions sourced to the third party to express the editorial writers' own attitudes (Bonyadi, 2011: 6; Halliday, 1994: 355;), for the generic patterns include "knowledge verbs" (Fowler, 1986), which are "associated with some (often indirect) expressions of how accountable a writer is for knowledge content" (Malmström, 2007: 36). In other words, editorials' opinions are presented through the angle of beliefs which "feature an evaluation... and are the result of a mental judgement" (van Dijk, 1995a: 2-3). Evaluations and judgements expressed in editorials result from the editorial writers' attitudes towards events.

As the definition of subjectivity indicates, subjectivity is realized by means of modal operators, modal adverbs, evaluative adjectives, adverb phrases, generic patterns and adverb groups, which are involved in the system of modality, the system of engagement, and the system of judgement. All these realizations are classified into five categories: modality, propositional comment, speech-functional comment, judging appraisal① and engaging opinion②. The present study is designed by treating them as research objects, which can be shown in Table 2. 1.

Table 2. 1 Linguistic Manifestations of Subjectivity

Linguistic Manifestations	Examples
Modal operators	can, will, must
Modal adverbs	probably, possibly, certainly
Modal adjuncts in adjective forms	required, supposed, keen
Comment adjuncts	naturally, hopefully, truly
Valuative adjectives	lawless, credible, sufficient
Generic patterns	It is obvious that... All authorities on the subject are agreed that... No sane person would pretend that... not... The conclusion can hardly be avoided that... Commonsense determines that...

2.4 The Theoretical Framework

From what we have discussed above, we can see that subjectivity is realized in linguistic forms of modal assessment in the process of producing discourse. SFL

① Categories of modal assessment correspond to categories of appraisal defined in the system of appraisal. (Eggins & Slade, 1997; Halliday & Matthiessen, 2004; Martin & Rose, 2003) Judgement revises feelings in the realm of proposals which then get formalized as rules and regulations administered by church and state. The realization of organizing judgement certainly reflects grammatical distinctions in the system of modalization. (Halliday, 1994) Therefore, evaluative adjectives and adverbs expressing judgement are included in the category of judging appraisal.

② Engagement is one system in appraisal, which refers to the resource for writer to engage with others in the process of expressing attitude (Martin & White, 2007; Martin & Rose, 2007). Generic patterns with knowledge verbs are the textual strategies which engage the opinions of the third party to account for the opinion that the writer intends to express. Therefore, the term engaging opinion is given.

regards discourse as a dynamic process of enacting social activity, in which the speaker realizes his subjective opinion while expressing attitudes and feelings. The realizing process reflects the speaker's conscious action of choosing lexico-grammatical resources to express his subjective stance, finally represented in intention-driven choices of proper linguistic subjectivisation.

Being argumentative and persuasive, editorials have chances to influence the thinking of the reader. In other words, editorials are written as argumentative texts mainly to influence the opinions of the audience. van Dijk (1995a: 1) emphasizes the role of editorials in the formation of public opinion in that they help to build the reader's thoughts about the events in the world. This function is fulfilled in the process of creating editorials, in which the editorial writer encodes his subjective stance in modal assessment in accordance with the intentionality of persuading readers to embrace his opinion with reasonable argumentation and effective persuasiveness.

In editorials, subjectivity is thought to be associated with the intentionality of forming argumentation and persuasiveness by means of linguistic forms of modal assessment. The editorial writer constructs argumentativity from four aspects: modal orientation, modal value, subjective judgement and subjective expectation, by which the writer can regulate the strength of argumentativity and negotiate with the reader. Also, the writer can construct persuasiveness in discourse from three aspects: expressing his assessment of modalized propositions and modulized proposals in terms of subjective modalization; delivering his emotive evaluation to activate the reader's conative reaction in terms of affective judgement; and, intensifying the persuasiveness by resorting to other opinions in terms of perspectivation. According to Finegan's(1995: 5) designation of encoding subjectivity in subjectivisation from three aspects, the theoretical framework in SFL is established in line with the principle of studying realizations of subjectivity by turning to the linguistic resources of the modal assessment. The system of modal assessment covers a wide range of interpersonal evaluations, ranging from a whole text (e.g. "I swear to tell the truth, the whole truth and nothing but the truth") to an element realized by a word (e.g. "detailed" in "an impressively detailed account") (Halliday & Matthiessen, 2004; Matthiessen, 2007). Accordingly, the system of modal assessment covers the linguistic resources involved in the system of modality, the system of engagement, and the system of judgement. Finegan (1995) develops his study of subjectivity from three areas: a locutionary agent's perspective in discourse realized in linguistic forms; a locutionary agent's expression of affect towards the propositions contained in utterances; and, a locutionary agent's expression of the modality or epistemic status of the propositions contained in utterances. In this study, these three areas correspond to the system of engagement, the system of affect and the system of modality, respectively. Judgement is regarded as the institutionalized affect, which deals with the speaker's judgement of propositions and proposals; that is, judgement concerns modalization and modulization from the ethic perspective. Thus, the system of judgement is chosen here to replace the system of affect according to the research purpose. Correspondingly, the linguistic resources are defined and diagrammed as shown in Figure 2.1.

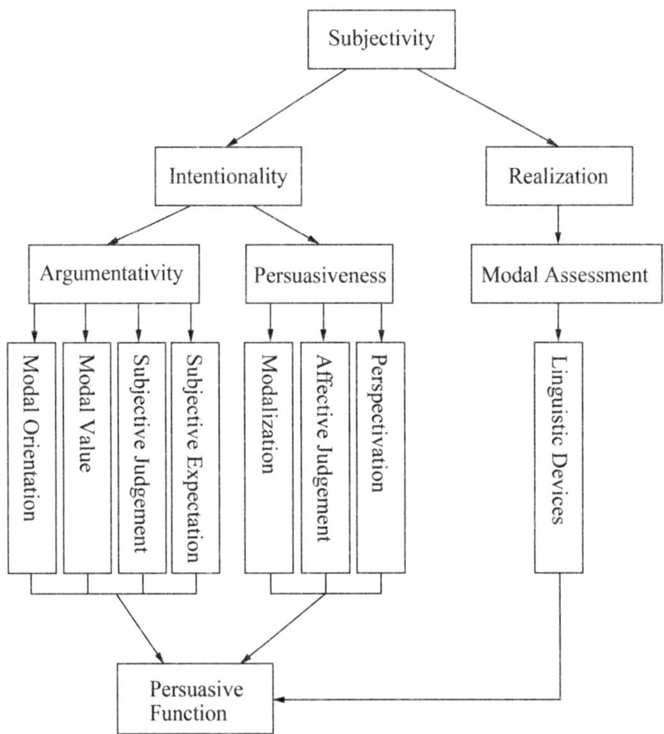

Figure 2.1 The Theoretical Framework for Studying Persuasive Function in Editorials

2.5 Summary

This chapter explains the process of building up the theoretical framework in detail within the realm of SFL. Subjectivity is expressed in modal assessment in the process of producing the discourse. As SFL holds that language is the metaphor of social actions, expressing subjectivity in language aims to do certain social action. This framework is therefore oriented to the subjective stance that is identical to the communicative intention, to some extent.

As this theoretical framework demonstrates, it carries out the study of expressions of subjectivity mainly from three areas, namely the system of modality, the system of engagement, and the system of judgement, setting the system of modality as the leading line of the network, and the other two systems as the ancillary lines. With the help of this framework, annotations done to the materials are implemented. In the following chapters, the corresponding analysis will be carried out step by step in line with these three areas.

Chapter 3
Methodology

This chapter talks about the key aspects of the methodology adopted in this study. It begins with a brief description of how the data of editorials is collected and how the corpus of editorials is compiled and processed. Then, it introduces the corpus tool—brat, which is a web-based tool that can be used to add notes to text documents. In this chapter, the focus is mainly on the annotation procedures illuminated with typical examples.

3.1 Corpus Description

A corpus is a collection of texts stored in an electronic database (Baker, Hardie & McEnery, 2006: 48). It is an area that enables the researcher to study language with a set of procedures, or methods. Corpus techniques are no more the preserve of a clearly delimited field of specialists, but rather tend to become a critical resource across linguistics as a whole and even beyond. As McEnery & Hardie (2012: xiv) state, "we might argue that the future of the field is in 'corpus methods in linguistics' rather than 'corpus linguistics' standing independently". The use of corpora will spawn explorations of linguistic phenomenon because tools are used to permit researchers to work efficiently and reliably. Up to date, using corpora has become the major trend of studies concerning machine-readable texts which are deemed as a basis to a set of research questions. It is self-evident to some extent that a corpus is properly planned and designed to meet research requirements and is used in a more systematic way. McEnery & Hardie (2012: 12) point out that "the importance of our findings from a corpus, quantitative or qualitative, depends on the general factor: the corpus data we select to explore a research question must be well matched to that research question".

As we aim to study how the writer expresses subjectivity in editorials, the research questions raise concerning their realizations and distributions with the aim to serve the persuasive function. The corpus is named as Sept. 11 Attack Editorials Corpus (hereinafter SAEC), including editorials out of *The New York Times* (hereinafter *NYT*), which is well known for its features of dependability and authenticity. Editorials concerning Sept. 11 Attack come from *NYT* whose official website is http://www.nytimes.com/. All the editorials in SAEC are adopted in their entirety. Their length, however, varies considerably due to the angles and aspects that the writer chooses.

The editorial is an article that presents the newspaper's opinion on an issue, and it is usually current, interesting, and has a purpose. The editorial writers sets up an argument and tries to persuade the readers to think in the same way as they do. Therefore, editorials are meant to influence public opinion, promote critical thinking, and even sometimes motivate people to take action on the issue. Generally speaking, an editorial is essentially an opinionated news story. It thus has developed its stylistic features. An editorial does not solely contain the writer's opinion, and it also represents the opinion of the entire staff which get the support from the objective reports and researches, so it is a mix of facts and opinions. The self-reference "I" is seldom used to make an argument in editorials, because it may diminish the strength and credibility of the newspaper and sounds informal. Various kinds of information coming from different sources will be used to sustain overtly or covertly the opinion explained here. A good editorial will surely contain point of enlightenment which can be described as an observation that is fresh and original. Information of this kind covers facts, quotations from relevant sources, or literary allusions. Usually, the opinion is stated out with accurate facts or quotations. In this way, the writers can express their attitudes and beliefs in the subjective or objective forms with strong supports.

The sampling is always purposeful. (Li & Wang, 2010: 48) It is also valid because texts are largely treated as artifacts in a small corpus. (Halliday & Matthiessen, 2004: 1) A carefully-designed sample corpus, constructed according to a specific sampling frame, reflects the language at a certain point in time (Biber, 1993; Leech, 2007; McEnery & Hardie, 2012). In this study, SAEC is the sample corpus consisting of texts opinionated about Sept. 11 Attack published within a given time span. Although all texts in SAEC are about Sept. 11 attack, they indeed hold different attitudes towards it, which may be reflected by the editorials' titles. (see Appendix I: Information about Data) SAEC includes 57,238 words which all together make up 87 editorials. Such a minor, specialized corpus is located at the second point in the the framework, whereby discourse semantic systems can be dealt with (Bednarek, 2010: 249). It is used to investigate the relationship between the functions of linguistic devices and formal phenomena by analyzing these features across a set of instances resulting from a corpus search and obtaining outcomes of this work from quantitative analysis regardless of correlation or regression (Arnold et al. 2000; Hollmann, 2005; Temperley, 2003).

3.2 Corpus Processing

The editorials in this study are complete texts which are collected together to make up the small corpus. All the texts are numbered from 1 to 87 and stored in one folder. The texts are converted from HTLM format to DOC format. In the meanwhile, the figures, tables and pictures in the original text are omitted. Each text only contains the title, the published date, and the editorial itself. After the proofreading, the texts are transformed from DOC format to TEXT format with the help of Microsoft Word 2010. All of the texts in the TEXT format are encoded in UTF-8.

All the texts are acquired in the machine-readable form downloaded from the *NYT* website. This eliminates the costs of capturing data but needs more time to parse, reformat and restructure the texts in line with the corpus conventions. Problems have arisen during the format transforming process, especially the forms of punctuation marks (e. g. quotation marks, commas and parentheses), numbers, special codes, and unnecessary spaces. Proofreading is necessary before creating the corpus, and it has been done in the following two steps: firstly, the preliminary work is done on the screen with the help of of Microsoft Word; secondly, the texts in SAEC are printed out and checked out carefully. Mark-up has been done in a separate EXCEL file to document.

3.3 Corpus Tool

3.3.1 Designation and Practical Usage of Brat

As most corpus-based researches must depend on corpus tools to deal with text annotation, search and statistics, a new corpus tool "brat" is introduced in this study. Brat is a web-based tool for text annotation. It is used to add notes to existing text documents created entirely on standard web technologies, with no need to install local software or browser plug-in to use it. Brat is a user-friendly web-based annotation tool that aims to enhance annotator productivity by using NLP techniques (Stenetorp et al., 2012), which is free under the open-source MIT license from its homepage at http://brat.nlplab.org.

Brat has been designed and implemented on the basis of early well-produced annotation tools and approaches, such as the search capabilities of the XConc tool (Kim, Ohta & Tsujii, 2008), the web-based system MyMiner (Salgado et al., 2010), and GATE Teamware (Cunningham et al., 2011), and the fast annotation mode of Knowtator (Ogren, 2006). Since it was created, brat has been used to create more than 50,000 annotations by academic institutions, covering the domains of genemutation-phenotype relation, cancer biology, verb frame annotation and so on (Stenetorp et al., 2012). And it proves workable when used to make semantic role labeling (Gildea & Jurafsky, 2002; Carreras & Marquez, 2005), chunking (Abney, 1991), dependency annotation (Nivre, 2003) and BioNLP Shared Task 2011 (Pyysalo et al., 2012).

3.3.2 Features of Brat

Brat displays its distinctive features from four aspects, which helps maintain the quality of annotations and makes annotation accessible to non-professional users.

First of all, brat has comprehensive annotation visualization, based on the concept of "what you see is what you get". All aspects of the underlying annotation are visually represented in an intuitive way. Brat is designed on the basis of STAV text annotation visualiser (Stenetorp et al., 2011), which enables users to make an understanding of complex annotations, including dense, non-projective sets of connections between annotations, and partially overlapping text annotations. Brat has gotten graphics-based visualization function by adopting PNG image format that can be used in publications as shown in Figure 3.1.

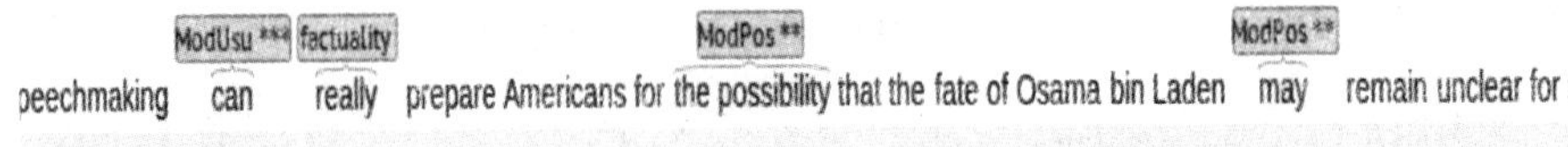

Figure 3.1 Visualization Examples: Modal Verbs and Modal Adjuncts

Brat has not merely been used to create annotations, but it has also been used to visualize annotations output for manual analysis and evaluation purposes.

Secondly, brat provides users with the intuitive annotation interface. Its capabilities are extended in contrast with STAV, by implementing annotation editing that is done by adding functionality for identifying intuitive interface gestures which are familiar to text editors. Brat is also browser-based and is designed systematically by taking standard web technologies into accounts, so it is unnecessary to install any additional annotation software or use browser plug-ins. Moreover, brat can help identify annotations made by Uniform Resource Identifiers (URIs) that is always used to link individual annotations in e-mails, documents and on web pages.

Thirdly, brat has a set of annotation primitives that can be defined in annotation configuration. Brat annotation configurations are controlled by text-based configuration files and stored as "annotation. conf" that can be created and edited in any text editor. The files use a simple line-oriented structure and a syntax similar to many other text-based configuration systems, of which the top-level is organized into sections marked as [section-name]. Configuration file includes four sections, namely [entities], [relations], [events] and [attributes], concerning different categories of annotation: text-span markings, n-ary associations, equivalence classes, binary relations and attributes respectively, which can be applied in any combinations to do specific annotation tasks (Stenetorp et al., 2012). Each section needs to be presented in the configuration file, though they are allowed to be empty. Within sections, each non-empty line demarcates one configuration item, with the first non-space sequence naming the item and the rest prescribing the specific content. Blank lines and lines beginning with the hash character "#" are ignored as comments. Figure 3.2 displays the visualization of this entity annotation targets.

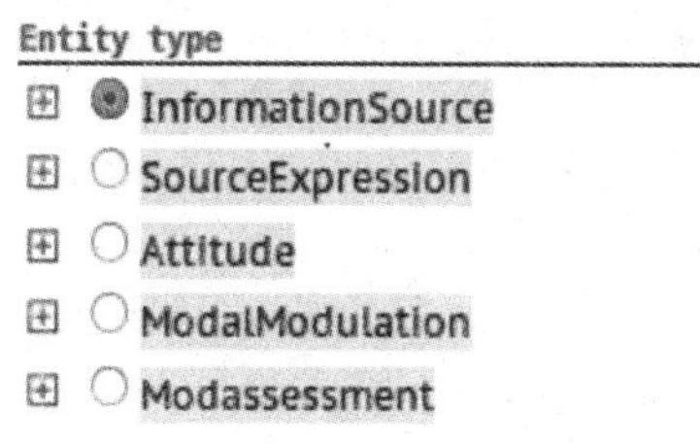

Figure 3.2 Visualization of Entity Annotation Targets

Fourthly, brat can implement searching and concordance functions because it has a concordancing tool that can be activated by pressing "Ctrl + F". Sophisticated as it seems, it does not provide counts of concordance lines and very often breaks down due to minor errors in texts. To settle these problems, we have designed a tool: brat-aid, a concordance tool for this brat-annotated corpus. Brat-aid is helpful to do text processing and make concordance statistics. Text processing is to prepare at first text files on Windows for Linux. The searching result will then be gotten, and Figure 3.3 shows the result of searching the entity "ModPos".

aardio form

Text Processing | Search

Text | Entity | Attribute | Value | Relation | Event

data loaded | Search | save

ID	LeftPart	Entity	RightPart
1	esday morning, before it began to become clear who	might	be missing, who might be presumed dead and who, i
2	it began to become clear who might be missing, who	might	be presumed dead and who, in the case of the pass
3	e passengers and crew on the four hijacked planes,	must	certainly have died. The streets around the hospi
4	sengers and crew on the four hijacked planes, must	certainly	have died. The streets around the hospitals near
5	s spread, so did the obituaries, which are now, as	certainty	sets in, beginning to radiate outward from the ep
6	rning. Some had been through the 1993 bombing and	probably	thought about it every day. Some had never gotten
7	twin towers, and some no longer saw it at all. You	could	have found people living in nearly every neighbor
8	how interchangeable these Tuesday morning stories	might	have been if the timing of the attacks and the ul

Figure 3.3 The Result of Searching the Entity "ModPos"

The result is provided with counts, concordance lines, and text-file names, which are not supplied by the built-in brat searching tool. When it comes to "Relation" search, the result highlights different entities with different colors. All the results can be stored as html files by clicking the save button for future reference. See Figure 3.4.

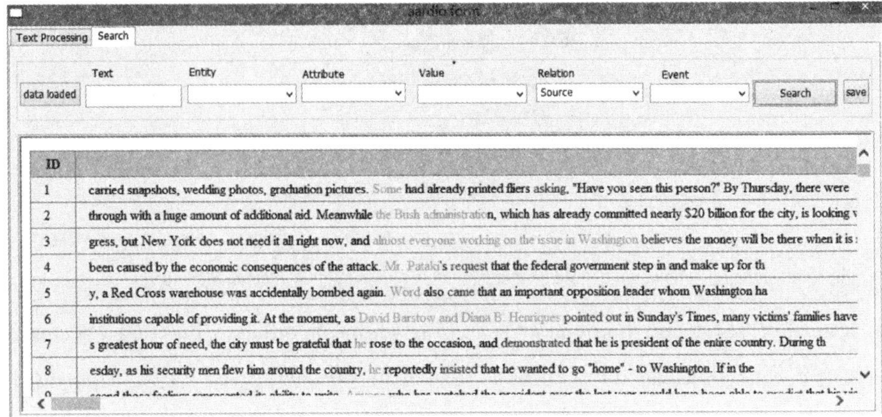

Figure 3.4 The Result of Searching Relation "Source"

3.3.3 Brat Used in Our Research

Theoretically, brat can be adopted as the evaluation and training of state-of-the-art tools for most natural language processing tasks. It has been successfully applied to the English and Dutch financial newswire corpus to do explicit sentiment annotations (Stenetorp et al., 2012), and has further been developed to detect explicit as well as implicit expressions of sentiment at a sub-sentential level under the guidance of polar sentiment annotation scheme (Kauter el at., 2015). With this scheme, brat can be used to annotate explicit and implicit linguistic forms expressing sentiment in natural textual data, thus making the created corpora a useful resource for the sentiment study.

This research is a case study that takes the discourse components of editorials into account. As we all know, an editorial is a short piece of writing that expresses the newspaper's position on an issue that it deems important. (Le, 2010: 39) Discourse studies of editorials include different cases of language use, transmission of beliefs, and social interaction. The study of editorials suggests how ideas cascade downward from the government's first public expression on an issue. Activation of thoughts and feelings in the mind of journalists and leaders almost immediately stir up conversations that spread ideas between participants. (Entman, 2004: 9) These thoughts and feelings exactly indicate subjectivity at the semantic level, which is realized explicitly or implicitly in editorials. The linguistic phenomena chosen rely on the specific research goals. In last chapter, the theoretical framework is created, which is used here as the annotation scheme for identifying the key components and properties of opinions and emotions in editorials. According to this framework, three types of modal assessment realizing subjectivity are annotated in the context at the word and phrase levels, which involve explicit or implicit mentions of modality, and positions engaged in or brought in discourse to contract or expand subjectivity and judgment expressing subjectivity.

The high-level goal of this research is to investigate the use of linguistic devices to express subjectivity through a corpus annotation study. A focus of this study is to recognize subjectivity expressed in editorials, which is realized in different linguistic forms in accordance with the context. Correspondingly, a range of words and constituents are marked, such as adjectives, modal verbs, adverbs and nouns.

To our knowledge, no annotation scheme exists for the fine-grained annotation of explicit as well as implicit expressions of sentiment below sentence level (Kauter et al., 2015). Our study of subjectivity is carried out in the realm of SFL (Halliday, 1994a) and under the appraisal systemic framework (Martin & White, 2005). The linguistic resources are concerned with construing interpersonal meanings in the course of producing editorials, which function to construe the sentiment in the context. Therefore, the theoretical framework studying subjectivity is put forth as the annotation scheme, by referring to Wiebe et al. (2005), Stenetorp et al. (2012), Kauter et al. (2015).

McEnery & Hardie (2012: 14) note that corpus annotation is a commonplace of linguistics; i. e. the most important thing in corpus study is to annotate the data to match the research questions. Corpus annotation is largely the process of providing the well-annotated materials with a systematic and accessible form, which is necessary to reach the research goal. Each annotation project will typically define its own configuration files as "annotation. conf" stored in the brat data directory. Each of these sections concerning [entities], [relations], [events] and [attributes] has been redefined with the detailed information presented in the configuration file in Appendix Ⅲ. Besides listing the entity types, the [entities] section is of a hierarchical nature by revealing the optional realization of entity organization, which is manifested in the process of realizing [ModalModulation] as modulation and modulization items shown in Figure 3.5.

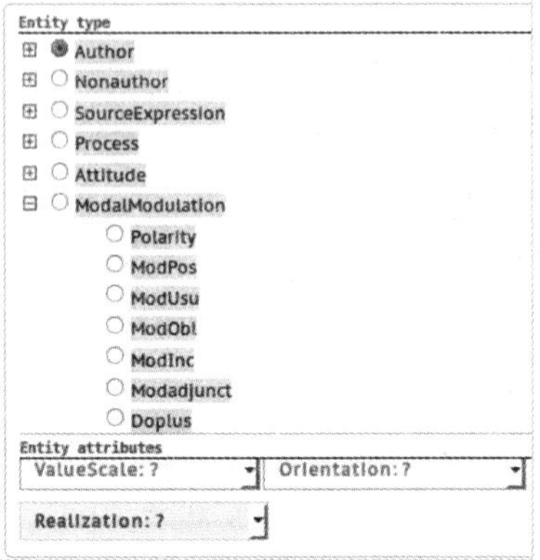

Figure 3.5 Hierarchical Realization of Entities

3.4 Annotation Implementation

The main goal of our annotation is to detect and analyze modal assessment of subjectivity, which is annotated and assessed at the expression level. Realizations of subjectivity pertain to modality, speech-functional comment, propositional comment, judging appraisal and engaging opinion.

3.4.1 Annotation of Modality

Expressions of modality contain those of modalization and modulization, which can be identified at different levels. This means that a modality expression can be realized in different forms in a concrete context. When annotations are made to modality expressions, several related variables are involved, because the system of MODALITY involves the sub-systems such as the type of modality, the orientation of modality, the value of modality and the polarity of modality. As designed in this annotation files, all these variables are divided into [entities] and [attributes] that are not treated as two strictly distinct categories of expressions but rather as two overlapping features by using [attributes] to describe [entities]. Similarly, the same annotation procedure can also be used to make annotations to the other two types of subjective expressions. This makes the annotating work more consistent and easier.

If all variables are considered, there are technically 144 categories of modality.

However, as one category of modality may contain many realizing variants, tens of thousands of modality expressions are actually adopted in the concrete context. That is to say, it is impossible to have some defined rules about the boundary detection of modal expressions when they are isolated from the context. Thus, some typical ones are identified by judging from their contexts. As the annotated examples shown in Figures 3.6, 3.7, 3.8 and 3.9, modality expressions can take different forms: they can be modal adjuncts (Figure 3.6), modal verbs (Figure 3.7), verbal constructions (Figure 3.8), and nominalization forms (Figure 3.9).

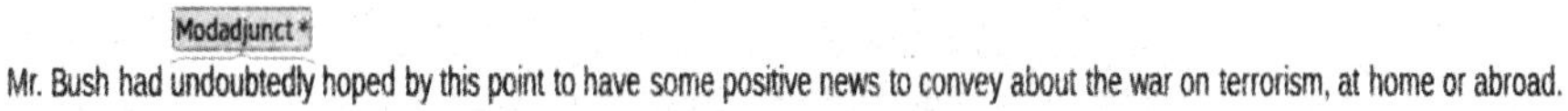

Figure 3.6 Realization of Modality in Modal Adjunct

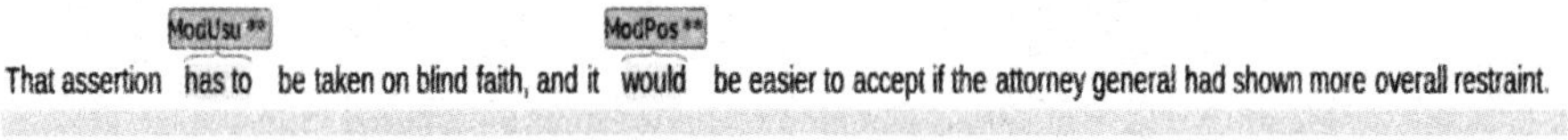

Figure 3.7 Realization of Modality in Modal Verb

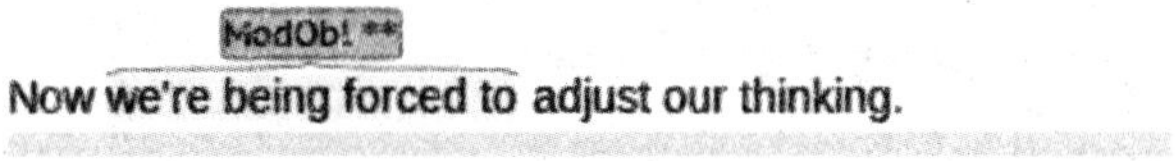

Figure 3.8 Realization of Modality in Verbal Construction

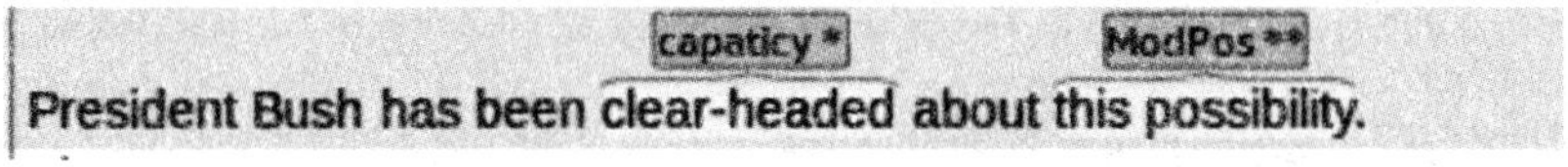

Figure 3.9 Realization of Modality in Nominalization

As shown in Figures 3.6, 3.7, 3.8 and 3.9, different realizations of modality are encoded in the configuration files as [entities], whose linguistic representations are annotated in attractively green chunks as "Modadjunct", "ModUsu" and "ModObli" respectively. The other features of modality, such as orientation, polarity and value are regarded as [attributes] in the configuration files. In this study, [attributes] is marked by adding the asterisk signs, like "Modadjunct*" in Figure 3.10.

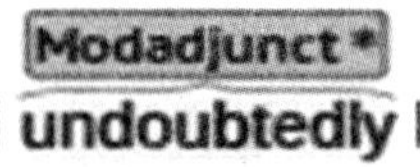

Figure 3.10 An Example for Annotating [attributes] with Asterisk Signs

As soon as the mouse is put on the asterisk signs in the brat environment, the information behind the asterisk signs will appear automatically, as shown in Figure 3.11.

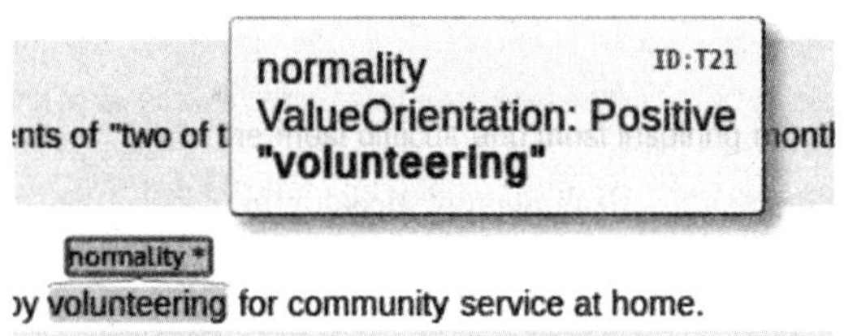

Figure 3.11 The Representation of Information by Asterisk Signs

Hence, variables of modality can be marked independently or with other features. Usually, the variable of orientation co-occurs with polarity and/or value. Figure 3.12 is a typical example to show this.

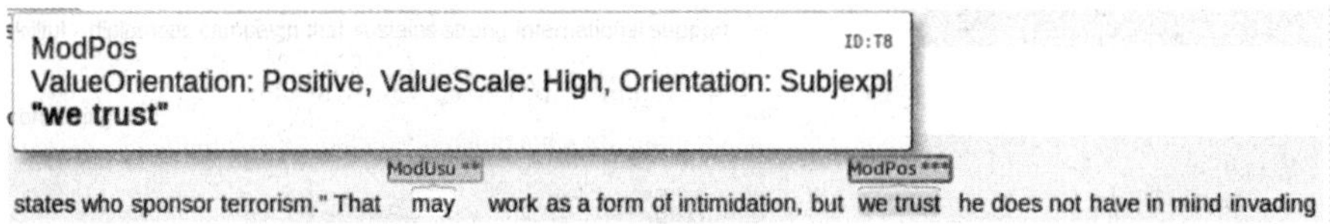

Figure 3.12 Combination of Subjective Explicit Orientation with Orientation and Value

Figure 3.12 explains the case of taking the subjective explicit orientation, with "Orientation" clearly marked as "Subjexpl" here. Moreover, the two asterisks obviously indicate that it is the very example of combining two variables which appear respectively as "Orientation: Subjexpl" and "ValueScale: High". As this example can make it clear that different variables can combine, it's unnecessary to do more explanations to other similar cases.

3.4.2 Annotation of Judgement

The judgement expressions are also regarded as ways of realizing subjectivity.

The five branches are normality, capacity, tenacity, veracity and propriety.

In this study, the system of judgement is encoded as "entities", which is correspondingly demonstrated as the hierarchically visible interface as shown in Figure 3.13.

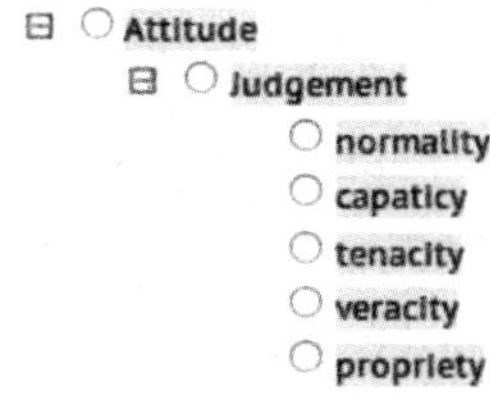

Figure 3.13 Annotating Interface of the System of Judgement

Moreover, the system of judgement involves positive or negative orientation, which is encoded as "attributes" and marked by the asterisk (Figure 3.14).

Figure 3.14 Annotation of Judgement Expression

Then, the patterns of annotating judgement expressions are paradigmatically given in Figure 3.15. It deals with the case of judging the "capacity", which is marked in the green chunk with implying information complemented in one pop-up window as "ValueOrientation: Positive". Similarly, other branches in the system of judgement can be annotated in the same way with positive or negative feature marked by the asterisk.

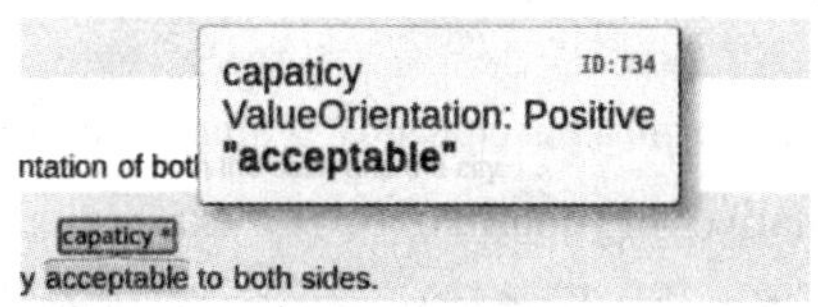

Figure 3.15 Annotation of "Capacity" Judgement in Negative Value

3.4.3 Annotation of Engagement

As we can see from Sections 3.4.1 and 3.4.2, the procedures of annotating the modality expressions and the judgement expressions are mainly relevant to two features, namely [entities] and [attributes]. However, to annotate the system of engagement is to reveal what acts as the source and how it is intruded into the discourse. Besides the information source that is encoded as [entities] in the configuration file, a new annotation parameter [relations] is designed.

Annotation editing is mouse-based and user-friendly. To mark a span of text is to select it with the mouse by dragging or by double-clicking on the targeted word. The feature named "relations" is figured by adding a relation between two annotations, clicking with the mouse on one annotation and then drag a connection to the other in the arc line with the arrow head, as shown in Figure 3.16.

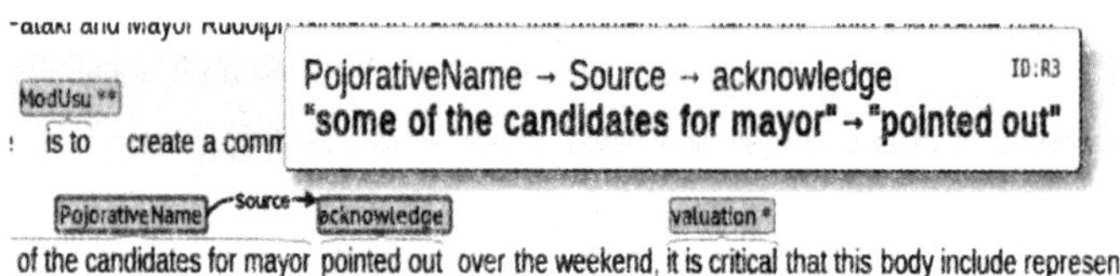

Figure 3.16 Annotation of [relations] by the Arc Line

As shown in Figure 3.16, the feature of [relations] is labeled as "Source" occurring almost in the middle part of the arc. [relations] is used as effective strategies to highlight the position, by which the writer either expands the range to strengthen the propositions by leading in external positions, or contracts the argumentation so as to highlight some certain point by disclaiming or proclaiming alternative positions.

3.5 Summary

Methodologically, the corpus-based study typically uses data and findings from a corpus, whether quantitative or qualitative, to explore a hypothesis in order to validate it, refute it or refine it. That is to say, it is reasonable to have the corpus data match to the research question and to serve a specific type of result in line with the scientific method under certain theoretical framework.

In this chapter, data collection and analytical procedure are described to explain the fundamentals and background of the analysis. The detailed description is made as to the corpus construction, the annotation software brat and the annotation procedure, based on the theoretical framework built up. The corpus of this study is collected as a purposive sampling, which aims to investigate the data of editorials concerning the event of Terrorism Attack Sept. 11 published in *NYT*. Brat, capable of absorbing advanced IT techniques of NLP and user-friendly for operating easily, is adopted to annotate the explicit and implicit forms of subjectivity-realizing. The annotation procedure is explained with configuration files supplied and illuminated with typical instances.

Chapter 4
Realizations and Characteristics of Subjectivity

This study of subjectivity is conducted in the realm of SFL, involving the system of modality, the system of engagement, and the system of judgement. Realizations of subjectivity are classified in the category of modal assessment, which covers five subcategories: modality, propositional comments, speech-functional comments, judging appraisals and engaging opinions. Correspondingly, the research objects in this study include modal operators, modal adverbs, evaluative adjectives, adverb phrases, generic patterns and adverb groups. When subjectivity is realized by these linguistic resources, there appear different distributing patterns with respect to these five subcategories, which are characteristic of conscious choices in accordance with the persuasive function of editorials.

Distributing patterns represent the dynamic process of realizing subjectivity in editorials and reflect its property of intentionality of serving the persuasive function. Distributing patterns are created on the basis of statistic analysis of data collected by the concordance tool, brat and brat-aid, in line with these five defined subcategories.

4.1 Realizations of Subjectivity in Terms of Modality

According to Halliday (1994a) and Halliday & Matthiessen (2004), the system of modality consists of three subcategories: modality, speech-functional comments and propositional comments. This section just deals with the subcategory of modality, which is studied with respect to the variables of type, orientation and value.

4.1.1 Statistics of Realizations in Modality

The variants of orientation determine distinctively how each type of modality is realized in the system network of modality (Halliday, 2004:619), and variants of type and orientation are usually put together. Table 4.1 summarizes the distribution patterns in the combination of types and orientations of modality used in SAEC. Correspondingly, the proportion of each pattern is displayed with percentage in the table.

Table 4.1 Distribution Patterns of Realizations in Terms of Type and Orientation

Orientation / Type	Subjective: explicit		Subjective: implicit		Objective: implicit		Objective: explicit		Total	
	Num.	Ratio	Num.	Ratio	Num.	Ratio	Num.	Ratio	Num.	Ratio
Possibility	28	1.72%	410	25.22%	136	8.36%	20	1.23%	594	36.53%
Usuality	0	0	315	19.37%	90	5.54%	0	0	405	24.91%
Obligation	6	0.37%	334	20.54%	79	4.86%	2	0.12%	421	25.89%
Inclination	8	0.49%	136	8.36%	62	3.81%	0	0	206	12.67%
Total	42	2.58%	1195	73.49%	367	22.57%	22	1.35%	1626	(100%)

As is shown in Table 4.1, the horizontal columns show different distribution patterns of realizations in accordance with orientation matching to each type of modality, with the totality given in the right tandem. Taking the type of possibility for instance, 594 (36.53%) cases are used in SAEC, among which 28 (1.72%) cases occur in the subjective-explicit orientation, 410 (25.22%) in the subjective-implicit orientation, 136 (8.36%) in the objective-implicit orientation and 20 (1.23%) in the objective-explicit orientation, respectively. The vertical lines show various distribution patterns in terms of the type matching to one variant of orientation. Taking the feature of subjective-explicit orientation for instance, 42 (2.58%) cases are adopted in SAEC, including 28 (1.72%) cases of possibility, none of usuality, 6 (0.37%) cases of obligation and 8 (0.49%) cases of inclination.

Orientation and type, two variables of modality, can be used as two angles from which we can do the research about distribution patterns of realizations of subjectivity in modality. From the angle of the variant of orientation, the study mainly focuses on the way that the speaker chooses proper linguistic resources of modal assessment to express subjectivity, no matter whether it is metaphorical or congruent. From the perspective of the variant of type, the study deals with the nature of the commodity being exchanged. As the exchanged commodity is divided into propositions and proposals, the study can be carried out along with modalization and modulization, with the former referring to the degree of possibility or usuality relevant to a proposition and the latter referring to the degree of obligation or inclination of a proposal. With these two perspectives combined, a bird's-eye-view of distribution patterns of realizations in modality is formed.

Distribution patterns of realizations of subjectivity in terms of value are presented in Table 4. 2. The horizontal column and the vertical column represent different angles to account for different realizations of subjectivity in terms of value variables. Thus, the study can be carried out pertaining to distribution patterns of each of the three values matching to types of modality along the horizontal column or each type of modality along the vertical column. Correspondingly, the percentage of every distribution pattern of realizations with respect to each value variable is calculated. Thus, three types of percentage-reflecting numbers come into being.

Polarity isn't regarded as the variable of modality, but it has a close relationship with the value variable. It suggests the speaker's judgement when the validity of a proposition "is/isn't", or "do/don't" performs the actualization of a proposal. (Halliday, 1994a: 88-89; Halliday & Matthiessen, 2004: 75) The value transference happens to negative polarity, which often leads to the identical change between the high value and the low value. In a sense, polarity plays a very important role in construing the realization of subjectivity, and will be further discussed in the following chapters when it is necessary.

Table 4.2 Distribution Patterns of Realizations in Terms of Value① in the System of Modality

Type (T) / Value (V)	ModPos			ModUsu			ModObl			ModInc			Total	
	Num.	V/T (%)	V/G (%)	Num.	V/T (%)	V/G (%)	Num.	V/T (%)	V/G (%)	Num.	V/T (%)	V/G (%)	Num. (T)	T/G (%)
High	77	21.71	4.75	39	10.86	2.38	221	62	13.57	19	5.43	1.19	356	21.89
Medium	282	35.75	17.26	236	29.92	14.45	166	21.37	10.32	101	12.95	6.25	785	48.28
Low	226	46.54	13.88	139	28.72	8.57	40	8.18	2.44	80	16.56	4.94	485	29.83

Note: Num. = Number.

① V/T, V/G, T/G are also put in brackets, as is shown in Table 4.2, representing the formula that work out the percentages of the usage of modal expressions consistent with the value variable in this study. The capitalized "V" refers to the numbers of the uses of modality expressions with respect to three values, thus including 12 numbers. "T" is the totality of adding up the numbers of the same value-variable case occurring in four types of modality, here represented by the numbers "356, 785 and 485" specifically. And, "G" indicates clearly the only general number "1626" here.

4.1.2 Realization Features of Subjectivity with Respect to Type and Orientation

Table 4. 1 summarizes different distribution patterns of realizations in SAEC with respect to type and orientation. The research will go along with orientation in order to describe what distribution patterns are adopted in line with these four types of modality, and then move on to distribution patterns in terms of value.

Generally speaking, distribution patterns of realizations in modality with respect to four types of modality are strikingly uneven, as is shown in Figure 4. 1. The pattern of the subjective-implicit orientation occurs most frequently no matter whether it is considered from the perspective of orientation or type of modality. This pattern appears 1195 times, rating as 73.49% (1195/1626) to the totality of realization in the system of modality. Among this subjective-implicit pattern, the type of possibility occurs 410 times, ranking the highest ratio as 25. 22% (410/1626), followed secondly by the type of obligation as 334 (20. 54%), thirdly by the type of usuality as 315 (19. 37%), and by the least frequency of the type of inclination as 136 (8.36 %), as is shown in Figure 4. 1.

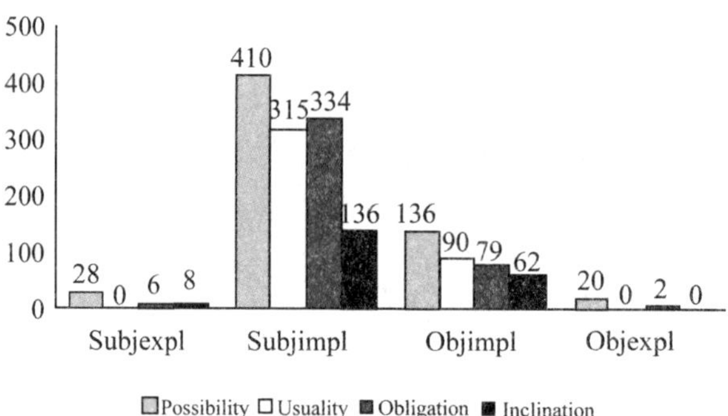

Figure 4. 1 Distribution Patterns of Realizations with Respect to Type and Orientation

As is shown in Figure 4. 1, the subjective-implicit pattern occurs the most frequently among the four patterns, which is realized particularly in congruent forms. According to Halliday (1994a), Halliday & Matthiessen (2004) and Matthiessen, Teruya & Lam (2010), the modal operators are the congruent forms to realize subjectivity in the subjective-implicit orientation. They include five subcategories: marginal modals, semi-auxiliaries, modal idioms, central modals and catenatives

(Quirk, 1985). For example:

(1) You **could** have found people living in nearly every neighborhood in New York and much of northern New Jersey, people who had grown up or gone to school in nearly every state in this country. (Text 6)

Besides the modal operator that is drawn on to express subjectivity in the implicitly subjective orientation, the verbal form that is cognate to the modal operators is often utilized to fulfill the same function. There are cases that the modal operator together with the cognate verbal form delivers the speaker's subjectivity. For example:

(2) A more reliable way of persuading the old businesses to return **would be to** deploy the traditional array of economic devices—tax credits, loan guarantees and the like—that states and cities use to lure businesses. (Text 13)

(3) John Whitehead, the corporation chairman, **is going to** have to figure out how to give these many views their rightful due, while still coming up with an inspiring and unified proposal for the area. (Text 38)

The implicitly objective pattern is second to the subjective-implicit pattern, which is used 367 times, taking up merely 22.57% (367/1626). Within this pattern, the type of possibility occurs 136 times (8.36%), and 90 cases (5.54%) occurring in the type of usuality, 79 cases (4.86%) in the type of obligation and 62 cases (3.81%) in the type of inclination. The linguistic forms that realize this pattern are various, ranging from the lexical to the phrasal rank, mainly using the congruent forms as modal adverbs and verbal phrases, just as Halliday (1994a) and Halliday & Matthiessen (2004) state. For example:

(4) As a pivotal front-line organization in the war against terrorism, the agency **is supposed to** detect and prevent new terror attacks, help locate and perhaps even kill Osama bin Laden and let President Bush know if the anthrax in the mail comes from Iraq—to mention only a few of Washington's expectations. (Text 15)

However, the linguistic forms that are derived metaphorically from or relate closely to the modal adverbs are also included. Therefore, some nouns, adjectives and even verbs indicating the speaker's subjectivity are regarded as linguistic realizations of modal assessment. For example:

(5) The United States will have to engage in some delicate diplomacy to keep these groups from collapsing into the kind of chaotic warfare that has engulfed Afghanistan in the past. **The need** to crush the Taliban and Al Qaeda is clear. (Text 33)

As Table 4. 1 indicates, the subjective-implicit pattern (73. 49%) and the objective-implicit pattern (22. 57%) have taken up predominantly the largest part of realizations in modality with the proportion of 96. 06%. However, this doesn't mean that the other two patterns are not important because they also play very critical roles in their own ways. Although the subjective-explicit pattern appears only 42 times and occupies the least proportion (2. 58%), they reveal the subjective stance that the speaker upholds clearly and explicitly. However, there is no case of usuality occurring in the subjective-explicit orientation in this corpus, for "there are no systematic forms for making the subjective orientation explicit in the case of usuality or inclination in that no coded expression stands for 'I recognize it as usual that...' or 'I undertake for... to...'" (Halliday, 1994: 357-358). As for the other two cases in this pattern, the type of possibility occurs 28 times (1. 72%), which is more than two and half times than that of obligation which appears only 6 times (0. 37%). All of them have the plural pronoun "we" acting as grammatical subjects or its cognate form "us" or "our" as logical subjects. In the former case, they exist in the clauses, with the plural pronoun "we" as the subject, and mental verbs or word groups or even phrases acting as the main predicates that are sometimes modified by auxiliary verbs alone or even along with other modal adjuncts. For example:

(6) Inevitably, **we imagine** those people surrounded by choices that might or might not have saved their lives, choices they did not make or perhaps did not even notice. (Text 69)

(7) But for now **we have a remarkably precious opportunity** to witness a portrait of this nation assembled out of memories and pictures, out of the efforts of everyday people to explain in everyday words who it is they lost on Tuesday. (Text 6)

(8) But there are many other things **we still cannot be sure of. We do not know** whether the president has the ability to trim his early impulse toward unilateral thinking and conservative ideology in ways that will allow him to maintain an international alliance against terrorism. (Text 30)

In Example (9), the pronoun "us" acts as the logical subject whereas the pronoun "it" as the formal subject. In Examples (10) and (11) the adjective pronoun "our" is used as the logical subject to encode the subjective orientation explicit in the phrasal forms.

(9) **It was instinctive in us** to choose from among the dead that day the ones whose behavior we would emulate if we could. (Text 69)

(10) **In our minds** he will always be standing at ground zero, his back to the towering shards and smoke from the World Trade Center. (Text 32)

(11) When our homes, schools or neighborhoods are exposed to elements like asbestos, we want the air cleaned until every single particle is gone. The only acceptable risks, **to our modern way of thinking**, were the ones we deliberately courted ourselves. (Text 81)

The pattern of the objective-explicit orientation, as is seen in Table 4.1, is of the least frequency (22 cases, 1.35%). None of this pattern appears in the case of usuality and inclination well. 20 cases (1.23%) of this pattern occur in the type of possibility and merely 2 (0.12%) cases in the type of obligation. Generally speaking, most realizations of this pattern exist in the projecting clause, e.g. "it is *adj.* ...", as Halliday (1994a: 358) indicates. For example:

(12) When it comes to sheer memorability, **it would be impossible** to top the public performances in drag, when he appeared as a blond bombshell, an Italian grandma or, most recently, a leggy Rockette. (Text 32)

(13) ... but New York does not need it all right now, and almost everyone working on the issue in Washington believes the money will be there when **it is required**—either from the original appropriation or through the Federal Emergency Management Agency. (Text 85)

Besides such familiar clausal expressions, the grammatical construction of "there be" structure is also thought of as another way to encode subjectivity when it conveys modal assessment followed by the indefinite projected clauses. It is regarded as the variant of, in certain contexts, the projecting clause "it is *adj.* ...". For example:

(14) That disbelief was telling us something from the very beginning. **There was no reason** to expect that a civilian nation, going about its Tuesday, should be able to take in the magnitude of what had just happened. (Text 69)

4.1.3 Realization Features of Subjectivity with Respect to Value

Halliday (1994: 358) observes that besides the variants of orientation and type in the system of modality, the variant of value is the third variable of modality. It is necessary to clarify the value variable from two aspects: distribution patterns in each type of modality; and the forms labeling different values as high, medium or low. Obviously, Table 4.2 outlines distribution patterns of realizations of subjectivity in terms of the value variable in each type of modality, shown in Figure 4.2.

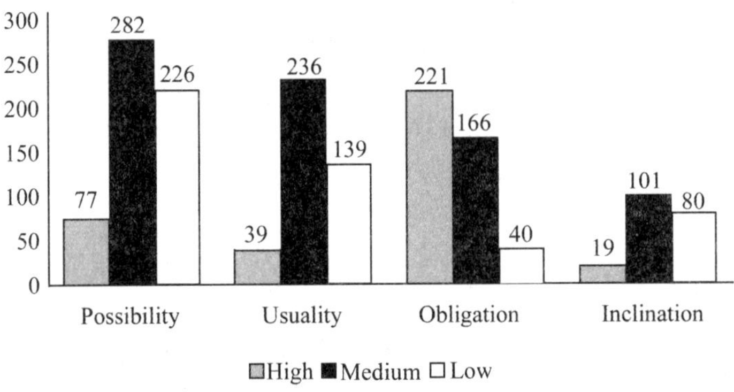

Figure 4.2 Distribution Patterns of Realizations in Terms of Value

Generally speaking, realizations of subjectivity in the medium value occur 785 times (48.28%), more than those in high and low value which are 356 times (21.89%) and 485 times (29.83%) respectively. This general trend is identical to those of types of possibility, usuality and inclination, whose frequencies in medium value are predominantly higher than those in high and low value. Moreover, like the general trend, realizations of subjectivity in high value of types of possibility, usuality and inclination are of the lowest frequency. However, when it comes to the type of obligation, things become quite different, because its frequency in high value (221 times) is the highest, and the second is the medium value (166 times), and the lowest is the low value (40 times).

As for the forms labeling values of realizations in modality, the medium value is set apart from the other two "outer" values by the system of polarity. That is, the negative can be freely transfered between the proposition and the modality in the medium; however, for the "outer" values, they switch either from high to low, or from low to high if the negative is transferred (Halliday & Matthiessen, 2004: 620-625). Then, the forms labeling values include mainly two variants in this study: values expressed by the different modal operators, namely high, median and low; the non-modal-operator forms, such as category labels indicating high, median or low value. Moreover, every variant involves positive and negative properties of the polarity. When the negative feature needs to be expressed, it can be realized by means of either transferred negative or direct negative. Theoretically, this generates a set of 144 basic categories of modality; however, the actual number of systematic distinctions runs well into tens of thousands. (Halliday, 1994: 359; Halliday & Matthiessen, 2004: 621)

Then, to convey one value is to choose proper forms in accordance with the contextual factors. For example:

(15) This work **cannot** all be on American shoulders. Afghanistan must be a multilateral project, as the January conference in Tokyo on rebuilding made clear. Yet the United States **must** lead the way. (Text 46)

Here, the modal operators "cannot" and "must" are both labeled as high value. The former gets the high value due to the negative transference from its cognate form "can" that is labeled as low value. In Examples (16) and (17), the modal assessments are labeled as medium and low respectively.

(16) Some had been through the 1993 bombing and **probably** thought about it every day. Some had never gotten over the view from the twin towers, and some no longer saw it at all. (Text 10)

(17) About a dozen or so test cases **are expected to** be filed in a week or so. (Text 53)

In Example (16), the modal adverb "probably" is used in medium value. The verb phrase "are expected to" in Example (17) is adopted to express the modality like "be wanted to" (Halliday & Matthiessen, 2004: 618), which belongs to the inclination type and is used in low value.

4.2 Realizations of Subjectivity in Terms of Propositional Comments

Propositional comments are annotated in this study by referring to the linguistic resources of modal assessment given in Halliday & Matthiessen's book *An Introduction to Functional Grammar* (3rd) (2004).

4.2.1 Statistics of Realizations in Terms of Propositional Comments

The category of propositional comments covers seven aspects, and is subdivided into 14 varieties, precisely as commenting either on the proposition as a whole or on the part played by the subject. (Halliday & Matthiessen, 2004: 609-611) The full range of propositional comments is shown in Table 4.3.

Table 4.3 Categories and Sub-varieties of Propositional Comments

Domain	Category	Sub-variety
On Subject	wisdom	wise
		unwise
	morality	moral
		immoral
On Whole	asseveration	natural
		obvious
		sure
	prediction	predictable
		unpredictable
	presumption	hearsay
		argument
		guess
	desirability	desirable
	undesirability	undesirable

When making the assessment on the whole proposition, the comment may be either asseverative ("it is so") or qualificative ("this is what I think about it"). Contrastively, as commenting on the part played by the subject, its role is evaluated for its wisdom or morality. (Halliday & Matthiessen, 2004: 131) Figure 4.3 shows distribution patterns of realizations of subjectivity in varieties of propositional comments.

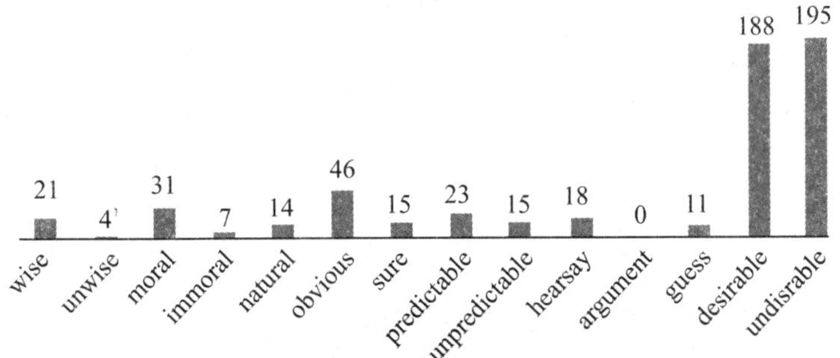

Figure 4.3 Distribution Patterns of Realizations in Propositional Comments

Table 4.4 Sub-components in the Varieties of Desirability and Undesirability

Variety	Sub-component
Desirability	luck
	reaction
	composition
	valuation
	security
	satisfaction
	hope
Undesirability	undesirable
	N① reaction
	Ncomposition
	Nvaluation
	insecurity
	dissatisfaction

① Capitalized N symbolizes the negativization of the following nouns, namely reaction, composition and valuation, for there are no antonyms for them.

As is shown in Table 4.4 and Figure 4.3, a special variety of desirability, which consists of two subcategories as desirability and undesirability, occupies more than 50% of all the propositional comments in SAEC. According to Halliday & Matthiessen (2004), the variety of desirability has 7 sub-components. Except for the sub-component "hope" merely being desirable, the other 6 sub-components are further evaluated as "desirable and undesirable". Evidently, there are 13 sub-components in the variety of desirability and undesirability. (see Table 4.4) Distribution patterns of these varieties of desirability are statistically and visually summed up in Figure 4.4.

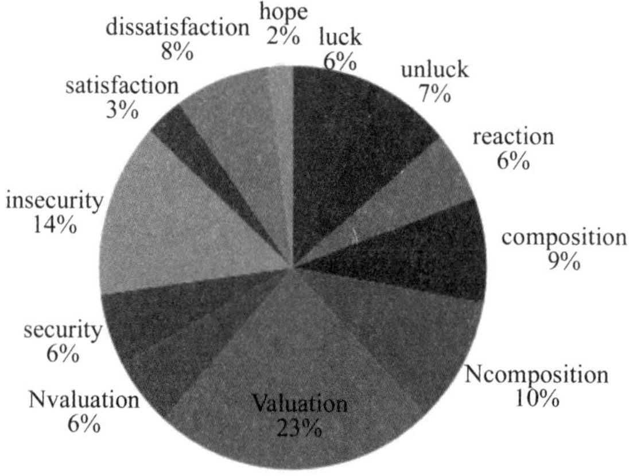

Figure 4.4 Distribution Patterns of Realizations in Terms of Desirability*

4.2.2 Realization Features of Subjectivity in Terms of Propositional Comments

Based on the findings of Halliday & Matthiessen (2004), the description about propositional comments is carried out systematically, focusing on propositions made on the properties of the subjects or on the whole propositions. In the former case, the comments, with properly chosen forms, focus on the wisdom or morality of subjects. Those comments can be realized by modal adjuncts in forms of adverbs, such as "wisely, cleverly, foolishly, correctly, wrongly, unjustifiably, etc.", or in forms of relational clause with the adjectives derived cognitively from the modal adjuncts

* The percentage of Nreaction is 0.

acting as the predicative adjectives, e. g. "it is wise...", or even in forms of nominal groups with the corresponding adjectives acting as the epithet, e. g. "correct decision". When the modal comment is realized by adverbial modal adjuncts or adjectives in the nominal groups, both manifestations enacting the interpersonal functions take the orientation implicit. However, when the modal comment is realized in the relational clause with "it" acting as the formal subject, it is by nature the experiential manifestation, which makes the orientation of the assessment explicit. For all these realizations make no use of the speaker-referring pronoun "I", they are fundamentally of objective orientation. In this corpus, there are 63 linguistic forms used to make modal comments on the subject's properties of wisdom and morality. According to Figure 4. 3, 56 of them appear in the objective implicit forms, and only 7 take on the objective explicit forms. Please look at Examples (18) and (19):

(18) **It remains presumptuous for the United States** to think that it can, by itself, carry out such a task in Afghanistan. (Text 33)

(19) Even though the risks are great, President Bush made the **right** choice in selecting this limited, clandestine form of warfare rather than attempting a full-scale invasion of Afghanistan by thousands of American ground troops. (Text 83)

In Example (18), the comments on the property of the subject, especially on its unwise property, is made by the clausal form "It remains presumptuous...". The adjective "right" in Example (19), however, is used as the epithet of the nominal groups "the right choice", which makes indirect comment pertaining to the wise property of President Bush.

When the propositional comments are made on the whole propositions, the comment occurs merely in the form of declarative clauses, which are either asseverative or qualificative. Correspondingly, the forms realize the propositional comments ranging from the clausal rank to the lexical rank, including the mental, verbal and relational clause, the adverbial group, the adjective and the prepositional phrase. When the adverbial group or the adjective is chosen to realize the propositional comment, the expressions of subjectivity regularly manifest the objective explicit orientation. However, when the mental, verbal or relational clause or the prepositional phrase is used, the variable of orientation becomes much more complicated. If the mental, verbal or relational clause is used with the speaker marking pronoun "I" as the subject, e. g. "I rejoice/argue/am anxious" or the cognate variant as the logical subject, e. g. "It fascinates me that", it surely takes the subjective explicit orientation. The corresponding prepositional phrases like "to my pleasure" are also regarded as making the subjective orientation explicit. If the relational clause uses the pronoun "it" as the formal subject, it then makes the objective orientation implicit. However, forms with a passive verbal, such as "it is said that" and "it is rumored", and the verbal clause with the second or third personal subject such as "they say" and the prepositional phrases, such as "according to their words", can't be discussed in terms of the variable of orientation, for "in the realm of propositions, the line between explicitly objective propositions and modal assessment seems to disappear" (Halliday & Matthiessen, 2004: 630). They are then regarded as discourse strategies which will be discussed later.

Then, as far as the variable of orientation is concerned, the general sketch about the way that the subjective assessment is realized is continued. As for the cases that the propositional comments are asseverative, there are generally 75 variants to express the modal comments related to the natural, obvious and sure aspects. (see Figure 4. 3) All of them uniquely take the objective orientation, with 10 realizing forms manifested explicitly and the other 65 forms implicitly. Please look at Examples (20) and (21):

(20) Every week **it becomes clearer** how difficult a task it will be to balance the concerns of all those who believe they own a part of Sept. 11. (Text 56)

(21) **Obviously**, the most important defense against smallpox is better intelligence on just who has samples of the virus. If they are tightly guarded in the United States and Russia, the danger is minimal. (Text 76)

Examples (20) and (21) show that the asseverative type is used to comment in terms of the "obvious" aspect on the proposition following it. In Example (20), the clausal form "it becomes clearer" is adopted by the writer in explicit-objective orientation to make comments in terms of "obvious" aspect on the proposition projected by a "how-clause". In Example (21), evaluative adverb "obviously" is used as a comment adjunct in the position of interpersonal theme, which indicates the comment on the proposition made by the whole clause.

When the propositional comments are qualificative, they characterize as three processing aspects: prediction, presumption and desirability, which can be further subdivided into seven subcategories: predictable, unpredictable, hearsay, argument, guess, desirable and undesirable. (Halliday & Matthiessen, 2004: 609) Generally speaking, there are 450 variants that can be used to construe such kind of propositional comments. (see Figure 4. 3) Among them, only 9 forms take the explicitly subjective orientation, but all the rest 441 variants take the objective orientation of the propositional comments with 41 manifesting explicitly and 400 implicitly. Please look at Examples (22) and (23):

(22) As the nation moves into 2002, **we no longer worry about** whether George W. Bush has the gravitas to lead the country in time of crisis, or whether his foreign policy team has the skill to protect the nation's interest in a global conflict. (Text 30)

(23) That was the **unmistakable** message delivered by President Bush in his State of the Union address when he labeled Iran, Iraq and North Korea an "axis of evil" that he would not permit to threaten the United States with chemical, biological and nuclear weapons. (Text 37)

Both Example (22) and Example (23) explain the case that subjectivity can be realized in the qualificative type, which show that the comment is made concerning different aspects of a proposition and taking on different froms. Example (22) is to express the writer's desirability through the reaction towards the proposition projected by a "whether-clause", which is in explicitly subjective pattern with "we" as the subject. The epithet "unmistakable" in Example (23) indicates the writer's desirability of the proposition, for it shows that the proposition is valuable.

4.3 Realizations of Subjectivity in Terms of Speech Functional Comments

A proposition can be evaluated in its meta-lingual function, which reflects the speaker's interpersonal attitude to particular linguistic markers. The speech-functional comment acts as such linguistic markers, which represents the speaker's assessment of a proposition with respect to its meta-lingual function.

4.3.1 Statistics of Speech Functional Comments

The speech functional type also falls into two sub-types: qualified and unqualified. The qualified type is closely related to projection and can be followed by "... speaking". While the unqualified, which cannot be modified extensively like the qualified by "... speaking", are either claims of veracity or signs of assurance or admission (Halliday & Matthiessen, 2004: 131). Distribution patterns of realization of subjectivity in speech functional comments are illustrated in Table 4.5. Moreover, the corresponding percentages of each case involved in the speech functional comments are also displayed clearly and vividly in Figure 4.5.

Table 4.5 Distribution Patterns of Realization of Subjectivity in Speech Functional Comments

Type	Variety	Number	Ratio (%)
Unqualified	assurance	16	12.90
	concession	33	26.61
	factuality	48	38.71
Qualified	validity	19	15.32
	honesty	1	0.81
	secrecy	0	0
	individuality	1	0.81
	accuracy	5	4.03
	hesitancy	1	0.81
	totality	124	100

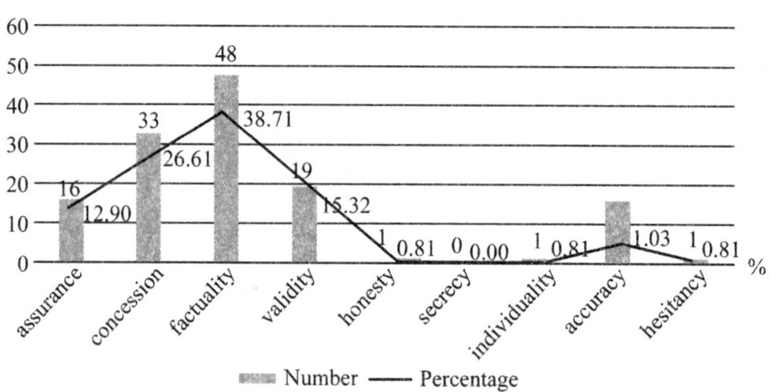

Figure 4.5 Distribution Patterns of Realizations in Speech Functional Comments

4.3.2 Realization Features of Subjectivity in Speech Functional Comments

According to Halliday (1994a) and Halliday & Matthiessen (2004), the comments on the speech functional property enact fundamentally interpersonal function. They may occur with either declarative or interrogative clauses by changing the modal orientation properly. When they occur with declarative clauses they represent the speaker's attitude, while with an interrogative clause they stand by the listener's side. Halliday (2004: 611) studies speech functional comments in three ways: the verbal or mental clause with the subject made up of the speaker-referential pronoun "I" acts as the projecting clause, e. g. "I assure"; the prepositional phrase, e. g. "for my part" and "in tough term", works as an extra-subjective or an extra-objective option to manifest the modal comments explicitly; and the adverb, e. g. "admittedly", "truly", "generally", and their expanding adverbial group of the qualified type like "generally speaking", are usually drawn on as speech functional comments to express subjectivity in the implicitly objective orientation.

Both the qualified and unqualified types can be used as speech functional comments. As far as the unqualified type is concerned, altogether 97 (78.22%) variants of the speech functional comments appear in SAEC, with 48 (38.71%) variants indicating claims of veracity concerning the factual aspects, 16 (12.9%) variants acting as signs of assurance and 33 (26.61%) variants acting as signs of admission. (see Table 4.5) All these variants occur as the adverbs to make the objective orientation of the speech functional comments implicit. For example:

(24) These demands are almost **certainly** not going to be met, and the president vowed that the "hour is coming when America will act". (Text 6)

(25) If **in fact** the government is treating its detainees fairly, why not be more forthcoming? Timely release of the facts would help dispel concerns about unfair treatment. (Text 82)

Both Examples (24) and (25) illustrate that speech functional comments are used to make claims of veracity concerning the factual aspects. In Example (24), the adverb "certainly" acts as the linguistic sign of assurance, and "in fact" in Example (25) acts as the linguistic marker of concession.

Besides, 27 (21.77%) variants of the qualified type are taken advantage of to express the speech functional comments. Among them, 19 (15.32%) variants deal with the degree of the validity, and the other 8 (6.45%) signify aspects of the personal engagement. All these variants take the objective orientation of these speech functional comments, with 23 occurring implicitly in adverbs or adverbial groups expanded by "... speaking", and 4 explicitly in prepositional phrases. Please look at Examples (26) and (27):

(26) But it will be the new authority's job to steer Mr. Silverstein in the right direction, **aesthetically speaking**, and to make sure that whatever he does fits the city's larger needs and is linked to the surrounding neighborhoods of Battery Park, Chinatown, Little Italy and Soho. (Text 23)

(27) As Mr. Cheney **accurately** noted, Saddam Hussein has twice attacked his neighbors. (Text 66)

In Example (26), the adverbial group "aesthetically speaking" is used to evaluate the validity in terms of its aesthetic property from the writer's perspective; and, the adverb "accurately" in Example (27) claims for the accuracy of the proposition from the writer's point of view, just as "I tell you accurately".

4.4 Realizations of Subjectivity in Terms of Judging Appraisals

It has been described clearly that categories of modal assessment correspond to categories of appraisal. (Halliday & Matthiessen, 2004: 607) The judgement system revises feelings in the realm of proposals which then get formalized as rules and regulations administered by church and state. Then, the study of judging appraisals will shed significant light on the realization of subjectivity in modal assessment.

4.4.1 Statistics of Judging Appraisals

The system of judgement includes five sub-types: normality, capacity, tenacity, veracity and propriety. (Martin & White, 2005: 52) In SAEC, all these sub-types occur and are realized in judging appraisals.

When we discussed the modal comments on propositional subjects and on the whole proposition, wisdom and morality properties of the subject correspond respectively to the variants of capacity and propriety in the system of JUDGEMENT, and the natural aspect of the asseverative sub-type is consistent with the normality of judgement. Then, all these cases are included when statistics of judging appraisals are made.

Patterns of realizing subjectivity in judging appraisals are statistically enumerated with respect to five sub-types. As judgement features the positive and negative distinction, every realization in judging appraisals is of positive or negative property. Their percentages to the totality of judging appraisals used in SAEC are calculated accordingly, as is shown in Table 4.6.

Table 4.6 Distribution Patterns of Realizations of Subjectivity in Terms of Judging Appraisals

Types / Value (V)	Normality		Capacity		Tenacity		Veracity		Propriety		Totality	
	Num.	V/G	Num.	V/G	Num.	V/G	Num.	V/G	Num.	V/G	Num.	V/G
Positive	24	2.25%	313	29.36%	100	9.38%	17	1.59%	151	14.17%	605	56.75%
Negative	6	0.56%	122	11.44%	52	4.88%	11	1.03%	270	25.33%	461	43.25%
Total	30	2.81%	435	40.8%	152	14.26%	28	2.62%	421	39.49%	1066	100%

Note: Num. = Number; G = 1066.

4.4.2 Realization Features of Subjectivity in Judging Appraisals

As is shown in Table 4.6, distribution patterns of realizations in judging appraisals are uneven as far as the five sub-types of the system of judgement are concerned. Theoretically, linguistic resources that the writer chooses to express the tropism of judgements will then construe his subjective assessment in the course of producing discourse, in which the writer introduces various kinds of attitudes and enables them to be negotiated so as to obtain some certain communicating goal.

Generally speaking, it is the whole discourse not any part of it that constructs different tendencies of judgements. Then, some ideational meanings can be invoked to express judgement meanings in certain context (Li, 2004: 4), and it is important to take co-text into account, instead of simply analyzing items one by one (Martin & Rose, 2003: 37). The realization of judgements should not be discussed merely at the lexical level; instead it can take advantage of all kinds of linguistic resources, such as lexical items, grammatical structures, and even discourse structures. (Hu, 2009; Thompson & Hunston, 2001) However, judging appraisals are studied limitedly in this study from the lexical level to the clausal level. Please look at Examples (28), (29) and (30):

(28) If New York is going to get the help it needs, its leaders are going to have to be both restrained and politically **canny** in what they ask for.

(Text 100)

(29) New York City and George W. Bush were never a natural couple until last week. Now Mr. Bush has managed to reach out in ways both symbolic and practical. In its greatest hour of need, the city must be grateful that he **rose to the occasion**, and demonstrated that he is president of the entire country. (Text 11)

(30) **The administration takes the spread of nuclear, chemical and biological weapons dangers extremely seriously.** (Text 68)

All these three examples explain that the lexico-grammatical forms ranging from the lexical item to the clause can be drawn on directly to realize judgements. Besides, some linguistic forms or devices are consciously adopted to invoke meanings of judgements in discourse that the writer wants to convey to the reader. For example:

(31) Helping New York survive Sept. 11 was a mission that actually occupied only a few months of Mr. Giuliani's eight years in office, but it seems as if he had been in training for it all along. He always ran the city **like a warrior king.** (Text 40)

Example (31) shows that the lexical metaphor—like a warrior king—implicates a judgement of a person acting in this way. It functions superficially the ideational meaning, but in fact it would provoke an attitudinal response in the reader. The indirect realizations of judgements are much more sensitive to the context and the reading position for interpretation rather than depending on lexical metaphors and direct inscriptions. Similarly, a range of mechanisms can be used to evoke attitude, all of which function to afford or indicate an attitude in the context. (Martin & White, 2005: 67)

As far as distribution patterns are concerned, there appears a unique feature: the frequencies of capacity and propriety are much higher than those of the rest three types. Capacity is of the highest, which occur 435 times (40.8%), with 313 of them being positive and 122 being negative. Second to capacity, propriety is 39.49% in proportion to the totality, appearing 421 times with 151 of them being positive and 270 being negative. The tertiary is tenacity which occurs 152 times (14.26%), with 100 of them being positive and 52 being negative. Normality is the fourth one, and it occurs 30 times (2.81%), with 24 of them being positive and 6 being negative. The last is veracity with the lowest proportion of 2.62%, occurring only 28 times with 17 of them being positive and 11 being negative. Therefore, as is shown in Figure 4.6, the positive is preferred in the cases of normality, capacity, tenacity and veracity, and reaches to the peak point in the type of capacity. Contrastively, the negative value of propriety is the highest, which is clearly proven by the highest point of the negative line in Figure 4.6.

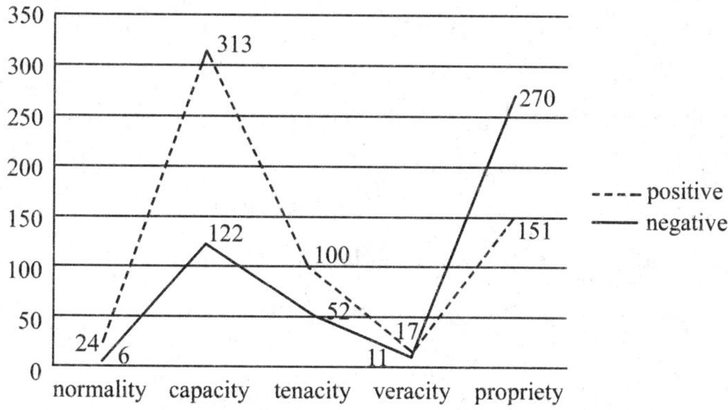

Figure 4.6 Distribution Patterns of Realizations in Terms of Value Property of Judging Appraisals

The system of judgement is divided into two major groups: social esteem and social sanction. (Martin & Rose, 2003) Judgements of esteem include three subtypes: normality, capacity, and tenacity. Judgements of sanction consist of veracity and propriety. As is shown in Table 4.7, in this corpus, expressions of social esteem appear 617 (57.87%) times in total. Among them, 437 (40.99%) cases occur in positive, while 180 (16.88%) cases are evaluated negatively. Expressions of social sanction are used 449 times totally, among which 168 (15.76%) cases are of positive value and 281 (26.36%) cases are of negative value.

Table 4.7 Distribution Patterns of Realizations in Judging Appraisals in Terms of Social Esteem and Social Sanction

	Social esteem		Social sanction	
	Num.	Ratio(%)	Num.	Ratio(%)
Positive	437	40.99	168	15.76
Negative	180	16.88	281	26.36
Totality	617	57.87	449	42.12

The parameters for disposing subjectivity in the system of judgement can be justified by connecting to the system of modalization. (Halliday, 1994) To be precise, normality is to usuality, capacity is to ability, tenacity is to inclination, veracity is to probability, and propriety is to obligation, respectively. (Martin & White, 2005) Correspondingly, modulization covers normality and veracity; modalization consists of capacity, tenacity and propriety. As is shown in Table 4.8, as far as SAEC is concerned, expressions indicating modalization are only 58 (5.43%), with 41 (3.84%) cases being positive and 17 (1.59%) being negative. Contrastively, expressions indicating modulization amount to 1008 (94.57%), with 564 (72.89%) cases being positive and 444 (21.68%) being negative.

Table 4.8 Distribution Patterns of Realizations in Judging Appraisals in Terms of Modalization and Modulization

	Modalization		Modulization	
	Num.	Ratio(%)	Num.	Ratio(%)
Positive	41	3.84	564	72.89
Negative	17	1.59	444	21.68
Totality	58	5.43	1008	94.57

Evidentially, there appear two typical features with respect to modalization and modulization: firstly, expressions of modulization are much more than those of modalization; secondly, expressions occurring in positive are much more than those in negative, whether it is the case of modulization or modalization.

4.5 Realizations of Subjectivity in Terms of Engaging Opinions

An information source usually refers to forms that might inform a person with something that may be observations, speeches, pictures, names of organization, documents, websites, etc. These sources bring into discourse opinions attributed to the third party by means of some proper linguistic resources. These linguistic resources introduce heteroglossic viewpoints and are thought of as patulous propositional comments extending the writer's judgement or strategically strengthening the writer's stances.

4.5.1 Statistics of Engaging Opinions

From the perspective of subjectivity, we regard the way that the alternative voice is chosen into the discourse as the strategies that the writer uses to support his opinions or challenge the opposite opinions. In SAEC, the writers draw on various such ways to express their individual opinions, and they are termed as: entertain, pronounce, endorse, acknowledge and distance in this study.

In this section, we focus on how the writers introduce the proposition into the discourse by studying collocating relations between strategies leading into the proposition and sources taking charge of the proposition.

Information sources include common noun, proper noun or (personal) pronoun. Common nouns include persons, other living things, collectives, objects and institutions, which are typically accompanied by a deictic. Proper names consist of names of particular persons, institutions of all kinds, and places. The referent of the personal pronoun is defined interpersonally in accordance with the context. Usually, personal pronouns and proper names are used without any other elements of the nominal group. In SAEC, personal pronouns, common nouns and proper names appear in proper forms as information sources leading various propositions into discourse. Information sources are classified into six types: the third person single form, institutional name, non-known person, pronoun, collective and organization.

Correspondingly, these relations have been annotated involving three sub-types: cases with clear sources referring to one of the six types; cases with sources informed from the context being labeled as the context-source; and cases with no sources informed from the context but contextually in other contexts, which is termed as the non-source here. Then, matched patterns are displayed clearly in Table 4. 9.

Table 4. 9 Matched Patterns of Sources and Importing Strategies

	Entertain	Pronounce	Distance	Acknowledge	Endorse
The third person	0	0	29	92	11
Pronoun	0	1	20	44	7
Organization	4	1	12	17	4
Institutional name	1	18	3	38	43
Non-known person	0	0	2	3	0
Collective	1	1	4	19	2
Nonsource	0	0	18	6	0
Context-source	0	1	2	1	5
Total	6	22	90	220	72

From Table 4. 9 we can see that it is obvious that information sources do not match with importing strategies evenly. Then, detailed analysis about this phenomenon is made in accordance with the three strategies used to bring the proposition into discourse.

4.5.2 Realization Features of Subjectivity in Terms of Engaging Opinions

The terms of engaging information come from the system of engagement, but their connotations are changed in this study. The type of acknowledge is of the highest frequency, occurring 220 (53. 66%) times. Second to this type is the distance, which is used 90 (21. 95%) times. The endorse type is tertiary and appears 72 (17.56%) times. The final two types (entertain and pronounce) are used 28 times altogether, with the entertain type occurring only 6 (1. 46%) times and the pronounce type occuring 22 (5. 37%) times. Those features can be seen in Figure 4. 7.

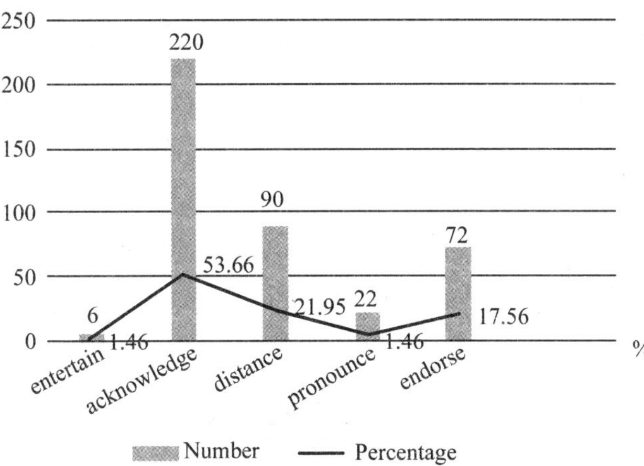

Figure 4.7 Distribution Patterns of Engagements in External-Sourced Opinions

They are classified into three kinds of strategies of bringing external-sourced opinions in discourse. That is, entertain and pronounce deal with the way that the writer indicates covertly his individual position; acknowledge and endorse refer to the strategies that the writer resorts to to emphasize his position indirectly; and distance deals with the evidence that the writer uses to go against the opposite opinions, by which the writer gets away from the responsibility. They are used in discourse by the writer consciously to align or disalign with the proposition sourced externally in order to indicate his individual proposition. Generally speaking, these strategies embody evidentially how the writer operates the linguistic devices in the course of creating the discourse in order to get his opinion expressed. Please look at Example (32):

(32) If in fact **the government** is treating its detainees fairly, why not be more forthcoming? (Text 82)

Example (32) shows that rhetorical questions can be used by the authorial voice to entertain those alternatives. This type of questions is employed in singly-constructed, non-interactive context to entertain, but they do not assert any proposition, by which the reader is positioned to supply a particular answer. (Sadock, 1974) This type of questions can be frequently used as an effective persuasive device by the writer to influence the reader to get the desired responses. Similarly, pronounce indexes authorial emphases or authorial interpolations into the discourse, by which the writer directs against some assumed or referenced counter position.

Frequently, the writer would ask for propositions of external sources to establish the basis of arguing the correctness of his stance. Acknowledge and endorse are the strategies to play this function. For example:

(33) But **the report** released by Britain, in a move coordinated with the White House, **demonstrates** that the Bush administration has enough information about the links between Mr. bin Laden, the Taliban leadership of Afghanistan and the terrorist assaults to make a strong case. (Text 75)

In Example (33), the writer attributes the proposition that "the Bush administration has enough information about the links between Mr. bin Laden, the Taliban leadership of Afghanistan and the terrorist assaults to make a strong case" to the report released by Britain in order to prove the conviction of the deduction that "Mr. bin Laden and his terrorist network were responsible for the Sept. 11 attacks". In fact, the writer often resorts to examples and statistical numbers to support his arguments to endorse individual position in editorials.

However, the strategy of distance involves formulations in which the writer departs explicitly from the attributed material through the semantics of the framer. In most cases, it is typically realized by means of the reporting verb, e. g. say, report, believe, and according to, etc. and by certain uses of scare quotes. Therefore, the writer disaligns with the position being advanced when it is imported into discourse as the target hit consciously. Contrastively, the position that the writer insists on in the context will be implied. For example:

(34) **Among New York's senior political figures**, there is an emerging consensus that a special commission or authority should be created to oversee the reconstruction. (Text 13)

In Example (34), the content of "an emerging consensus" is clearly attributed to "New York's senior political figures", which appears as the circumstantial element here. Thus, the writer distances himself from taking the responsibility of the proposition "that a special commission or authority should be created to oversee the reconstruction".

As to the parameter [relation], acknowledgement and endorsement are used highly to 247 cases with 206 cases of acknowledgement and 41 cases of endorsement, almost involving in all kinds of sources. Distance is adopted about 83 times in the database, collocating with all these sources. However, there are only one case of entertainment and one pronouncement. Bearing such statistical consequences, we will then make the analysis of source expressions.

4.6 Realizations of Subjectivity in Terms of Metaphorical Operations

By definition, grammatical metaphor is a re-coupling of a congruent realization within the grammatical zone construing additional layers of meaning and wording, which virtually involves semantic junction dealing with an inter-stratal relationship between semantics and lexico-grammar. (Halliday & Matthiessen, 1999) Grammatical metaphor is either interpersonal or ideational, and interpersonal metaphor can be subdivided into metaphor of modality and metaphor of mood. (Derewianka, 1995; Halliday, 1998; Halliday & Martin, 1993; Halliday & Matthiessen, 1999, 2004)

4.6.1 Metaphorical Realizations of Modality

Systemically, metaphor makes an expansion of the meaning potential by creating new patterns of structural realization. Thus, it opens up new systemic domains of meaning. In fact, the pressure to expand the meaning potential results from the development of metaphorical modes of meaning.

Within the realm of modality, it is true that certain grammatical environments prefer metaphorical realizations of modality. The semantic domain of modality is thus extended metaphorically to include explicit indications of subjective and objective orientation. That is to say, a modal proposition or proposal can be realized by means of a projection sequence with a nexus of two clauses instead of a single one. The modal assessment itself is given the status of a proposition metaphorically as the projecting clause of the nexus, and a modal adjunct similarly realize the proposition or proposal at the same time. Therefore, the orientation is expanded by adding a systemic contrast in manifestation between explicit and implicit. To be specific, the difference between subjective and objective orientation comes from the difference between a projecting mental/verbal clause with a senser/sayer and a relational clause without such a projector. Hence, the ideational manifestations make it possible to encode explicitly the orientation: the logical manifestation is explicitly subjective, e. g. "I regret", but the experiential manifestation is explicitly objective, e. g. "it's regrettable" (Halliday & Matthiessen, 2004: 614-615). Therefore, the metaphorically realization of the assessment in terms of orientation and manifestation can be formulated. For example:

(35) **We trust** the Bush administration is not seriously considering torture—an idea that seems more interesting to radio talk shows and columnists than to government officials. (Text 18)

(36) While he may elude capture for a time, and Taliban fighters may try to wage guerrilla warfare from the mountains, **it is unlikely** they can stage a military comeback. The Taliban regime is effectively finished. (Text 27)

Metaphor of modality works as the discourse strategy to upgrade the interpersonal assessment from an adverbial group or prepositional phrase serving within a simple clause to a clause serving within a clause nexus of projection. This metaphoric strategy reveals an essential relationship between modality and projection, and thus can be extended beyond modality and applied to subjective assessment, e. g. "I regret" and "It is regrettable that". To bring this out, we can regard this kind of linguistic resources as exposing metaphorically the speaker or addressee as "projector", such as "I think", "I say", "do you think", "do you say".

4.6.2 Metaphorical Realizations of Propositions and Proposals

As a fundamental relationship involved in modal assessment includes modality and projection, subjective assessment is regarded as an interpersonal projection. However, the notion of interpersonal projection is not limited to modal assessment. It also works in the field of mood. Usually, imperative clauses and modulation are closely connected, because modulation is always treated as the imperative type of modality. That is to say, an imperative clause imposes an obligation and the imperative tag checks the addressee's inclination. (Halliday & Matthiessen, 2004)

Just like modality, speech function can be encoded as a substantive proposition which is realized as a figure of sensing or saying that can project the original proposal or proposition. Thus, the imperative which usually enacts the speech function is now realized metaphorically by a hypotactic clause nexus typically as if it is a report of what the speaker says. This metaphorical realization fundamentally characterizes the transition of mood and is called metaphor of mood. (Halliday & Matthiessen, 2004)

Metaphors of mood are based on the ideational projection and involve typically a shift in the realization domain of commands from imperative to indicative clause. (Halliday & Matthiessen, 2004: 627-635) Although there are several realizations of mood of metaphors, only two types are relevant to this study. The first type is that the extensive resources of the lexico-grammar of verbal and mental clauses are clearly presented in ideational projection, which then make the subjective orientation of the speech functional selection explicit. Example (37) is the corresponding manifestation of the first type.

(37) Sooner or later, **we all wonder** if we have it in us to be brave when bravery is needed. (Text 4)

In Example (37), the original proposal or proposition is metaphorically dressed up as a projected proposal in a projection nexus, and the speaker-plus subject "we" makes the subjective orientation of modulation explicit. Besides, the newly-born layer of ideational projection can have more modifying elements, as is shown in Examples (35), (36) and (37).

The second type involves in a shift from imperative to indicative clause so as to realize commands. The indicative clause can be either declarative or interrogative. However, in SAEC, only modulated declarative is used to enforce the commands. For example:

(38) **You could have found** people living in nearly every neighborhood in New York and much of northern New Jersey, people who had grown up or gone to school in nearly every state in this country. (Text 6)

In Example (38), due to the metaphor of mood, the command is realized by the indicative clause with the indicator of addressee "you" acting as the subject person and modality acting as modulation. According to the context, the subject "you" doesn't only refer to the addressee, but means the generalized person.

Therefore, by metaphor of mood, proposals are realized in the indicative, which results in the effect of generalizing the rule as propositions which describe how the world ought to be, instead merely bringing proposals directly to the addressee. Therefore, the presence of the mood element not only provides a range of more delicate ways of commanding but also expands the potential for negotiation.

4.6.3 Metaphorical Realizations of Nominalizations

In this study, nominal forms cognate to certain modal expressions are regarded as the way of sticking out the objective orientation explicitly. Why are they looked as modal expressions, and also, why the way to manifest the objective orientation explicitly?

The reasons lie in their nominalization process with the help of ideational metaphor. Ideational metaphor is a resource for construing relevant experiences of the world, which characterizes to be shifted "downwards": a sequence is realized by a clause, a figure is realized by a group, and an element is realized by a word (Halliday & Matthiessen, 2004: 639). It is an experientialization of experience. (Halliday & Matthiessen, 1999: 264) Nominalizations are typical consequences of ideational metaphors, by which processes and qualities are construed as entities with their own epithets or qualifiers. The metaphorical entity fundamentally acts as the value of a proposition in an identity existing in discourse, which must be interpreted against the background of its congruent variant contextually. (Halliday & Martin, 1993; Halliday & Matthiessen, 1999, 2004)

As Halliday (1994a: 353) points out, it is a significant feature of our present-day world that a large number of newly-born entities are metaphorically created. Thus, a group of nouns that are used to express the writer's attitudes are just in this case. They belong to the category of fact nouns, two of which are always used to express the writer's attitudes. The first one is chance (nouns of modality) which is related to modalized propositions and can be paraphrased as "it may be (the case) that...", such as "chance", "possibility", "likelihood", "probability", "certainty", "off chance" and "impossibility". The second one is need (nouns of modulation) which is related to modulated proposals and inherently means "it is necessary for... to...", e.g. "requirement", "need", "rule", "obligation", "necessity", "expectation" and "duty". (Halliday, 1994: 266-268; Halliday & Matthiessen, 2004: 471-478)

In SAEC, some fact nouns resulting from nominalization are thought of as the modal expressions which help to make the objective orientation explicitly. Such fact nouns include obligation, possibility, chance, readiness, inclination, impossibility, need and likelihood. Contextually, they refer back anaphorically to the preceding text or refer ahead cataphorically to the following text. The understanding of those nouns must rely on the contextual situation in which they are occurring. For example:

(39) If the United States is to combat terrorism effectively in the weeks ahead it will have to act in concert with other nations, including a number of Islamic countries. President Bush has recognized the **need** for international cooperation in his public statements and conversations with foreign leaders since the terror attacks on New York and Washington. (Text 2)

In this passage, the noun "need" is a metaphorical variant of the above modulation clause, particularly corresponding to the modal process of the clause. The deictic is the definite article "the", which refers back anaphorically to the modal operator "have to" in the preceding text. In this way, the nominalization "need" is used to express the writer's acknowledge of obligation, which must be interpreted based on the proposal "it will have to act in concert with other nations, including a number of Islamic countries".

Although fact nouns are not nominalizations of projection nexuses, they always appear as they have already been packaged in projected form. In other words, their occurrences usually predicate a presupposing proposition or proposal. In most cases, they appear alone without their congruent forms, but need to be triggered semantically in the context. For example:

(40) But it imposes upon the people responsible for distributing the money a powerful **obligation** to spend it wisely, equitably and efficiently. Failure to meet that **obligation** would not only shortchange the victims but sour the good feeling that has sprung up between the city and the rest of the country in the weeks following Sept. 11. (Text 80)

Here, "obligation" is an inherently modulated fact noun, which can be interpreted in this context as "it is necessary for the people responsible for distributing the money to spend it wisely, equitably and efficiently". The second "obligation" refers back to the first one anaphorically, which is also proven by the demonstrative "*that*". From this point, both of the two fact nouns in Example (40) share the same function. Then, by choosing the fact noun "obligation", the writer indicates successfully his attitudes towards the proposal: it is obligatory to spend the money wisely, equitably and efficiently.

Obviously, fact nouns of chances and needs are the result of ideational metaphor, which reflect the normalizing process or are just used as the normalization in the text. The usages of them really help express covertly the writers' attitudes towards the written proposition or proposal. Contextually, they can be generally paraphrased as "it is possible" for chances of modalization, and "it is necessary" as to needs of modulization. Therefore, it is reasonable for us to regard fact nouns as taking the objective orientation of modal assessment explicitly.

Above all, grammar metaphor plays a very important role in realizing the writers' attitudes towards what they have expressed in words. Then, they display four significant features in this process. Firstly, with the help of the interpersonal metaphor, the expression of modalization and modulization can occur in the independent projecting clause with the proposition or the proposal, or the projected clause. Then, the presence of the mood elements expand the potential meaning when they are delicately modalized, doubted, argued and negotiated interpersonally in numerous other ways. In the case of nominalization, it then extends the potential of having epithets and qualifiers. Secondly, grammar metaphor can serve as the discourse strategy to realign or re-map the configuration between meaning and figure. When modalization and modulization are in the form of independent clause, they can regulate the prosodic wave of the discourse. Besides, it is the same case when nominalization takes place to act as the theme or the focus of new information. Thirdly, pragmatically grammatical metaphor can realign the configuration so as to formally and politely accommodate to the social distance between the speaker and the addressee or construct the alignment among them. That is to say, interpersonal metaphor is part of the principle of interpersonal iconicity: the syntagmatic extension of the wording metaphorically reflects a greater semiotic distance between meaning and wording, and thus enacts a greater social distance between speaker and addressee. (Halliday & Matthiessen, 2004: 642)

4.7 Summary

In this chapter, data statistics of realizations of subjectivity have been carried out through the system of modality, the system of engagement, and the system of judgement. When subjectivity is realized by choosing these linguistic resources, five subcategories are covered: modality, propositional comments, speech-functional comments, judging appraisals and engaging opinions. Accordingly, distribution patterns are built up on the base of consequences of data statistics and analysis with respect to various variants related to these five categories. That provides helpful information to be drawn on for further discussion of the dynamic process of realizing subjectivity in editorials with the aim to serve the persuasive function.

Chapter 5
Construction of Argumentativity in Terms of Subjectivity

An editorial is a type of newspaper articles, presenting the opinion of the editor on some issues, whose object is to persuade the reader with the invalidity of ideas. Argumentativity is a fundamental property of editorials. It makes the editorials automatically credited a strong presence in the newspaper as argumentative texts. In the course of producing the text, subjectivity is constructed along the scale between the positive and negative pole, which covers the intermediate ground between the positive and negative polarity. At the intermediate ground, the writer can use different ways to indicate the way that he appears in the text, how he graduates the strength of subjectivity and how to express the expectation in the process of expressing modal evaluations, which is closely related to the strength of argumentativity.

5.1 Understanding Argumentativity in Terms of Subjectivity

Subjectivity is one basic property of language, which affords users chances of expressing their attitudes and beliefs in discourse. In fact, language is responsible for subjectivity in all its parts. In editorials, subjectivity is realized in the writer's act of forming reasons and of drawing conclusions, in which argumentativity is fully explained. In communication, argumentativity works as argumentative direction and argumentative strength, which help to define the four aspects of argumentativity: direction, negotiation, value and evaluation.

5.1.1 Subjectivity and Argumentativity

According to Benveniste (1958), subjectivity is the "psychic unity" which transcends the totality of the actual experiences and then makes the permanence of the consciousness. Therefore, subjectivity can be regarded as the property of language that is associated with human beings' consciousness and capacity of using language, which is construed in the communication when the speaker says "ego". Language provides the linguistic forms appropriate to the expression of subjectivity; the discourse, however, provokes the realization of subjectivity. Therefore, the speaker obtains the capacity of choosing proper language forms to construct himself as "subject" in the process of communication consciously.

Argumentativity, as an essential feature of editorials, refers to the state of being argumentative, which is constructed in the process of developing or presenting an argument. (Anscombre & Ducrot, 1989) These processes of realizing subjectivity and constructing argumentativity are by nature from the historical perspective. It is the acts of reasoning elaboration, which characterizes the writer's self-consciousness of choosing proper linguistic forms to have his subjective stance argued with the aim to convince the reader. That is to say, ordinary communications are basically argumentative, not merely delivering information, which makes it difficult for meanings to evolve in the direction of increased subjectivity. (Verhagen, 2005: 22-23)

"The consciousness of self is only possible if it is experienced by contrast." (Benveniste, 1958: 224) Intentionality is a core content of the human being's consciousness, which extends itself in the whole communication into intentional content and intentional attitude, with the latter representing the speaker's assessments on and attitudes towards the proposition expressed by intentional content. (Xu, 2013) Besides, intentional attitudes include three subcategories: psychological state, psychological evaluation and psychological orientation. They are expressed by certain grammatical forms, e. g. "I believe", "I presume" and "I suppose", or by lexical forms in different values, e. g. "easily" in "The wall paints easily", or by arranging the flows of information in the course of producing discourse.

Hence, intentional attitudes are consistent with subjectivity in that the speaker intends to express his opinions the moment he utters these words. What the speaker wants to do by expressing intentional attitudes is to perform the intentional act, as is proven by the formula "A = F(p)" (Searle, 1969). The process of expressing intentional attitudes indicates intentional force which can be realized by choosing language forms with certain psychological evaluation and psychological orientation. In other words, intentional force can be measured in the property of delicacy with respect to the qualitative on the scale or with respect to the orientation of the speaker's appearances.

5.1.2 Construction of Argumentativity with Respect to Intentional Force

Communication is the primary process for the speaker to regulate the opinion and assess the behavior of others. (Owings & Morton, 1998) An editorial is such a communication process, whereby the writer tries to influence the reader's thoughts, attitudes, or even immediate behavior. Argumentativity of editorials is adopted to realize intentional force that is used to serve the communication intention due to two features: argumentative direction and argumentative strength. (Verhagen, 2005) Argumentative direction includes "direct of fit" (Searle, 1969) in the sense that editorials direct the reader to infer which conclusions are invalid; and, argumentative strength represents the scale that the writer adopts when he makes a subjective assessment, which means that an assessment is made by the writer through evaluating judgement in ethics or scaling it according to a given criteria in the act of reasoning elaboration to negotiate with the readers to have them persuaded. In this sense, argumentativity can be constructed from four sides: direction, evaluation, scale, and negotiation.

Intentional force is indicated when intentional attitudes are expressed. Intentional force functions as a property of intentional attitudes and manifests the intensity of intentional attitudes. That is to say, intentional force is conveyed when psychological states, psychological evaluation, and psychological orientation are delivered. In other words, the performances of these three subcategories of intentional attitudes directly determine the manifestation of intentional force.

These three subcategories are realized in the process of using language to express subjectivity, for they reflect the relationship that the speaker adopts different language forms to represent different psychological characteristics. Psychological states deal with the speaker's psychological modes, say, "believe", "know", "doubt", "wish", when the utterances that are usually realized by using such grammatical forms as "I believe", "I presume", and "I suppose", take place. For example:

(41) **I believe** that Tom is at home.

Psychological evaluation conveys the speaker's evaluation towards the quality of the entities or the importance of the information expressed, which is encoded by choosing the words indicating different scales of value, e. g. "Tom is certainly/possibly at home." As to the modalized possibility of the proposition "Tom is at home", the speaker uses modal adverbs "certainly" and "possibly" with high and low value respectively to convey his evaluations. Moreover, psychological evaluation can be realized by the textual arrangement, which highlights the focus of information by regulating the flow of information. For example:

(42) I fired at the enemy the moment I saw them approaching when I was on duty. At last, I beat them off.

(43) I beat off the enemy's attack by opening fire the moment I saw them approaching when I was on duty.

Both Example (42) and Example (43) represent a series of events, which can be narrated in a chronological order as "I was on duty. I saw the enemy approaching. I opened fire. I beat the enemy off." Rearranging the events series like Examples (42) and (43), the speaker should re-evaluate the importance of all events in order to make the information "fired at the enemy" and "beat off the enemy's attack" prominent. Psychological orientation, however, describes attitudes that the speaker holds to the target objects, which are identical to the attitude in the appraisal system. To be specific, it is categorized in the subsystems of appreciation and judgement, because valuations made on something imply positive or negative judgement of the behaviors that someone performs to create the objects. (Martin & White, 2005) For example:

(44) It was a responsible inning.

(45) He was a responsible player.

In Example (44), the word "responsible" is used to appreciate the quality of "innings", by which certain evaluation is made. It judges the propriety of the behavior that is performed by someone who plays the inning, as is shown in Example (45).

Intentional force is realized in the process of expressing intentional attitudes, and this process, in turn, reveals various aspects involved in the transmission of intentional force, which can be measured by means of the subjective magnitude that is indicated as the speaker delivers his modal assessment. Theoretically, the magnitude is indicative of common processing mechanisms rooted in human beings' need of obtaining information about the structure of the external world, and it can be measured in terms of amount, numerosity, duration, or even in terms of the decisive variable in the course of "action-time" duration. (Brannon & Roitman, 2003; Rossetti & Pisella, 2002) In this sense, magnitude reflects the speaker's evaluations when making assessments, and then acts the interpersonal metafunction. They disperse in discourse, for modal assessments are manifested in different textual environments: the clause, the nominal group, and prosodic patterns created in passages of texts or whole texts. (Halliday & Matthiessen, 2004)

As argumentativity includes intentional force, it can be defined when it works in different scales of the subjective magnitude. Correspondingly, its four aspects, namely negotiation, scale, evaluation, and direction, are reflected with respect to: how the speaker negotiates with the reader; to what scale the speaker makes evaluation; what is the attitude the speaker holds in ethics; and, how the speaker steers discourse information as expected. Answers to such questions involve four aspects: orientation, value, subjective judgement and subjective expectation.

5.2 Construction of Argumentativity in Terms of Modal Orientation

In the system of modality, orientation determines the way each type of modality is realized. Within the system of orientation, the basic distinction exists between subjective and objective modality, cutting across the distinction between the explicit and implicit variants. Choices of different orientations reflect the writer's awareness of making his opinion expressed by engaging the reader in the discourse in order to argue with. In editorials, modal orientation acts as linguistic signs of negotiation reasoning, which reflects the typical feature of argumentativity.

5.2.1 Reasoning Elaboration of Continuum Cline of Subjectivity

Subjective assessment stands for the speaker's understanding on the validity of the assertion or on the rights and wrongs of the proposal, and is usually realized by an adjunct in its congruent form. As far as orientation is concerned, subjective assessment is presented as the act of distinguishing between subjective and objective manifestations, which are further classified by the distinction between explicit and implicit variants. When the four variants appear together, they define the expression of subjectivity. Therefore, the system of orientation is extended by adding a systemic contrast between explicit and implicit expressions.

The realization of subjectivity is expanded by grammatical metaphor and contains explicit manifestations of subjective and objective orientation. It is realized in modal assessment like the projecting clause of the nexus, which thus is given the status of a proposition, functioning as a modal adjunct in the clause expressing a proposition or a proposal that delivers an interpersonal assessment of modality. (Halliday & Matthiessen, 2004) Metaphorical realizations of subjectivity are used together with congruent realizations, which increase the delicacy of manifesting differentiation. A continuum made along this cline ranges from the explicitly subjective orientation, transmitting the middle interim stages between the implicitly subjective orientation and the implicitly objective orientation, to the explicitly subjective orientation. All these forms associated with orientation are linguistic devices that the writer can choose to realize subjectivity in communication. However, they differ in the degree of subjectivity. As a cline might be glossed as scales in systemic linguistics (Halliday, 1961), the continuum thus will reflect the scales of the subjective magnitude of subjectivity. Chen Zheng (2014) defines this continuum in terms of the strength of subjectivity by four scales: from the weakest represented by (a) to the strongest point represented by (d), with (b) and (c) standing for the sub-weak and the sub-strong points respectively, as is shown in Figure 5.1.

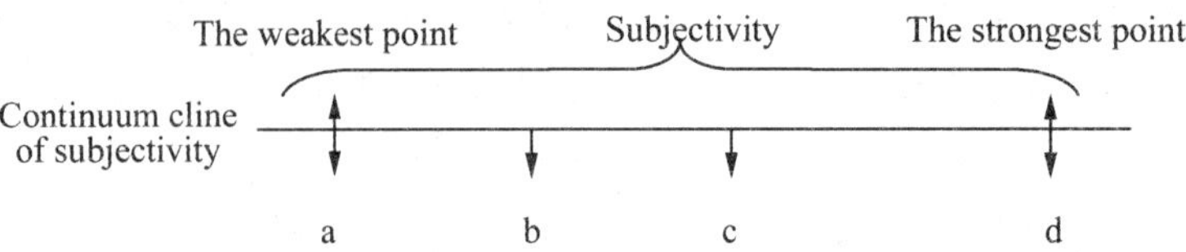

Figure 5.1 Scales of Strength of Subjectivity (Chen, 2014: 90)

Since semantic meaning is realized in lexico-grammatical forms in SFL, various degrees of the strength of subjectivity are correspondingly realized in linguistic forms, and they are identical to the expressions of modal orientation. Sign (a) corresponds to the explicitly subjective orientation, (b) to the implicitly subjective orientation, (c) to the implicitly objective orientation and (d) to the explicitly objective orientation. Thus, the four scales of subjective magnitude are defined with respect to modal orientation.

This continuum of subjectivity is constructed by treating orientation as the cline extending from subjective to objective, which reflects the fact that subjectivity can be realized by resorting to various lexico-grammatical resources. This concept of the continuum reveals that language, on the one hand, has evolved to satisfy human being's needs of expressing subjectivity; i. e. language is like the potential reservoir that can provide linguistic resources which indicate different orientation to realize subjectivity. On the other hand, as SFL regards choices as meanings, by which the speaker makes choices in the network of interlocking options, he chooses consciously to express, for his own purpose, subjective opinions effectively.

In SFL, comment adjuncts and fact nouns are two main categories that can also function to express subjectivity. (Halliday, 1994a; Halliday & Matthiessen, 2004) Both of them can be regarded as study targets with respect to modal orientation and can be positioned in the continuum. Comment adjuncts scatter at various but functionally significant places in the clause, and are usually analyzed as a part of mood and carry the burden of the clause as an interactive event. Both comment adjuncts and modal adjuncts relate closely to the system of mood by functioning as interpersonal adjuncts. Figure 5.2 is a good case in example.

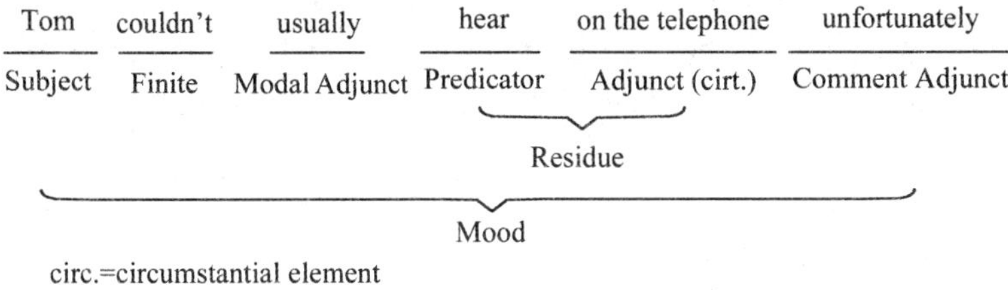

Figure 5.2 An Example for the Clause with Mood Adjunct and Comment Adjunct

Then, two categories build up a continuum with comment adjuncts paradigmatically extending from modal adjuncts. (Halliday, 1994) Moreover, comment adjuncts can be integrated into this continuum, and all of them take the implicitly objective orientation. Semantically, comment adjuncts express the speaker's attitude to the proposition as a whole or to the particular speech function, and is subcategorized into propositional and speech-functional comments. Both of them are implicitly objective in terms of orientation. In SAEC, comment adjuncts occur 718 times, with propositional comments occuring 588 times and speech-functional comments 130 times respectively. Comments adjuncts, like modal adjuncts, function as forms of realizing subjectivity. There are altogether 1085 cases in SAEC that express subjectivity by taking the implicitly objective orientation.

Fact nouns are effective mechanisms to represent fact type as they have ready been packaged in projected form. According to Halliday(1994), fact nouns can be subcategorized into four types. The chance type refers to nouns of modality, e. g. "chance", "certainty", "likelihood", etc., which are used to express modalized propositions; the need type are nouns of modulation, e. g. "necessity", "requirement", "obligation", "rule", etc., which are employed to realize modulated proposals. A fact is a kind of idea that acts as a source of pleasure, displeasure, fear or some other emotion. And, the linguistic form that is used as the act noun has been so fully semanticized that it is already wrapped and packaged to take its proper place in the linguistic structure. That is to say, fact nouns result from normalizing facts by wrapping them as embedded postmodifier clauses. For example:

(46) There is a slim chance that such a resolution could bring renewed **inspections** that would at least slow down Iraq's unconventional weapons programs. (Text 77)

(47) The restrictions on the designers included a **requirement** that the site be packed with a full 11 million square feet of office space, 600,000 square feet of retail space and another 600,000 square feet for a hotel.

(Text 69)

Both Example (46) and Example (47) embed projections, occurring as postmodifier to fact nouns in the clauses. This embedding insertion makes facts objectified and enters as constituents into the structure of clauses. In this sense, fact nouns can be used to express subjectivity in explicitly objective orientation.

As comment adjuncts and fact nouns are included in the scope defined in terms of orientation, the totality of modal expressions in terms of orientation increases to 2344 cases in SAEC. Judging from the feature of orientation, distribution patterns of modal expressions in terms of orientation can be shown in Table 5.1.

Table 5.1 Distribution Patterns of Modal Expressions in Terms of Orientation

Orientation	Subjective: explicit	Subjective: implicit	Objective: explicit	Objective: implicit	Total
Number	42	1195	22	1085	2344
Percentage	1.79%	50.98%	0.94%	46.29%	100%

As wording realizes meaning, wording then has subjective assessments realized directly by means of modal expressions. Then, the four scales of the subjective continuum are defined in accordance with linguistic resources of subjectivity in terms of modal orientation. In other words, the four scales of this subjective continuum represent four cases of linguistically-encoded subjectivity, situating relations between the subject of conception and the target of conception illustrated in Figure 5.1 (Athanasiadou, 2006: 226), which are expressed subjectively or objectively in accordance with modal orientation. This proves that orientations deal with subjectivity expressions in the lexico-grammatical strata, and constitute the system network that makes subjectivity expressed by combining types and orientations of modality. From this point, the four scales of the continuum can be regarded as corresponding to the four kinds of expressions coming from modal orientations, with the latter realizing the former.

5.2.2 Construction of Argumentativity as Negotiation Reasoning

Negotiation is a dialogue process intended to reach a beneficial outcome, which is conducted by putting forward a position and making small concessions to achieve an agreement. An editorial is of a central feature of negotiations, by which the writer makes his subjective stance expressed and the reader understands what the writer is getting at. It functions as an instruction to engage in a reasoning process of integrative negotiation, whereby a set of techniques that attempt to improve the quality and likelihood of negotiated agreement are used to create value in the course of the negotiation. (Saner, 2000)

Integrative negotiation approaches negotiation as a shared problem and adheres to objective, principled criteria as the basis for agreement. (Brazeal, 2009) Fisher & Patton (1984) provide techniques that can effectively improve the chance of reaching an agreement. Those techniques include: to discuss each others' perceptions; to find opportunities to act inconsistently with one's own views; and to save face. These three techniques work in editorials systematically for the writer to make integrative negotiation with the reader, which are explained in terms of modal orientation from three aspects. Firstly, when implicitly subjective orientation and implicitly objective orientation are drawn on, the writer adopts modal operators to imply that he openly and honestly shares his perceptions by empathizing with the perspective of the other. Secondly, in explicitly subjective orientation, the writer expresses his personal opinion clearly and permits the reader to find opportunities to act inconsistently with his intended views. Thirdly, when the implicit objective orientation is taken, the writer takes the face-saving approach by justifying a stance based on the previously expressed principles and values so as to have the stance understood from the reader's perspective. Each choice of orientation reflects the way that the writer has his subjective stance expressed, and also spares some space to bring in the readers so as to negotiate with them. This reasoning process involved in negotiation can be construed cognitively.

To evaluate the scales of subjective magnitude, it is necessary to determine the relative relationship among evidence, speaker, and proposition. Langacker (1985, 2002) discusses such relationship pertaining to the inherent asymmetry between the tacit conceptualizing presence and the targets that are waiting for conceptualization. An entity is said to be objectively construed when it appears onstage as an explicit, focused target of conception. On the contrary, when an entity goes offstage as an implicit, un-self-conscious target of conception, it is subjectively construed. The distinction between subjectivity and objectivity is a matter of degree. (Langacker, 2006) The asymmetry is maximal when the subject of conception takes the form of lacking self-awareness of remaining himself offstage, and the target of conception is totally absorbed in apprehending the onstage situation. However, when the subject of conception and the target of conception are both going inside the onstage situation, the asymmetry is correspondingly minimal. The former case is maximally subjective, and the latter is maximally objective or minimally subjective because all situations that Langacker (1990, 2002, 2006) thinks of as subjective or objective are thought of as subjective in Traugott's (1989, 2003, 2010) opinion. Thus, the continuum is formed between maximally and minimally subjective referring to the vantage point of the subject and the target of conception. Correspondingly, Athanasiadou (2006: 226) scales this continuum into four situations, as is shown in Figure 5.3.

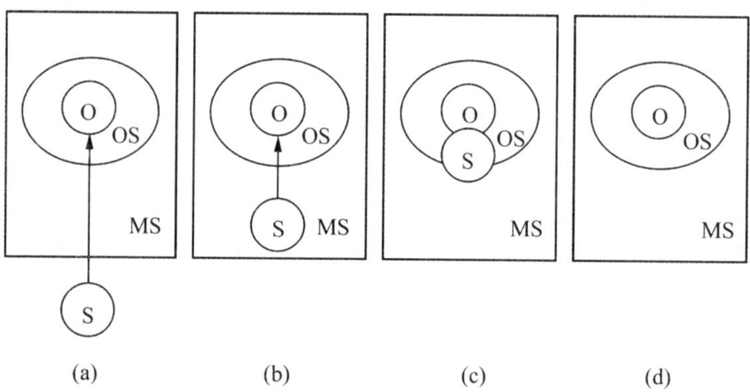

Figure 5.3 Four Scales of Subjective Continuum[①]

Here, four scales come into being in accordance with the relative relation of the subject of conceptualization and the target of conceptualization. Firstly, the speaker is totally external to the onstage region of the conceptualized entity. Secondly, the subject goes towards the inner area of the maximal scope and makes an evaluation from within, which then diminishes the objectivity of the conceptualized target. Thirdly, the subject is closer to the target of conceptualization. Fourthly, the subject is implicitly treated as one experiencer indicating this kind of individuating uses from the point within a privileged vantage place (Athanasiadou, 2006: 226-228).

① MS: maximal scope of conception; OS: onstage region; O: focused object of conception; S: subject of the subject; ↑ : apprehension by the subject.

These four scales categorized in the subjective continuum are identical to the four kinds of modal orientations: scale (a) corresponds to the explicitly subjective orientation; scale (b) to the implicitly subjective orientation; scale (c) to the implicitly objective orientation; and scale (d) to the explicitly objective orientation. Cognitively-construing processes explain the negotiation reasoning when the writer plans to express his subjective stance in modal orientation.

5.2.3 Construction of Negotiation in Terms of Modal Orientation

Different expressions indicating different orientations are chosen for the purpose of demonstrating different strengths scaled in this subjectivity continuum. Meanwhile, the attitudes that express communicating intention are realized by consciously choosing lexico-grammatical forms that are unique for their orientations. Thus, the two sides of subjectivity come together in this choosing process. This mapping correspondence between the four scales of the subjectivity continuum and the four kinds of realizations in terms of orientation reveals the significance of negotiation between the writer and the reader in editorials.

Firstly, the distinction between the construing of the maximally subjective and that of the minimally subjective leads to the demarcation of the strength of subjectivity, with the strongest subjectivity concordant to the minimally subjective and the weakest one to the maximally subjective. This mapping mode shows that the writer has various ways of delivering his opinions by dressing him up subjectively or objectively. That is to say, the cline of expressing subjectivity in line with orientation provides the writer with various ways that enable him to take or get rid of responsibility. When the writer tries to distance himself from taking responsibility, the explicitly subjective orientation of the proposal or proposition is adopted in order to shift the modal responsibility that is embodied in the subjecthood to somebody or something else. (Halliday & Matthiessen, 2004) In the same way, the explicitly objective orientation also dissimulates modal expressions as an assertion. However, the explicitly objective metaphorical realizations of subjectivity neutralize individual opinions as facts, which dress up the writer's viewpoints as if they are not his points of view at all. Thus, the existence of the writer is experientialized and he would not take any responsibility at all. (Halliday, 1994a; Halliday & Matthiessen, 2004)

Modal verbs in SFL typically signify the adoption of the implicitly subjective orientation and imply the speaker-orientation feature conventionalized in the course of subjectification. Modal verbs evolve along with the attenuation of subject control and the development of grounding predication (Langacker, 1998, 2003), and their meanings are primarily focused on the internal world of the writer and and become increasingly based on the writer's subjective attitudes (Traugott, 1989). In the process of subjectification, meanings of modal verbs tend to shift in the direction of increasing the feature of speaker-orientation which refers to an orientation towards the speaker and the speech situation. (Narrog, 2005) In this sense, the implicitly subjective orientation indicated by modal verbs shows that the speaker expresses his confidence in the truth of inferences having been made in the direct situation logically (Traugott & Dasher, 2002; Coates, 1983), for which the speaker must take responsibility at length. Contrastively, the implicitly objective orientation is typically marked by using modal adjuncts and comment adjuncts which become increasingly associated with the speaker's attitude resulting from the process of subjectivisation. To be specific, modal adjuncts and comment adjuncts can express the writer's attitudes resulting from the process, and whereby meanings come over time to index, encode and externalize the writer's perspectives and beliefs. (Schwenter & Traugott, 2000) Thus, they are free from some fixed positions and involve the development of marking function towards the ideational component of discourse structuring and towards text-structuring functions, which enable them to acquire meanings that express elaboration and clarification of the writer's intent. (Traugott, 1995; Defour, 2010) As syntactic changes indicate the degree of subjectivity that modal adjuncts and comment adjuncts express, they become rigid and their usual syntactic capacity weakens due to the speaker's consciously neglecting his presence. (Company, 2006) Accordingly, their functional development from meanings based on the external situation transfers to meanings inferred from the textual situation. These subjectivized meanings associate closely with the epistemic-evidential sense, in which the writer's assessment of the proposition is based on the fact that a subjective belief of how things happen in this world is conceived of as the shared knowledge. Then, the implicitly objective orientation demonstrates that the writer expresses this subjective assessment through the epistemic-evidential inference objectively based on the contextualized situation, which departs him from taking the responsibility of making opinionated assessment.

There exists an obvious inverse correlation between scales of the continuum in orientation and scales of the strength of subjectivity; i. e. the more subjective a form of expressing subjectivity is in terms of orientation, the weaker it is in lines with the strength of subjectivity. In terms of the interpersonal property, modality has the function of bringing the proposition down to earth and relating to context by reference to the judgement of the speaker; and it becomes the topic that can be argued about. (Halliday, 1994) Modal assessment has the property of enacting the interpersonal function, by which the speaker gains a space to negotiate with the hearer. When the speaker expresses subjectivity in the explicitly subjective orientation, he gives his attitudes directly and affirmatively, leaving almost no space to be argued about, e. g. "I think that Tom knows". He just speaks out the words from his own perspective and is ready to take the responsibility for making the stance without hesitation. When the explicitly objective orientation is adopted, the speaker packages his stance and expresses it as an assertion of a proposition or proposal as if he doesn't make any intrusion at all. Therefore, the speaker just gives out the statement and waits for the hearers to make their own interpretation freely in lines with the context. In a word, it is a way that the speaker opens enough space to negotiate with the hearer so that he can ask the hearer to align with him.

Then, the modal orientation adopted when the speaker expresses the subjective assessment relates closely to the responsibility that the speaker will take for doing so. When the explicitly subjective orientation shifts to the explicitly objective orientation via the implicitly subjective orientation and the implicitly objective orientation, it implies that the responsibility that the speaker should take is on the decrease, but the space spared for the reader to take part in the negotiation becomes larger and larger. Accordingly, more and more spaces are given for the reader to make his own interpretation or construe (in Langacker's term) of the writer's opinion in accordance with the situation, which works as the most effective way to get the reader to be aligned with.

As illuminated in Table 5. 1, in SAEC, the writer usually doesn't want to express attitudes affirmatively or take direct responsibility, as there are only 42 (1.79%) cases of subjectivity realized in the subjective explicit orientation. He does not want his attitudes encoded as the statement of propositions or proposals without leaving his traces, which can be seen from the 22 (0. 94%) cases that realize subjectivity in the objective explicit orientation. On the contrary, in SAEC, the editorial writer tends to express subjectivity in the implicitly subjective orientation or in the implicitly objective orientation. Through choosing the implicitly subjective orientation, the writer tends to express subjectivity indirectly and takes the responsibility implicitly as a result of the speaker-orientation inference. All the writers in SAEC use 1195 (50.98%) cases expressing subjectivity in the implicitly subjective orientation to deliver their subjective stances in an indirect but arbitrary way, so they leave little chance to let their beliefs to be argued about by resorting to speaker-orientated modal verbs. Since modal verbs permit alternative voices to give a suggestion or claim (Halliday, 1994b; Martin & Rose, 2003), there is some room for the writer to invite other voices to take part in the course of negotiating services or information. The editorial writer prefers to use facts, figures and examples etc. to form subjectivity as an informed, well-placed authority by employing 1085 (46.29%) cases of subjectivity coded in the implicitly objective orientation. Hence, the writer pretends to be off the present situation and makes understanding of subjectivity by referring to the contextualized situation, which owes subjectivity to the situated evidence and permits alternative voices to reevaluate this transferred subjectivity. Thus, more space is spared for other voices to make their own interpretations on this kind of intended subjectivity or for them to negotiate with the writer.

Secondly, different nodes in the subjectivity continuum not only represent different patterns of orientation that can be used to express different scales of the subjective strength, but also reflect identical matches between the patterns of orientation and the scales of the strength of subjectivity. As patterns of orientation occurring at the lexico-grammatical strata realize or represent semantically the strength of subjectivity, the realizing processes are conscious choices that the writer intentionally makes to express subjectivity in proper lexico-grammatical forms. Fundamentally, patterns of orientation are conscious and intentional choices when the speaker takes advantages of them to encode subjectivity.

In SFL, language is regarded as a kind of social phenomenon and functions when the system of the network working as resources makes meanings. This definition conceives the forms of a language as means to an end, rather than as ends. Then, the way language is organized is functional with respect to satisfying human being's needs. Modal assessment is the fundamental component of the interpersonal function, which reflects that the writer is active to act on the others in the environment. (Halliday, 1994a) In other words, the writer is active in the process of choosing some lexico-grammatical forms to express subjectivity by adopting properly to the situation. Essentially, properties of subjectivity emerge in choosing processes. Although choice doesn't, in most cases, imply that the selection of an option is either intentional or conscious (Halliday, 1969; Matthiessen & Bateman, 1991), choices of realizing subjectivity are the active actions with conscious awareness. As meaning resides in systemic patterns of choices in SFL, patterns of orientation are the outward realizations by systemic choices; that is, choices of orientation are selections among certain sets of contrasting features.

Subjectivity is the interpersonal component reflecting the writer's activeness in the course of producing the editorial. This activeness embodies as the writer's choices to realize his stance with intentional or conscious awareness, which involves the option that the writer makes among modal verbs, modal adjuncts, comment adjuncts and fact nouns to give expression to subjectivity on the one hand, and the act of choosing a strategical operation to deliver subjectivity indirectly on the other. According to the definition of subjectivity upheld by Langacker (1998, 2003), when the subjective explicit orientation is chosen, it construes the case where the writer works on the stage. However, when the other three orientations are chosen, the writer always expresses subjectivity by operating off the stage. Specifically, in the explicitly subjective orientation, the writer appears overtly on the stage to express subjectivity. However, in the other three patterns of orientation, the writer is off the stage to realize subjectivity covertly.

For this reason, the subjectivity continuum can be divided into two parts according to the writer imprinting his existence in linguistic forms or not, to illustrate how the writer identifies himself in the process of expressing subjectivity. In the explicitly subjective orientation, the writer signs his appearance overtly with the first person pronoun "I" or its plural form "we" to express his attitudes and beliefs by working on the stage. In SAEC, the editorial writer adopts 42 (1.79%) times of the pronoun "we" to express subjectivity, which shows that the writer rarely communicates his attitudes and beliefs straightforward in overt forms in editorials. Comparatively, the writer hides his appearance intentionally and strategically by choosing the other three patterns of orientation when he conceals his appearance in the process of encoding subjectivity, which gives the cues of the writer's working off the stage to make beliefs and attitudes expressed covertly by choosing lexical forms such as modal verbs, modal adjuncts, or comment adjuncts, or by making use of metaphorical structures. The remaining 2302 cases, rating 98.21% to the total forms of subjectivity in SAEC, realize subjectivity in the implicitly subjective orientation, the explicitly objective orientation or the implicitly objective orientation, which make it clear that the writer tends to work off the stage to make subjectivity expressed in covert forms in editorials.

In sum, the writer's activeness in expressing subjectivity is demonstrated as the subjectivity continuum in terms of orientation is constructed. This continuum reflects the potential of the writer to make appropriate choices to express subjectivity, and functions as the interface that represents the different vantage points adopted in the conceptualizing presence, indicates different degrees of responsibility taken in evaluating subjectivity, and spares different spaces for the writer to argue with the readers. The choices of different orientations are fundamentally the writer's conscious action with the aim to fulfill the persuasive function.

5.3 Construction of Argumentativity in Terms of Values

Argumentative strength concerns the magnitude of the "force which the warrant leads to the conclusion" (Toulmin, 2003: 99). An argument is regarded as a claim that is based on supporting data in accord with a warrant, the strength of which can be assessed based on the scales to which it is evaluated, as is reflected in the value variable of modality.

5.3.1 Regulation of Value Attached to Modal Expressions

As the variable in the system of modality, value has three ranks: high, medium and low, which is historically fossilized as an essential property of the modal expressions. This hypothesis has been proven true in one language or cross-linguistically by lots of studies and scholars: Horn (1972), Coates (1983), Steele (1975), Bybee, Perkins & Pagliuca (1994) etc. However, these kinds of researches have gone beyond the present discussion. Within the realm of SFL, value is firmly accepted as the third variable in modality. The modal expression must be chosen with value properties considered. The property of value is used to regulate the argumentative strength of editorials as the writer's subjective stance is expressed.

In this study, the expressions that can be labeled with the value property are classified into three types: the modal operators, the modal adjuncts and the driven forms out of the modal operators and the modal adjuncts. As the value is demarcated in terms of the modal operator and the modal adjunct in SFL (Halliday & Matthiessen, 2004: 116; Halliday, 1994: 76), it is easy to identify values by referring to these standards. The three values of modal operators have been exemplified in Table 5.2.

Table 5.2 Values of Modal Operators

	Low	Medium	High
Positive	can, may, could, might, (dare)	will, would, should, is/was to	must, ought to, need, has/had to
Negative	needn't, doesn't/didn't need to, have to	won't, wouldn't, shouldn't, (isn't/wasn't to)	mustn't, oughtn't to, can't, couldn't, (mayn't, mightn't, hasn't/hadn't to)

Besides, the derived forms out of the modal operators and the modal adjuncts include adverbs, adjectives, nouns and phrases involved in this sort of adjectives or nouns or both. Similarly, we can resort to the standards that help to mark the values of the modal operator and the modal adjunct. Therefore, it is not very hard to confirm their values.

The value variable of modality is differentiated in three levels, but is not rigidly changeless. Under some certain circumstances, it can admittedly be weakened or strengthened so as to regulate the argumentative strength through adopting to the context.

Historically, the modal expression evolves to be endowed with values of different levels. Their values, especially the two "outer" values in the system of polarity—high and low, are influenced deeply by the negative. The negative can transfer freely between the proposition and the modality at the medium level, but the value switches correspondingly from high to low, or from low to high with the outer values. In SAEC, the value transfers due to the negative outlines like the following three types.

Firstly, if the negative is transferred, values of the modal operator will switch properly, as is shown in Table 5.3.

Table 5.3 Value Switches Due to Transferred Negative

	From low to high				From high to low	
Cases	cannot, can't, can never	could not	might not	may not, may never	need not, do not need to	be not going to
Number	33	7	4	5	2	1

According to Table 5.3, there are altogether 52 cases of value transference happening to the modal operator. Surprisingly, 49 cases among them switch from low to high, and only 3 cases switch from high to low.

Secondly, as to the case that the negative transference happens to the verbal group of modulation, there are 10 cases altogether. Similarly, 9 cases switch from low to high, but only 1 switches from high to low. It is cited by Examples (48), (49), (50) and (51).

(48) Yet terrorism **must not be allowed to** turn the so-called information superhighway—to reach for a term from more carefree days—into a series of private information culdesacs. (Text 84)

(49) A cap, however, is **not permissible** under the statute. (Text 36)

(50) Many families are waiting for others to go first, partly to see how much they get, while others **are not yet emotionally ready to** translate grief into dry actuarial statistics. (Text 53)

(51) But the country ought not to be led into war on the basis of information the American people **are not allowed to** share. (Text 64)

The third type is not directly relevant to the transferred negative, but the value switches to some modal expressions only because they are influenced by the words indicating the negative meaning, such as "no one", "nothing", "none", "not one" and "nor". And there are just two modal operators "can" and "could" involved in this type. There are altogether 10 cases belonging to this type, and their values switch from low to high. For example:

(52) Six months ago, **no one could** have begun to hope that ground zero would look the way it does today. (Text 43)

(53) **None** of these groups **can be permitted to** control the future of this site. (Text 56)

(54) But what these proposals demonstrate most conclusively is that **nothing memorable can** be done in Lower Manhattan if the Port Authority insists on reclaiming every inch of commercial space that it controlled before Sept. 11. (Text 58)

(55) **Nor can** America and its allies abruptly close the Saudi oil spigot. (Text 79)

Besides the value changes due to the negative transference, there are other strategies that can help to regulate the value. The variants of the verb "do" are added so as to stress the strength of the modal judgement, e. g. "does need to". For example:

(56) The United States **does need to** protect itself and its citizens from the possibility that smaller nations will gang up on Americans just because they suddenly find they can. (Text 57)

Moreover, some certain linguistic resources are chosen as the epithets of the modal expressions in order to regulate the degree of the assessment. In this study, intensive adverbs, such as "more than", "almost", "too", "quite", "especially", "still", "also", etc., quality adjectives, such as "slim", "simple", "dire", etc., and comparative forms, such as "more", "the most", "less", etc., are used to strengthen or weaken the degrees of the modal assessments. For example:

(57) Americans are **more than** ready to rise up and give him their support. (Text 1)

(58) The first is that Afghanistan remains in **dire** need of an expanded international security force, something the administration has flatly rejected. (Text 46)

(59) There is a **slim** chance that such a resolution could bring renewed inspections that would at least slow down Iraq's unconventional weapons programs. (Text 66)

5.3.2 Construction of Argumentative Reasoning in Terms of Value

As modal assessment refers to the intermediate area of meaning between positive and negative polarity, its value variable represents a scale on which modal expressions can also occupy in-between positions. The value variable has historically evolved to be the subjectivized property of modality. In this sense, the modal expression, no matter whether it is the modal operator or the modal adjunct, provides various forms like the reservoir of linguistic resources to realize values in practical utterances. In this study, various variants of the modal expression are chosen to realize values in the actual uses. Then, we exploit the reasons for the interpersonal effect and the rhetoric effect.

The modal expression relates closely to the mood element and mainly carries out the interpersonal function. Besides, the value gives an index to the speaker's intention of enacting the interpersonal function. The interpersonal effect prominently underlines that the realization of the value fulfills the interpersonal function successfully. Typically, an act of producing the discourse is an interactive process, by which the producer sets up proper linguistic devices in order to forestall a set of intentional anticipation. (Halliday, 1994a; Halliday & Matthiessen, 2004) The modality system is to some extent a part of these devices. Accordingly, the value system in modality mirrors exactly the intermediate degrees between the positive and negative poles. By depending on the value system, the speaker can express his judgement on the modalized proposition and the modulated proposal, and ulteriorly makes quantitative differentiation of them as high, medium and low. In return, when producing discourse, the speaker can properly choose, by complying with the context, modal expressions with due values so as to express his modal assessment. For example:

(60) Mr. Bush need not reshape his government, but he **does need to** reach across the aisle to Democratic Congressional leaders for ideas as well as support. (Text 1)

In Example (60), the modal expression with the high value—does need to—is used to covertly convey the speaker's judgement towards the modulated proposal; i. e. the speaker personally thinks that it is very necessary for Mr. Bush to ask for Democratic

Congressional leaders' ideas as well as support. This interpretation can also be proven from other side: this high modal assessment is also highlighted by the stressing verb "do", which is contextually ratiocinated by being compared with another modulated proposal "Mr. Bush need not reshape his government". Effectively, the speaker succeeds in transmitting his modal assessment of the proposition or proposal. In this way, he efficiently steers the information flow. Generally speaking, the interpersonal function would be completed in this process.

The way that the speaker chooses to express the modality value is connected with the rhetoric effect of the discourse. Rhetoric is actually an art of discourse, and is thought of as a technique of using language effectively and persuasively in the process of creating discourse. (Caballero, Dickinson & Townsend, 1984; Lindqvist, 2008) The transferred negative works as a discourse strategy to regulate the values of modality. Opposite to the formally unmarked positive, the negative is distinctly marked by some additional element. (Halliday & Matthiessen, 2004) Since the negative is formally marked, the value switch that is related to the negative is then regarded as conscious wording. For example:

(61) **None** of these groups alone **can be permitted to** control the future of this site. (Text 56)

In Example (61), "none" as the negative element denies the two modal expressions "can" and "be permitted to", so that it causes their values to switch from low to high. Therefore, why not use the modal expressions with high values "these groups alone must be required not to control the future of this site" directly? By comparing these two expressions, we can analyze the advantages of the transferred negative from three aspects. Firstly, "none" is the theme loaded with the focus of information. Secondly, the low value "can be permitted to" is much milder than the high value "must be required to", and is much more polite and more easily acceptable. Thirdly, the clause here represents the accumulation of new information distilled by the whole passage. In a sense, the wording with the transferred negative just serves this function of working as the hyperNew because it is so markedly intensified and structurally coherent to the above that it is consciously arranged to strengthen the value of the subjective assessment and formally attract the reader's attention. Evidently, the speaker makes the best use of the transferred negative for the purpose of serving the rhetoric effect of the discourse.

5.3.3 Construction of Argumentativity in Terms of Value

An editorial is of great argumentativity, and involves a series of rhetorical devices to convey the writer's subjective stance to influence the reader. In SAEC, distribution patterns of modal assessment reflect typical characteristics in terms of value, which can be seen clearly in Figure 5.4.

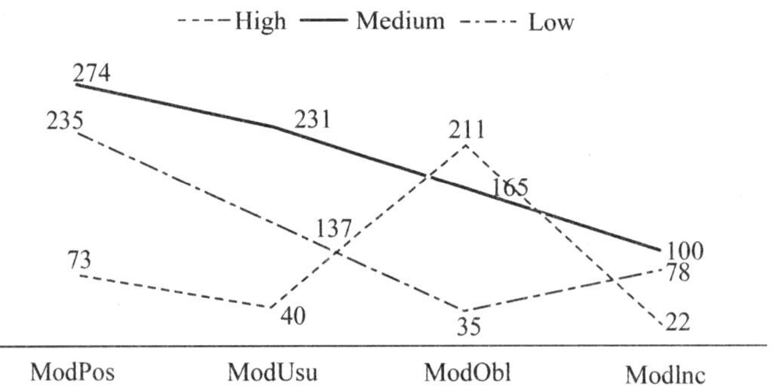

Figure 5.4 Distribution Patterns of Modal Assessments in Terms of Value

In terms of value variables, modal assessment can be interpreted as a resource to build up degrees of positivity and negativity, and can construct a guiding trend of evaluation as grading polarity. As is shown in Figure 5.4, distribution patterns in terms of value reflect these characteristics through their frequencies. Firstly, in general, the frequencies in the medium value (770 cases; 48.28%) are predominantly higher than those in the high (346 cases; 21.89%) except for the case of the obligation type, and those in the low value (485 cases; 29.83%). Secondly, the frequencies in the high value are the lowest on the whole, but it reaches to the highest peak in the type of obligation, appearing 211 cases (51.33% of all appearances of obligation). Thirdly, the frequencies in low value remain at the median level, but it descends to the lowest point in the obligatory type, occurring 35 times (8.51% to all appearances of obligation).

In view of these distribution patterns formed in accordance with the value variable, motivations are explored with respect to argumentativity. Argumentativity is of a typical feature of editorials, for which the writer takes advantage of language to influence the reader's emotions or to play with the language to reach desired goals.

The choice of words is vital in the process of persuasion because the writer uses them to negotiate with and play on the sensations of the readers. Modal assessment with less than maximal strength may leave some room for discussion and negotiation; that is, a strength of non-high value (medium or low value) will leave room for discussion. However, when the strength of the negation is high, no space will be left for cancelling the inference that it is not worth trying. (Verhagen, 2005)

In SAEC, the writer uses the medium value to indicate that the authorial opinions are expressed politely to be negotiated easily because the pertinent attitude is much more persuasive than the rough eloquence. However, as far as the type of obligation is concerned, the high value reaches to the highest peak, by which the writer indicates that the reader is obliged or expected to perform certain actions under certain conditions.

5.4 Construction of Argumentativity in Terms of Judging Appraisals

Judging appraisals are defined as resources to realize the judgement of appraisal, contrasting with affect and appreciation, which enact judgements in terms of the parameter of people, especially their behaviour. Judgement is made through depending on features of a character, such as "how special", "how capable", "how dependable", "how honest" and "how ethical". Grammatically, judgements are realizationally linked to modality. (Martin & Rose, 2003; Martin & White, 2005) The parameters in terms of which judgements are made are social esteem and social sanction.

5.4.1 Subjective Judgement: Social Esteem and Social Sanction

In essence, appraisal is one of the three major discourse semantic resources construing interpersonal meaning in SFL, and it works on evaluation in other models in various ways. (Martin & White, 2005) Hunston & Thompson (2000) make a useful distinction between opinions about entities and opinions about propositions. That is, opinions about entities are primarily attitudinal and carry positive and negative feelings, while opinions about propositions are canonically epistemic and deal with different degrees of certainty. By taking a choice of lexico-grammar as a meaning which creates resource rather than a set of forms, Martin & White (2005) note that the realization of an attitude scopes across a phase of discourse, regardless of grammatical boundaries. Martin (1992: 3) treats the grammatical systems of modalization and modulation as "epistemic" and "deontic" modality respectively, and this differentiation allows linguists to reason both semantically and grammatically.

As one subsystem of attitude, judgement is concerned with resources for assessing behavior and evaluating characters according to certain normative principles. Besides, the elements for constructing judgement manifest grammatical distinctions in the system of modality. (Halliday, 1994) According to Iedema, Feez & White (1994), the parameters defining the major types of judgement are closer to these modal oppositions, i. e. fate for normality, resolve for tenacity, truth for veracity, and ethics for propriety.

Martin & White (2005) put judgement under appraisal system, which deals with the writers' attitudes to people and their character in the way that they are measured up. In general, judgements are further classified into two types as those dealing with "social esteem" and those oriented to "social sanction". The former concerns how special someone is, how capable he is, and how dependable he is, known as "normality", "capacity" and "tenacity" respectively. While the latter, judgements of sanction, has to deal with "veracity", i. e. "how honest someone is" and "propriety", i. e. "how far someone's action is beyond reproach". Social esteem is apt to be policed in the oral culture, through chat, gossip, jokes and stories of various kinds. (Eggins & Slade, 1997) Sharing values in the scope of harmonious social esteem is critical to the formation of harmonious social networks. Moreover, the social sanction is usually codified in formal style, such as edicts, decrees, rules, regulations and laws. What's more, penalties and punishments act as levers against those who do not comply with the codes. Sharing values of social sanction underpins civic duty and religious observance formally and ritually to certain procedure. (Martin & White, 2005)

Halliday's study on modality and interpersonal metaphor provides a bridge between modality and appraisal. (Halliday, 1994a; Halliday & Matthiessen, 2004) A set of linguistic devices are chosen to realize probability, usuality and capacity, ranging from congruent forms and metaphorical ones to lexis which is clearly appraising in nature. For example:

(a) Tom's clever.

(b) Tom's certainly clever.

(c) It's certain Tom's clever.

(d) It's true Tom's clever.

(e) It's true, honest, credible, authentic... that Tom's clever. [judgement: veracity]

The above examples show that the writer realizes judgements towards the proposition "Tom's clever" by using the modal adjunct "certainly" or in metaphorically-formed objective implicit "It's certain" and "It's true", or by lexis "true, honest, credible, authentic" appraising the veracity of the action. Thus, modalizations of probability get a connection with lexicalized judgements of veracity.

Veracity is to probability what modalities of usuality are to judgements of normality. Similarly, capacity is to ability what tenacity is to inclination, and propriety is to obligation. (Martin & White, 2005) Since all these new terms are introduced, the relation between types of modality and types of judgement is established, as is shown in Figure 5.5.

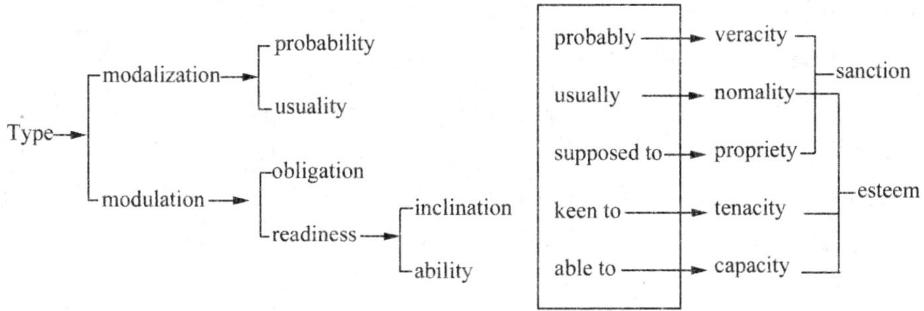

Figure 5.5 Relations between Modality and Types of Judgement

5.4.2 Management of Argumentative Evaluation in Terms of Judgement

van Dijk (1995: 2-6) has elaborated his opinions on newspaper editorials as "the result of a mental judgement"; i.e., the evaluations and judgements presented in editorials come from what the writer believes to be right or wrong. An opinion is like an evaluative belief, which is associated with individuals and is always deemed to be subjective in the sense that it is what someone thinks to be true. When an opinion is expressed in the discourse, it must be judged and justified according to the socio-cultural norms of a specific community. These socio-cultural norms lead to positive or negative judgements of social esteem and social sanction. In return, realizations of social esteem and social sanction are oriented to express editorials' opinions: positive judgements of social esteem and social sanction accumulate the strength to steer the discourse information flow at will; negative judgements, however, indicate that the discourse is arranged to unfold beyond expectation.

Judgement is always thought of as the institutionalization of feeling, concerning how people should behave, which involves making judgements on behavior from a positive or negative dimension. Judgements are expressed in the course of producing discourse, and they are presented by proper linguistic forms which explain the phenomena that some ideational meanings can be invoked to express judgement meanings in certain contexts. (Li, 2004) In return, the sensitivity of context underlines its importance of determining varieties of judgements at the discourse level; then, it is important to take context into account, instead of simply analyzing items on by one. (Martin & Rose, 2003) The realizations of judgements should not be discussed only at the lexical level, but all kinds of linguistic resources should be taken advantage of. (Hu, 2009; Thompson & Hunston, 2001) It is sure that all kinds of linguistic resources will be involved in, ranging from the lexical level to the discourse level. Based on the backdrop of value judgements, the authorial voice is positioned in terms of these attitudinal assessments against which all texts operate. (Martin & White, 2005) This raises the issue of how the authorial voice positions itself in accordance with the anticipated reactions and responses of the audience being construed for the text.

Judgements can be divided into two major groups: social esteem and social sanction. (Iedema et al., 1994; Eggins & Slade, 1997) Social esteem tends to be governed in oral culture through informal communicating forms with humor playing a critical role. Social esteem mainly comes down to admiration and criticism without legal implications, and pays attention to building up the social network of sharing identical values. Judgements of esteem deal with normality, capacity and tenacity. In contrast, judgements of sanction deal with veracity and propriety. It is encoded in writings, such as edicts, decrees, rules, regulations and laws. From this point of view, social sanction often goes along with praise and condemnation by depending on statute law as the judging criteria. As judgement deals with traits that the writer admires as well as those he criticizes, it can be evaluated as positive or negative accordingly.

When the positive judgement is denoted, the writer launches and/or reinforces a prosody that directs the reader in the evaluation of rationality at his will. For example:

> (62) The Bush administration has sharply **ratcheted up the pressure** on Pakistan this week, as well it should, and Pakistan indicated yesterday that it may cooperate. (Text 4)

In Example (62), the verbal group "ratchet up" means to increase by a fixed amount or degree, and unlikely to decrease again, and it is infused with a manner-connoted attitude as "increasing gradually and effectively". Contextually, this verbal group can be interpreted as the way that the writer connotatively flags his attitude of praising the Bush administration's capacity of effective actions. It acts as the marker to indicate that the writer aims to provoke a praising response in the readers. Evidentially, reading position for interpretation that Pakistan may cooperate is followed as it is expected in the context. Similarly, a negative judgement is one mechanism that construes some action or event in contrast with expectation (Martin & White, 2005), which functions as the sign of counter-expectancy in discourse. For example:

> (63) The administration spent much of yesterday to overcome the impression that Mr. Bush showed **weakness** when he did not immediately return to Washington after the terrorists struck. (Text 1)

In Example (63), "weakness" indicates negative evaluation on Mr. Bush's incapacity of dealing with the terrorists struck. As we all know, the president should stick to his post in the face of the emergency. The writer chooses "weakness" here to criticize Mr. Bush's incapability and to show the sign of his counter-expectancy revealing the unexpected action—he did not immediately return to Washington after the terrorists struck—which is recounted in the immediately following adverbial clause. In conclusion, social esteem and social sanction with the positive or negative value can act as the sign-post of expressing expectancy or counter-expectancy in discourse.

5.4.3 Management of Argumentativity in Terms of Judging Appraisals

An editorial is an argumentative opinion article, which spreads an ideology among the public in order to influence them. Opinions expressed in editorials are moral and righteous as they are judged and justified according to the socio-cultural norms of a specific community (van Dijk, 1995). According to Walton (2001), this kind of opinion comes from the popular belief of a society, and this source constitutes its reasonability in that it is taken for granted this kind of belief is true especially when it is used in a particular context. In this point, opinions are evaluative when they are related to a specific cultural community.

Besides, the evaluation of events or other people is accompanied by emotions and attitudes, and the verbal expression of such emotions at the same time expresses the subjective stance. (van Dijk, 1995) This evaluation is explored in the appraisal judgement in accordance with social esteem and social sanction and is realized in judging appraisals.

As far as SAEC is concerned, those three types, namely normality, capacity and tenacity, occur 617 (57.87%) times, with 437 of them appearing in positive type and 180 of them in negative type. Hence, we can see that judgements of esteem are much more preferred in editorials around Sept. 11 Attack. This tendency is explained with respect to the argumentativity of these arrangements from three sides. Firstly, editorials are supposed to reflect the opinion of the periodical, whose writers are always the senior editorial staff. Usually, a newspaper's editorial evaluates which issues are important for the reader to understand the newspaper's opinion. (Passante, 2007) The *NYT* often puts editorials under the heading "opinion". Editorials around Sept. 11 Attack reflect *NYT*'s opinion that the most important thing is to call on American victims to recover from the panic-stricken scar of terrorist attack. For this reason, the writers make most uses of judgements of esteem, in order to pacify American's panic emotion and calm down the manic mood of revenge. Secondly, the positive occurrences reach as highly as 70.83%, which results from 437/617. Therefore, it is clear that the writers tend to deliver positive values in the face of this kind of unexpected attacks, in order to persuade Americans to act reasonably as usual, to ask Americans to rise to the occasion resolutedly, and predict that all relevant people, institutions and the government and so on are able to pull up their slacks to get through this disastrous attack. Thirdly, opposite to the appearances in positive, there are 180 cases of social esteem occurring in negative, which rates lowly to 29.17% in judgements of esteem. Although this part is small, it still reflects that the writer has noted some problems exposed by the terrorist attack. These problems involve various fields, mainly covering individual incapacities, institutional fallbacks, administration confusion, and so on. However, the purpose of exposing all these problems is to analyze the reasons behind them and put forth suggestions for relevant people and institutions to take actions.

However, judgements of veracity and propriety, in SAEC, appear 449 (42.11%) times altogether, with 168 of them appearing in positive type and 281 in negative type. Compared with judgements of esteem, statistical results show that there are two features related to judgements of sanction used in editorials: judgements of sanction are used less frequently than judgements of esteem; and negative judgements of sanction appear much more frequently than positive ones, just opposite to cases of judgements of esteem. Further analysis is made about the characters revealed in SAEC and relevant to judgements of sanction. Usually, editorials are written to deliberately influence the social cognition of their readers by making good uses of different persuasion and argumentation strategies and devices. (Farrokhi & Nazemi, 2015) As a kind of media discourse, editorials aim to persuade their readers to take certain actions, or to influence their attitudes toward the issues just being discussed. (van Dijk, 1995) The writer prefers to express evaluations emotionally and tactfully by means of the cultural background, rather than speak out requirements directly. This can explain to some extent why the frequency of judgements of sanction is lower than that of social sanction. However, the editorial, by nature, belongs to the opinion discourse type, which requires the writer to express his judgements on certain persons involved in the issue being discussed: "how ethical they are", or "how truthful they are". Then, it is necessary that expressions of social sanction should be presented properly in discourse.

Editorials around Sept. 11 Attack are fundamentally texts of criticism, which no doubt give expressions of condemnation on the terrorist, and criticism in the course of finding out the causes and effects pertaining to this event. In this way, it is not surprising that expressions of negative sanction are much more preferred than those of positive sanction.

5.5 Construction of Argumentativity in Terms of Subjective Expectations

An editorial is an opinion text through which the writer aims to influence the reader by steering the discourse information flow with propositions supporting stated opinions. It is the writer's strategy to bring in a proposition sourced to the third party to support his subjective stance, as an argument is always composed of a proposition and a support. (Gauthier, 2007) Proposition, in this study, refers to an idea, a claim or a statement, which is used as the argumentative strategy to have the stance strengthened as the writer subjectively expects.

5.5.1 Categories of Subjective Expectations

Subjective expectation is elaborated based on the expectancy theory. Expectancy theory indicates that the speaker will act in certain ways if he is motivated to select a specific behavior instead of others due to the results of the selected behavior. Essentially, the motivation of the selection is determined by the desirability of the outcome. (Oliver, 1974) Subjective expectation is about the mental processes of choice, which explains what the writer undergoes to make choices oriented to goals. Then, there forms a positive correlation between efforts and performance: a favorable performance will result in a desirable reward in order to satisfy an important need, which in return makes the effort worthwhile.

Subjective expectation concerns consciously choosing processes by which the writer makes a decision on linguistic resources that can realize meanings when the writer produces a discourse. Subjective expectation includes two subcategories: expectancy and counter-expectancy. Expectancy refers to the ways that the writer depends on to flag his expectation to unfold a discourse. (Martin & Rose, 2003) Technically, conjunctions play an important role in letting the writer manage expectancy relations at each step of producing a discourse. Counter-expectancy is the strategy of using a key resource to lead to expecting one thing and then countering it with reality. Expectancy and counter-expectancy are outcomes of setting up logical relations or inter-connections between events, which is realized through wordings that include conjunctions, e. g. "and", "like", "finally", etc., and continuatives, e. g. "even", "still", "yet", etc. Conjunctions serve as logical connections between figures by comparing, sequencing, adding, or explaining them in discourse. Continuatives usually occur next to the finite verbs in the clause and function as a kind of source for evaluation, which can adjust our expectations in the discourse. In general, conjunctions and continuatives are characteristic of monitoring expectancy in discourse because they can engage alternative voice as heteroglossia to track the reader's expectation.

Heteroglossia stresses that all verbal communications are "dialogic", because it indicates that to speak or write is not only to take part in some way what has been said before, but also to expect the reader's responses. Bakhtin (1981) observes that all utterances exist against a background consisting of contradictory opinions, points of view and value judgements that are pregnant with responses and objections. In this sense, heteroglossia provides the means to characterize a writer's interpersonal style and his rhetorical strategies that are used to construct the heteroglossic backdrop for other voices and viewpoints in the discourse. This dialogic perspective concerns the signals that the writer provides to show how he expects the reader to respond to the current propositions.

5.5.2 Adjustment of Argumentative Direction in Terms of Engagement

In editorials, the writer operates to locate himself with respect to value positions that are referenced in the text against alternative opinions, points of view and value judgements. Those locutions represent the other voices and alternative positions expressed in the communicative context, and are grouped in the system of engagement. Engagement, in this sense, provides the means for the authorial voice to position itself with respect to the other voices and hence to engage with them.

Ego is he who says it, and it is where the foundation of subjectivity is determined by the linguistic status of person. (Benveniste, 1971) As the essential character of subjectivity is the capacity of the speaker to posit or construe himself as "subject", the first person designating ego obtains a status of transcendence which enables "I" to ask for the third person of evidence to persuade "you". Thus, the third person can function to bring alternative positions into the discourse to help to express the writer's proposition.

Engagement is orientated towards meanings in the context and rhetorical effects of the discourse, instead of grammatical forms. It uses a lexical and/or grammatical diverse selections of locutions in that they are used to operate so as to locate the writer with respect to the value positions expressed in discourse and with respect to, in Bakhtin's terms, the background of alternative opinions, points of view and value judgements against which all discourses operate. This selection includes wordings which have been dealt with under the heading of engagement. Besides, this kind of locutions can provide the means for the authorial voice to position itself with respect to, and hence to engage with, other voices of alternative positions construed in the current communicative context. Moreover, those selections will be demonstrated as overt markers of the point of views or attitudes of meanings and structures that bulge the self-expressive function of language while building up the authorial voice on the base of value judgements on the one hand, and concern their intersubjective property when presenting themselves as aligning with the value position advanced in discourse by turning to the communities of shared value and belief on the other hand. All these overt markers realize subjective expectation because they function as the linguistic signs of the way that the writer designs to unfold discourse to manage the discursive flow of information to meet to or counter against the reader's expectation.

Because of their rhetorical nature, editorials are distinguished by the characteristics in terms of various types of opinions used in them. (Elyazale, 2014) These opinions based on popular beliefs, emotions, facts, and evaluations are engaged in discourse in accordance with its persuasive function, which is brought into the discourse by means of strategies, such as entertain, pronounce, acknowledge and endorse, appearing as specific numbers, or in the form of rhetoric questions, or as quoting statements. Numbers are used as a linguistic tool to prove the strength of the argument (Shahri, 2010: 116); and, their introduction characterizes a strong rhetorical feature of editorials, for they suggest the precision of information and indicates its seriousness. Rhetoric questions are one of the most effective linguistic expressions in argumentation, which are adapted to stress the speaker's opinion. (Shahri, 2010) This kind of questions play an important role in argumentation because a question appearance requires a topic through which given possible agreement is expected and the potential answer embedded functions to emphasize this agreement. (Toulba, 2010) In editorial discourse, sayings or thoughts of weighty persons in economic, political or social areas are quoted directly or indirectly to strengthen the position taken. Quote and report are then used as argumentative strategies like "proofs" and "prepared arguments or witnesses", which helps in elevating the discourse producer into a higher rank because he obtains certain power from this reporting. (Shahri, 2010) Through quoting, religious texts, proverbs, wisdom statements are drawn on to strengthen the truthfulness of the arguments advanced and justify the morality of the text. In general, strategies of entertain, pronounce, acknowledge and endorse are drawn on by taking advantages of numbers, wisdom statements, religious texts, proverbs, etc. so as to strengthen the argumentative opinions upheld in discourse. These strategies are used by the writer to steer the discourse information as expected, which functions to increase the chances of realizing the subjective expectation. In this sense, strategies of entertain, pronounce, endorse and acknowledge are to raise the degree of the subjective magnitude in terms of satisfying the subjective expectation.

Comparatively, the strategy of distance opens up the space for alternative positions, for which the authorial voice is distanced from taking the responsibility. The positioning of the opinions based on popular beliefs, emotions, facts and evaluations is attributed to some external voices, among which the writer can choose to keep his position away from the proposition. The opinion thus introduced is regarded as being grounded on the subjectivity of an external voice, which is usually brought into the text by such kinds of distancing formulations as "X claims that", "it's rumoured that" etc. The authorial voice represents this proposition as the target, against which he advances his position as discourse unfolds. The effect is to invite the opposite alternatives and thereby to lower the interpersonal cost for anyone who would advance such an alternative. (Martin & White, 2003: 103) It follows that the strategy of distance is the way that the writer resorts to to develop his position advanced intentionally in discourse through suppressing the opinions that are wrongly upheld at that time. Thus, the strategy of distance fundamentally functions as the linguistic marks to introduce such kinds of information against expectancy or counter-expectancy. Then, it is reasonable to believe that the strategy of distance can be used to lower the chances of realizing the subjective expectation. Hence, distance is thought as the strategy to lower the degree of the subjective magnitude in terms of satisfying the subjective expectation.

5.5.3 Construction of Argumentativity in Terms of Engaging Opinions

Subjective expectation involves expectancy and counter-expectancy, and it works to promote events to take place as expected or regard events as countering expectation to impede them from happening. Subjective expectation presents the writer's intentional force to strengthen or weaken the chance of motivating the events under discussion to happen. In this sense, subjective expectation is motivated to reflect the strengthening or weakening aspect of subjective stance.

Engagements of alternative positions are the effective strategies that the writer uses to highlight the position. The taxonomy of engagement is orientated to recognize the particular positioning relevant to given meanings and to stress what is at stake when one meaning rather than another is employed. The writer contracts the argumentation by means of disclaiming or proclaiming alternative positions. However, to entertain or attribute external positions is the tactics that the writer deplores to strengthen the propositions expressed in discourse. The purpose of engaging other voices is to strengthen his viewpoint through supporting it by means of rejecting the opposite ones.

In this study, we just divide engagement into three categories with respect to strategies that the writer resorts to to express his opinions in discourse: entertain and pronounce refer to the strategies that the writer indicates his individual position covertly; acknowledge and endorse deal with the strategies that the writer resorts to to consolidate his position indirectly. However, distance concerns evidences that the writer uses to go against opposite positions, by which the writer can depart himself from taking responsibility. Entertainment, pronouncement, acknowledgement and endorsement are strategies through which the writer seeks help to drive the position to go as expected, which in this sense function as linguistic devices marking expectancy. However, distance provides the position that is opposite to the viewpoint constructed in discourse and thus works as the target to be fended off so as to strengthen intentional propositions from the opposite side. Then, distance occurs as the linguistic marker rejecting a certain position of counter-expectancy.

All these three strategies of engagement are drawn on to lead facts, evidence, and/or alternative positions into discourse, by which the writer acts consciously to align or disalign with the proposition owed to the external source so as to transfer his intended proposition. In SAEC, 410 cases of these strategies are used. Entertainment and pronouncement covertly indicate the writer's position. The former cares evidence and/or appearance-based postulations, e. g. "it seems", "the research suggests", "it appears", and rhetorical questions. The latter is a discourse—semantically, rhetorically motivated category with lexico-grammatical diverse realizations, in which objective, implicit realizations are treated as study targets. Both of them amount to 28 cases with the lowest percentage 6. 83%. Acknowledgement and endorsement are used 292 times and occupy the highest rate 71.22%, which is the strategy of consolidating the writer's opinions indirectly by turning to the third party's position. Distance refers to the strategy of the writer distancing himself from responsibility by using the third party's position as an explicit opposition to positions advanced contextually. 90 cases of this strategy depart the writer from taking responsibility, and the rate is a moderate 21.95%.

Entertainment refers to the wordings by which the writer indicates that his position is just one of a number of possible positions and thereby the authorial voice entertains those alternatives. Here, we concern "rhetorical questions" in the category of entertain. This type of questions is employed in the singly-constructed, non-interactive context to entertain instead of asserting some propositions, by which the reader is positioned to supply a particular answer. (Sadock, 1974) They are frequently used as an effective persuasive device by the writer to influence the reader to respond as expected. For example:

(64) If in fact the government is treating its detainees fairly, why not be more forthcoming? (Text 82)

The category of pronouncement covers formulations which index authorial emphases or authorial interpolations into discourse. Pronouncing formulations delivering facts constitute a typical intervention of the authorial presence so as to assert the value or insist upon warrantability of the proposition, by which the writer counters against some context-referenced position. As a rhetorically, discourse-semantically motivated category, realizations of pronouncement are lexico-grammatically diverse (Martin & White, 2005). The writer's opinion is brought into discourse in different ways. For example:

(65) **The fact** that most of the terrorists in the Sept. 11 attack, if not all, entered the country legally should not blind Congress to the need to block illegal entries by increasing security along its porous borders with Mexico and Canada. (Text 74)

In Example (65), the fact is projected as embedded nominalization functioning as Head, which frequently occurs as postmodifier to a noun of the "fact" class. It takes the explicit objective orientation with the writer operating covertly underground.

Frequently, the writers ask for the propositions sourced to external voices to establish the basis for them to argue the correctness of their positions. In this study, endorsement and acknowledgement are regarded as strategies to play this function. According to Martin & White (2005), endorsement refers to the formulations by which the writer imports propositions attributed to external sources but believed by the writer as correct, valid, undeniable or otherwise maximally warrantable. In this way, the writer constructs a heteroglossic backdrop of multiple viewpoints to support the target proposition. Simultaneously, endorsement functions to exclude any other alternatives from the ongoing argument by means of the writer's judgement of the proposition. Realizations of endorsement are often embodied by such verbs as "show", "prove", "demonstrate", "find" and "point out" etc. (Martin & White, 2005: 126). For example:

(66) But **the report** released by Britain, in a move coordinated with the White House, **demonstrates** that the Bush administration has enough information about the links between Mr. bin Laden, the Taliban leadership of Afghanistan and the terrorist assaults to make a strong case. (Text 75)

In Example (66), the writer attributes the proposition that "the Bush administration has enough information about links between Mr. bin Laden, the Taliban leadership of Afghanistan and the terrorist assaults to make a strong case" to the report released by Britain in order to prove the conviction of the deduction that "Mr. bin Laden and his terrorist network were responsible for Sept. 11 attacks". In fact, the writer often resort to examples, statistical numbers as arguments to endorse individual positions.

Acknowledgement functions as the other way of leading into discourse the propositions of external sources, which views the writer as a sort of "informational fair trader" who simply retells others' viewpoints. Therefore, the writer seems not to be implicated in any relationship of solidarity which the reader would enter into with the quoted source whose viewpoint is being reported. In this way, the writer may align the reader into a particular position where the writer acts to advance in discourse. A series of reporting verbs, such as "say", "declare", "report", "announce", "state", "believe" and "think" etc. are always used as the way of indicating acknowledgement. For example:

(67) Pointing out that citizens of 80 other countries had died with the American victims of the World Trade Center assault, **Mr. Bush emphasized** that neither Muslims nor Islamic nations were the enemy, and underlined his respect for their religion. He also noted that America respects the people of Afghanistan. (Text 6)

As Example (67) shows, the writer attributes the source of the proposition "neither Muslims nor Islamic nations were the enemy" to the internal source "Mr. Bush", which can be indicated by the reporting verb "emphasized". Clearly, the writer effectively aligns with the reader to support this position by means of acknowledging Mr. Bush's proposition, by which the writer develops the idea of "not all Muslims or Islamic nations were the enemy".

However, when fending off some opposite positions, the writer will also turn to the proposition of the third party so as to quietly distance himself from taking responsibility. The term distance deals with formulations in which the writer departs explicitly from the attributed material through the semantics of the framer. Under most circumstances, it is typically realized by means of reporting verbs, e. g. "say", "report", "believe", and "according to" etc. or scare quotes. Therefore, the writer disaligns with the position that is advanced in context when it is imported into discourse as the target consciously. Contrastively, the position that the writer insists on in the content will then be implied. For example:

(68) **Among New York's senior political figures**, there is an emerging consensus that a special commission should be created to oversee the reconstruction. (Text 13)

In Example (68), the content of "an emerging consensus" is clearly attributed to "New York's senior political figures", which appears as the circumstantial element here. Thus, the writer distances himself from taking the responsibility of the proposition "that a special commission should be created to oversee the reconstruction".

5.6 Significance of Constructing Argumentativity in Terms of Subjectivity

Argumentativity, concerned with reasoning processes, is one of the typical features of editorials, by which the subjective stance is encoded with the aim of persuading the reader. The construction of argumentativity is a self-aware process, which is to some extent identical with the process of realizing subjectivity in modal assessment. Then, it is significant to study the way that argumentativity is successfully constructed in the process of realizing subjectivity.

5.6.1 Study of Argumentativity in Terms of Intentionality

An editorial is a social process confused with the subjective stance manifesting the writer's intentionality orientated to the evocative goal. This process is a stage of constructing argumentativity, by which the writer dynamically successfully expresses subjectively-held viewpoints and fulfills the persuasion aim by applying various linguistic resources. In this process, subjectivity characterizes as argumentativity of intentionality that drives the discourse information to flow to serve the interpersonal function. Thus, argumentativity consists of purpose pulse, which works below the superficial linguistic context.

According to Finegan (1995), subjectivity involves three aspects, namely perspective, affect and modality. The intentional force of subjectivity can be also studied in lines with these aspects. In SFL, modality system is defined in terms of modal orientations that distinguish between subjective and objective modality, both of which cut across the explicit and implicit variants, and determine whether the writer appears overtly on the stage or covertly off the stage in the linguistic context. Modality has the value variable, by which the writer grades evaluations of the modal judgement. The modal judgement is also categorized into judgements of social esteem and sanction according to the positive or negative property attached that is dealt with in judgement subsystem of the appraisal system, which expresses the writer's desirability that given events should take place or not. Strategically, the writer will engage other voices to express the subjective expectation, by which he operates as the authorial voice by turning to facts, beliefs, emotions and evaluations in order to raise or lower the chances of enacting the events. Therefore, the subjective force can be described from the following aspects: whether the writers appear overtly to take the responsibility or covertly to departure themselves from taking the responsibility; how they should choose among high, median or low to assign to the modal judgement; should they judge the behavior that is encouraged positively or forbidden negatively according to social esteem and social sanction; in which way they subjectively expect to raise or lower the chances of enacting the event. Briefly, the subjective force involves four aspects, namely modal orientation, modal value, subjective judgement and subjective expectation, which drive the discourse to flow according to the exchanging purpose. Those four aspects of the subjective force work in the network system to serve the discursive purpose.

The subjective stance is realized by choosing appropriate lexico-grammatical forms with interpersonal meanings, which are consistent with the resources of modal assessment in the clause, and resources of attitudinal epithesis in the nominal group, and appraisal resources. (Martin & White, 2005) It enacts the interpersonal relations by scattering among sequences of discourse and organizing the discursive flow in accordance with the register. Editorials are written mainly to influence the opinions of large audience as the widest circulating forms of opinion discourse with the argument and information being their nerves. (van Dijk, 1996; Greenburg, 2000)

The realization of subjectivity in modal assessment provides a sharply-new angle to carry out the study on the construction of argumentativity in editorials. As the act of speaking is an interactive process, the writer wishes the listener to make desired responses. In this course, argumentativity is linguistically realized when these four aspects function as purpose pulses to serve the discursive purpose with subjective intentionality.

5.6.2 Study of Argumentative Negotiation in Terms of Subjectivity

Negotiation involves these kinds of attitudes that are expressed in a text, the strength of the feelings regulated and the ways in which evaluations are sourced and readers aligned. (Martin & Rose, 2003) Editorials are strongly presented in domains of human communication and credited typically as argumentative texts written mainly to influence the opinions of the audiences. (Alaoui, 2010) The persuasive purposes of editorials are negotiated as a part of interpersonal meanings. The writer regulates different kinds of interpersonal meanings to serve this persuasive goal by using the interpersonal resources of modal assessment in discourse.

As modal assessment represents the writer's point of view (Halliday, 1994), the writer dresses it up as if it was constituted as the assertion to give prominence to or ensconce the writer's own point of view. When the writer intends to protrude his angle, he chooses the subjective orientation, whether it is explicit or implicit, that gives almost no space of negotiation—it is exactly the point what the writer holds and permits the minimally subjective interpretation. Contrastively, the writer adopts the objective orientation when he attempts to hide his own opinion, and opens up larger space of negotiation which permits the maximally subjective interpretation within the scope of the linguistic context. As modality is a resource that sets up a semantic space between yes and no, and forms a cline running between positive and negative poles (Halliday, 1994a), modality can be used as a resource for negotiating information or services. Therefore, modality opens up a space for negotiation, in which different points of view can circle around an issue and construct a space for mediation and possible reconciliation. (Martin & Rose, 2003) In terms of its value variable, modality can be interpreted as a resource for building up degrees of positivity and negativity, which constructs a guiding trend of evaluation by grading polarity.

Judgement is regarded as institutionalized feelings, and concerns resources that help assess behaviour according to various normative principles of shared community values. (Martin & White, 2005) In these terms, judgement reworks to construct feelings about behaviour in order to resonate with members of the certain community. Then, the subjective judgement is employed to express the authorial evaluation, by which the writer can negotiate with the readers in order to align with them. As judgements in the relevant phase of discourse imply exactly how the writer wants the readers to judge the people, the subjective judgement is a rhetoric strategy to persuade the readers to accept the authorial stance by negotiating with them and asking them to be aligned with.

The subjective expectation is a strategy with which the writer negotiates with the reader in terms of certain opinions by introducing the third party's viewpoints. As the act of writing is an interacting process, the writer is not only doing something himself and also requiring some responses from the reader as expected (Halliday, 1984a; Martin, 1992). The writer himself plays a particular speech role, and also assigns to the reader a complementary role which he wishes him to play. Therefore, the writer asks for another voice to speak on behalf of himself while negotiating with the readers so as to stimulate a desired response from them. Negotiation opens up between the writer and the reader in terms of given engaged opinions, with the purpose of having the latter aligned with. Thus, the writer strikes out his subjective stance by negotiating with and convincing the reader strategically by means of supporting opinions of the third party or distancing himself from some opposite opinions.

5.6.3 Study of Argumentativity in Terms of Interpersonal Function

As language means action in terms of the interpersonal metafunction, enacting interpersonal relations linguistically while creating discourse is both interactive and personal. (Halliday & Matthiessen, 2004) In language, we attempt to enact our personal and social relationships with the other people around us in a proposition, or a proposal, by which we inform or question, give an order or make an offer, and express our appraisal of and also attitude towards anyone who we are addressing and anything that we are talking about. As the speaker adopts for himself a particular speech role and assigns to the listener a complementary role, the act of speaking is fundamentally an exchange matched by a sequence of desired responses, in which the subjective force functions actively in that giving implies receiving and demanding means giving in response.

Argumentativity is originated from the dynamic force of modal expressions, which is regulated by positive or negative property attached to judgements of social esteem and social sanction, and by supporting or opposing feature motivated by engaged voices. Modality, in SFL, refers to the intermediate degrees between the positive and negative poles, and functions as a dynamic force to present a proposition as likely or unlikely, desirable or undesirable related to its use context. According to Langacker (1998, 2003), the force-dynamic value of the modals does pertain to the evolution of the knowledge of reality, and also designates some kind of potency. This potency is defined as a sort of physical or mental force that tends to cause the process's occurrence (Langacker, 1990:333), which is subjectified and becomes more strongly grounded in the speaker's expectations than in those of a wider group. (Traugott & Dasher, 2002) As the result of subjectification, the modals become speaker-orientated and carry out illocutionary force. The space between the positive and negative poles has a different significance for propositions and for proposals. In a proposition, modalization refers to these scales of probability and usuality. In a proposal, modalization refers to the scales of obligation and inclination. The subjective force works as purpose pulse to combine and steer all expressions of modalization and modalization in discourse intentionally to influence the thinking of the audiences.

The editorials in SAEC are argumentative and persuasive, so they might have more chances to influence the thinking of the reader than any other newspaper text type. Based on their rhetorical nature, the *NYT* editorials are distinguished by certain characteristics in terms of the subjective force which leads us to carry out the analysis from four aspects. As to the aspect of modal orientations, the editorial writers mostly prefer to appear covertly (98.21%) rather than overtly (1.79%). (see Table 5.1) Despite operating off the stage, the writer implies his subjective operation in discourse in the implicitly subjective or objective orientation, both of which occur in varieties of the modal forms (97.27%). As the modals are speaker-orientated and full of illocutionary force, the use of them are primarily focused on the belief and knowledge covertly made in editorials from the authorial perspective, because these modals imply the attenuation of the role of the grammatical subject and indicate a diffusion of the source and target of the modal force on the one hand. On the other hand, the modals work as argumentative strategies to influence the linear arrangement and steer the discourse information aiming to fulfill the communicative intentionality, because the modal force predict modalization and modalization happening in a certain condition according to the writer's expectation. (Richardson, 2007)

As to the value variable (see Table 4.2), editorials takes on unique features in terms of the distinction between modalization and modulization. The modalization expressions occur 999 times rating highly as 61.29% and those of modulization appear 627 times (38.71%), to all the modal expressions. Statistically, it is obvious that the frequency of using modalization is much higher than that of modulization, which shows that lots of propositions are arranged in editorials to provide information for intended actions indicated by modulized proposals. This arrangement is reasonable, for certain conditions are needed for something to take place on the one hand; on the other, it also relates closely to the rhetorical structures of editorials, among which moves of presenting the case, discussing the alternatives and reaching a verdict would provide support with facts and background information in order to make the move of recommending action plausible and reasonable (Bhatia, 1993; Katajamaki & Koskelain, 2006; van Dijk, 1993).

For the subjective judgement, it works as institutionalized affect with respect to morality or ethics. As Figure 4.3 shows, although the frequency of the positive type (56.75%) is a bit higher than the negative one (43.25%), there occur distinctive features in terms of social esteem and social sanction. In the type of social esteem, the frequency of the positive (40.99%) is much higher than the negative one (16.8%), but in the type of social sanction, the case is completely reverse (15.76% < 26.36%). As judging resources scatter in discourse to construe the authorial attitudes to people and their character covertly, the writer chooses relatively much more expressions of social esteem in the positive property (i.e. positive normality, capacity and tenacity) than those in the negative property in order to build up the subjective stance intentionally advanced in discourse. However, as editorials chosen in this study are about the topic of Sept. 11 Attack, the crimes that the terrorist has done become the targets of condemnation, because they are actually against the international laws and should be punished according to these laws. That just explains the reason why expressions of social sanction in the negative property are used much more than those in the positive property.

As discussed in Section 5.5.3, the subjective expectation concerns the strategies that are drawn on entertain, pronounce, acknowledge, endorse and distance to engage in discourse popular beliefs, emotions, facts and evaluations so as to give some cues of the authorial expectancy and counter-expectancy. As is shown in Table 4.6, the forms that realize the authorial expectancy amount to 410 cases in the total, with the strategies of acknowledge and endorse occurring 292 times (71.22%) and those of entertain and pronounce appearing 28 times (6.83%).

The forms that imply the authorial counter-expectancy occur 90 times (21.95%). Generally speaking, *NYT* is characteristic of argumentative discourse by means of supporting expressed opinions with facts and evidences in order to make them plausible and acceptable. When engaging popular beliefs, emotions, facts and evaluations in discourse, the writer not only drives the information flows as he likes, but also prefers to make expressed opinions dressed up in a seemingly objective way by turning to facts, numbers and statements of the third party instead of speaking out directly. That explains why the strategies of expectancy are used more than those realizing counter-expectancy, and also provides the reason why the strategies of acknowledge and endorse are adopted much more than those of entertain and pronounce.

5.7 Summary

Subjectivity is realized by linguistic resources of modal assessment, which express the interpersonal meaning in the course of constructing the subjective stance from the authorial angle. Those resources of modal assessment are connected to set up an interpersonal conjunction between propositions and proposals in discourse. This interpersonal conjunction is a kind of logic-semantic relationship that forms the diminuendo-crescendo movement by combining theme and focus and imparts a small scale periodic or wave-like movement to the discourse. (Halliday, 1994)

Subjectivity represents the authorial perspective, and relates closely to argumentativity by involving in the four aspects: modal orientation, modal value, subjective judgement and subjective expectation. It functions to regulate the interpersonal relationship by agglomerating organizations of information at the clausal level and accumulate information in discourse for the interpersonal purpose.

Chapter 6
Construction of Persuasiveness in Terms of Subjectivity

Discourse is interpreted as the process of negotiating interpersonal meanings, by which some social activity is brought into force. Being argumentative and persuasive, editorials are credited as argumentative texts written mainly to influence the opinions of the public. In the process of writing editorials, persuasiveness is constructed as their fundamental property.

6.1 Understanding of Persuasiveness with Respect to Subjectivity

Editorials belong to persuasive discourses, which are intended to reinforce or change the responses of others. Persuasiveness is typically oriented to a successful motivation of persuasion, which is an intangible phenomenon involving both explicit choices of meaning and implicit choices of ways in which the writer transfers the authorial stance to the reader. It is characterized as intentional causation, which relates closely to subjectivity.

6.1.1 Subjectivity and Intentional Causation

Subjectivity is a fundamental property of language. The writer's attitudes and feelings can be constructed by choosing due lexico-grammatical forms with proper linguistic prints left consciously to indicate his presence explicitly or implicitly. In other words, the writer will and can be able to constitute his existence in discourse by choosing proper lexico-grammatical expressions among meaning potentials, which serve for planned communicating purpose. That is to say, subjectivity involves two aspects. Firstly, language is regarded as meaning potential just like impounding reservoir, from which subjectivity can be represented by various lexico-grammatical forms. Secondly, this realizing process reflects the writer's capacity of choosing consciously language resources to express subjective stance by adapting to the communicating intention. To some extent, whatever is chosen in discourse is one kind of consequence resulting from certain conscious actions with the aim to realize the communicative intention.

Since speaking is acting, no matter what attitudes and feelings are expressed the speaker will then transfer the communicative intention that would cause some identical consequences as expected if the communication goes on successfully. Hence, the writer is to make his opinions related directly or indirectly to the world created in language or the surrounding world, in which some social activity is enacted in that the mind of intentionality can be involved in objects and states of affairs in the world in linguistic forms. (Searle, 1998) This intentional causation concerns the representing capacity of the mind about the surroundings in lexico-grammatical forms and its corresponding causal relations to the world, in which such self-referential construction in discourse goes through the whole process of this linguistically-encoded mind-to-world direction of causation. Meaning thus created is referred to here as discourse semantics, to stress the fact that it is concerned with meaning intention carrying illocutionary act, which is then divided into representing intention and communicating intention. (Duan Kaicheng, 2004) As two distinctive but inseparable aspects, representing intention concerns the writer's self-consciousness and capacity of using language resources to construct the subjective stance in discourse to serve the communication intention.

As subjectivity is constructed in the process of producing discourse, it reflects the writer's ability and consciousness of taking advantage of language resources to enact interpersonal function. Intentional causation exactly explains motivations of choosing lexico-grammatical resources consciously to drive the discourse information to flow as expected to enact the social activity that is designed as the communication intention. Intentional causation reflects the dynamic feature of subjectivity, that is, to make the subjective stance constructed in discourse by means of the writer's consciously choosing due lexico-grammatical forms and turning to discourse strategies by adapting to communicating the intention of implementing certain social activity.

6.1.2 Persuasiveness and Subjectivity

Persuasiveness is the core character of editorials. It stresses the power to induce the taking of a course of action or the embracing of a viewpoint by means of argument. It is achieved through persuasive technology that is designed to change the reader's attitudes or behaviour in this interactively communicative discourse. (Fogg, 2003) As van Dijk (1996), Le (2004), and Murphy (2008) have put, editorials play a definitive role in the forming and altering of the public opinion, promoting social interaction between writers and readers in the language event, and influencing the social debate, decision making and other forms of social action. Editorials function to formulate the opinions of the newspaper, which are supported by a series of arguments intending to contribute to their persuasive function. (van Dijk, 1992) Albright (2006) even steps further to look at editorials as an effective way to change the world, especially with the new technology available.

Besides, the editorial writer attempts to reproduce his own attitudes, and ideologies by means of resorting to a series of persuasive technologies with the aim to legitimize the dominance and power of a specific group. (Gartner, 2005; van Dijk, 1992) Therefore, an editorial is a means for the writer to spread a certain ideology among the public so as to exert some power on it. (Elyazale, 2014) In other words, an editorial expresses the writer's opinion and aims to persuade the reader to agree to this opinion. As Richardson (2007: 86) points out, editorials are "opinion articles that will never qualify as objective reporting". Correspondingly, subjectivity is constructed from the writer's perspective, because the evaluations and judgements expressed in editorials come from what the writer believes to be right or wrong. Thus, subjectivity is realized through the lexico-grammatical forms used in discourse in accordance with the argumentative nature of editorials.

When the writer constructs subjectivity by putting himself in the position of expressing the ego in due linguistic subjectification, he also gives subjectification such power as an instrument of control in communication allowing attitudes and feelings to be conveyed and distorted, by which the writer has readers manipulated and informed, preferably manipulated when they suppose they are being informed. (Kress & Hodge, 2006) As language is never neutral, but it always carries the power that reflects the interests of the people who speak or write, subjectification in its nature is used as the linguistic marker for indicating the writer's existence and his control of the information flow in discourse. In this sense, subjectivity provides us with a new angle to study how the linguistic subjectifiction of editorials can function as a source of their persuasiveness.

6.2 Construction of Persuasiveness in Terms of Modality

The editorial is action-oriented in that what the writer thinks should be done. (van Dijk, 1996a) This action-oriented property relates closely to persuasive features. Persuasiveness refers to the power of persuading by reasons, which emphasizes its ability to produce certain perlocutionary effects. (Wekesa, 2012) Within SFL, modality is explored by depending on the underlying speech function of the clause and is categorized into modalization and modulization. Then, choices of modality in editorials reflect a rationalizing process, which is featured as persuasiveness of editorials.

6.2.1 Persuasive Rationalization with Respect to Modalization / Modulization

As the variants of orientation determine distinctively how each type of modality is realized in the network of modality (Halliday, 2004), both variants of type and orientation are put together for the convenience in this study. Concerning the nature of the commodity being exchanged, the study focuses on the types of modality that is further divided into modalization or modulization, with the former referring to scales of possibility or of usuality relevant to a proposition, and the later concerning degrees of obligation or of inclination relevant to a proposal.

Composing an editorial is a dynamic process that is "regarded as the newspaper's analysis, discussion, opinion or verdict on the issue of the day" (Bhatia, 1993: 170), in which communication intention is properly performed. Communication intentions are mainly to motivate and persuade readers to consider ideas or to give opinions that oppose or support the information provided in those editorials. As the discourse is often defined as a staged and goal-oriented social process (Martin, 1993), the way the writer chooses words to create favorable or unfavorable bias in the arguments characterizes its most significant aspect (Bhatia, 1993). In other words, the writer consciously chooses due lexico-grammatical resources to express his modal judgement in line with the intention of the editorial. However, most of the work will be done implicitly just like the writer operates off the stage.

In SFL, four types of modality are categorized as modalization and modulization which concern scales of propositions and proposals respectively. As is shown in Table 4.1, in SAEC modalization is used 999 (61.44%) times, with the type of possibility occurring in 594 (36.53%) times and the type of usuality 405 (36.53%) times. Modulization is adopted 627 (38.56%) times, with the type of obligation being used 421 (25.89%) times and the type of obligation 206 (12.67%) times. It is clear that modalization is used much more than modulization, which shows that the writer gives his recommendation after making full argument and analysis of the relevant information. As valid evidences speak much more eloquently, the writer supplies enough evidence in order to fulfill the task of persuasion. As everyone knows, to argue is not to quarrel. The force of the editorial comes from solid evidence, logical reasoning and careful analysis. An honest and friendly attitude also helps to win the trust of the readers and convince them of the rationalization of the editorial. Pragmatically, the writer designs to make evidence speak out directly and scatter his modal judgements in discourse covertly. In this way, the writer can guide the reader to ratiocinate to share valuation. It is not clever but still polite to let the reader reach an agreement with him.

As the composition of an editorial is a goal-driven process to motivate and persuade readers, the writer works in moves, namely, presenting the case, offering the argument, reaching the verdict and recommending action to reach the discourse goal. (Bhatia, 1993; Swales, 1990; Tongsibsong, 2012) It is commonly true that recommending action must be carefully proposed after all the relevant factors are considered and the full-fledged analysis is prepared. Therefore, the first three moves are in fact doing preliminary analysis about possible choices as well as a potential trend of intentionally suggesting the desired action. This to some extent explains why the modalized propositions appear more. However, as the final move indicates, the finial intention of the editorials is mainly to express strong opinions in order to stimulate some reaction from the reader or recommend action to the reader. For the communication intention, the writer expresses his recommendation firmly and clearly.

6.2.2 Persuasive Rationalization with Respect to Propositional Comment

Propositional comments are categorized as comment adjuncts, which express the writer's ideational attitude on the proposition as a whole or on the role played by the subject. When the comment is made on properties of the subjects of the propositions, it focuses on the wisdom or morality of the subject. When the comment is concerned with on the whole proposition, it is either asseverative or qualificative. They disperse in editorials by functioning as linguistic markers to signify the rationalization.

6.2.2.1 Persuasive Rationalization in Terms of Subject Comments

When it is reinterpreted in functional terms, the term "subject" implies a grammatical function, which is not an arbitrary grammatical category. However, "being the subject of a clause means something" (Halliday, 1994: 72). Usually, the writer makes an integrated choice of an item, which can realize the function of being subject of the proposition as well as theme in the message simultaneously.

Within the realm of SFL, the subject is given the position of the reference point to which the validity of the proposition can be evaluated. By making the judgement on qualities of the subject, the writer will then indicate his modal evaluation on the whole proposition covertly and convey the discourse intention consciously. Generally speaking, the judgement is made in term of wisdom or morality properties of the subject, which is often realized by means of the mental/relational clause, modal adverbs or modal adjectives as the epithet in the nominal group. (Halliday & Matthiessen, 2004)

As far as SAEC is concerned (see Figures 4.3 and 4.4), there are altogether 63 (11%) cases commenting on properties of the subject, among which 25 cases comment on the aspect of wisdom, with 21 cases being wise and only 4 cases being unwise, and 38 cases comment on moral qualities, with 31 cases being moral and 7 being immoral. Since wisdom property reflects the capacity of doing and morality property concerns the ethics of acting, the writer makes a positive or negative evaluation of them in order to indirectly express his modal judgement on the modulized proposal. (Martin & White, 2005) In other words, the writer makes evaluation on the properties of the subject's capacity or morality in the form of offering propositional information; however, the real intention of offering information is to enact modulized proposals. Examples (69), (70) and (71) explain how they work to realize modulated proposals. For example:

(69) **It is useless** to simultaneously tell Americans to get back to normal life, and then warn them that there is an imminent danger of another, unspecified terrorist attack. (Text 81)

(70) **Wisely**, it has recognized the importance of enlisting major Muslim nations like Pakistan, Indonesia and Saudi Arabia in the antiterrorist coalition. (Text 11)

(71) Even though the risks are great, President Bush made the **right** choice in selecting this limited, clandestine form of warfare rather than attempting a full-scale invasion of Afghanistan by thousands of American ground troops. (Text 83)

Examples (69), (70) and (71) embody various forms used to make the modal comments on the wisdom property of the subjects. To be concrete, they manifest that the assessment is realized in the relational clause (It is useless), the modal adverb (wisely) and the adjective (right) in the nominal group respectively, all of which are forms offering information. However, on second thought, the writer is planning on purpose to express the modal opinion on some modulized proposals, to be more specific, to advocate or oppose to enforce some actions. In Example (69), by the relational clause "It is useless" which reveals the writer's assessment, the writer, in fact, opposes to "simultaneously tell Americans to get back to normal life, and then warn them that there is an imminent danger of another, unspecified terrorist attack". In this way, this sentence can be interpreted with the denial intention expressed directly as:

(69′) Don't simultaneously tell Americans to get back to normal life, and then warn them that there is an imminent danger of another, unspecified terrorist attack.

Similarly, Examples (70) and (71) can be interpreted as follows:

(70′) Please enlist major Muslim nations like Pakistan, Indonesia and Saudi Arabia in the antiterrorist coalition.

(71′) I support President Bush to select the limited, clandestine form of warfare rather than attempt a full-scale invasion of Afghanistan by thousands of American ground troops.

What is revealed through this interpreting process is that the propositional comment as to the wisdom or morality of the subject can be thought of as the discourse strategy that the writer applies to enact modulized proposals. Such linguistic phenomena have been exploited in Halliday's work on mood, modality and interpersonal metaphor that theoretically build up the bridge between interpersonal grammar and appraisal system (Halliday, 1994; Martin, 1992b, 1995b; Lemke, 1998). Those propositional comments on the subject, in return, can be regarded as triggering elements that lead to an understanding of the persuasive effect.

6.2.2.2 Subjective Rationalization in Terms of Asseverative Comments

Comments on the whole proposition occur only in the declarative clause, which is either asseverative or qualificative. (Halliday & Matthiessen, 2004) Then, appropriate linguistic resources are chosen to disperse in discourse to meet this function and act as the guiding cues for the readers to touch on the writers. Correspondingly, they give the writer's attitude towards what is said, or convey the writer's evaluation on the text situation, or express their commitment to a proposition (Smith, 2003), which should be understood by referring to discursive context (Stein & Wright, 1995).

The asseverative emphasizes that comment is made by structures like "it is so", which are used to introduce a statement of truth and express a conviction in terms of its correctness. It usually involves three aspects: it is natural for the speaker to make this kind of proportional speculation; it is reasonable for the speaker to reach this kind of judgement; the speaker is sure of the proportion. Therefore, the writer always wields asseverative expressions in an attempt to make his propositions more credible.

As Figures 4.3 and 4.4 show, 75 (12%) asseverative cases are drawn on in SAEC, with 14 variants of them belonging to the natural aspect of asseverative expressions, 46 belonging to the obvious aspect and the rest 15 belonging to the sure aspect. These variants occur in relational clauses, modal adverbs, prepositional phrases, or assessing adjectives acting as post-deictic or epithet in nominal groups. In SAEC, new features occur when asseverative expressions are used to realize the modal assessment. In the following, we will talk about these features mainly from two parts. Firstly, the lexical copular verb "seem" replaces the copular verb; secondly, the strength of asseverative expressions is turned upside down. For example:

(72) It will be essential to get this right. A variety of designs should be solicited by city and state officials through an international competition. **It seems all but inevitable** that a memorial will have to encompass the footprints of the two trade center towers. (Text 52)

In Example (72), the writer chooses the lexical copular verb "seem" as the predicate in the relational clause and the lexical group "all but" collocating with negative prefix "in-" in "inevitable" intensifies the strength of its natural aspect. The connotation of the lexical copular verb "seem" is to give the impression of being in certain way, which is usually used to draw readers' attention to understanding that something will happen with proper evidence mentioned contextually or ensconced in cultural context. The writer provides relevant evidence in linguistic context so that he is able to impress the reader deeply in that the projected proposition is speculated naturally with sufficient information. Besides, the double negative collocation of "all but" and "inevitable" not only strengthens the modal judgement but also makes this intentional modal comment stick out. And, other intensifiers, such as "also", "still", "less", and linguistic structures, such as the comparative or superlative form, are frequently used to strengthen or weaken the degree of modal comments in editorials.

In sum, no matter why the writer uses the relational clause with the lexical copular "*seem*", or whether the degree of modal comments is regulated highly or low, the writer is to draw the reader's attention to the modal assessment expressed.

6.2.2.3 Subjective Rationalization in Terms of Qualificative Comments

Contrastively, when the propositional comment is qualificative expression, it is to highlight the way in which such proportion is ratiocinated, i. e. "this is what I think about it". It thus highlights the process of making such proportion from three aspects: prediction, presumption, and desirability. Generally speaking, the qualificative expressions indicate that the speaker makes the modal judgement in terms of the relevance of the message.

In SAEC, distribution patterns of the seven subcategories in the domain of qualificative expressions are contrastively presented. The type of desirability is at the highest level, appearing totally 383 times with 188 cases hinting desirable tendency but 195 indicating undesirable one. However, aspects of prediction and presumption are relatively at lower levels. Prediction occurs 38 times with 23 of them being predictable markers and 15 being unpredictable ones. Presumption emerges 29 times with 18 cases marked as hearsay and 11 as guess but no argument. (See Table 4.3 and Figure 4.3) Generally speaking, the sharply uneven distribution of these three aspects implies that the writer prefers to express his desirability in the editorial; and, under some circumstances, the writer gives his personal predictions on the tendency of the event; and, as to some given propositions on which the writer is lack of irrefutable evidence, he then gives his evaluative presumption to depart himself from taking the responsibility.

SFL is to study the functions that language enacts in the process of constructing social actions. In this sense, the aspect of desirability is clearly identifiable with social desirability. Social desirability that is defined broadly and ususally refers to the need of subjects to achieve approval by responding in a culturally appropriate and acceptable manner. (Crowne & Marlowe, 1960) From this perspective, social desirability is thought of as the tendency to respond in a manner, which expresses the speaker's purposes to make the reader look good. (Holtgraves, 2004) In SAEC, the writers make full use of all those 13 subcomponents to express his desirability of doing or not doing something according to the context. Whatever the writer chooses to express his desirability, desirable aspect or undesirable aspect, he really tends to ask the reader to take his side. For example:

(73) Mr. Bush has wisely made providing humanitarian assistance to the Afghan people an integral part of American strategy. **It is important**, for humanitarian and practical reasons, to minimize the suffering of innocent Afghan civilians. (Text 77)

(74) They mean that it should have a culturally and physically responsive connection to the rest of downtown. What that also means, and **this is**

more difficult, is that any commercial redevelopment of the World Trade Center site must also co-exist harmoniously with the memorial itself.

(Text 52)

Examples (73) and (74) manifest the writer's desirability from the valuable aspect and the non-valuable aspect respectively. Example (73) explains that the writer expresses his desirability by "it is important" so as to signify his positive evaluation on the projected proposal "to minimize the suffering of innocent Afghan civilians". In fact, the writer expects that this proposal can actually take place. In other words, the writer desires the target listener to "minimize the suffering of innocent Afghan civilians". However, although in Example (74) the writer makes the negative evaluation on the projected proposal by the undesirable comment "this is more difficult", he tends to desire the targeted listener not to hold the idea expressed in the text "that any commercial redevelopment of the World Trade Center site must also co-exist harmoniously with the memorial itself". Indubitably, the writer aims to ask for the reader's approval of doing or not doing a certain proposal. Of course, this is consistent with the style feature of English editorials, which "motivate and persuade their readers to conceive ideas that against or support the ideas presented in the editorials" (Tongsibsong, 2012: 171).

As a prediction is based on experience or knowledge, the proper linguistic resource should be chosen to mark it out. The intention of prediction related to attitudes is better construed under conditions. (Icek, 1991) By using the comment sign of prediction, the writer shows his modal judgement on a proposition or proposal in certain situations. For example:

(75) Under obsolete budgetary and bureaucratic arrangements established during the Eisenhower and Kennedy administrations, the Pentagon controls most of the nation's espionage machinery and manpower. **Not surprisingly**, its primary interest is using intelligence to help plan and fight wars.

(Text 15)

(76) The **surprisingly** swift successes of the American military campaign in Afghanistan have spurred talk about military action to oust Saddam Hussein from power in Iraq. (Text 24)

Example (75) tells that the proposition given in the clause "its primary interest is using intelligence to help plan and fight wars" is logically rooted in the linguistic context provided by the near above clause "the Pentagon controls most of the nation's espionage machinery and manpower". In this way, the writer indicates that the logical reasoning process is predictable. However, in Example (76), the commenting marker "surprisingly" is the epithet to modify the adjective "swift" in the nominal group, which is interpreted by referring to the knowledge that the American military campaign has achieved swift successes in Afghanistan by November 26, 2001. Thus, in the editorial of November 26, 2001, the writer expresses his opinion that swift successes obtained in such short period are indeed unpredictable.

A presumption is basically a special kind of inference, which can be interpreted at two levels: the inferential level and the dialectical level. At the inferential level, a presumption is considered as an inference to the rationalization of a proposition from two other propositions: a fact and a rule. At the dialectical level, a presumption is defined in terms of its function in a conversational context which is to shift an evidential burden from one side to the other in a conversation for the purpose of achieving the effect of persuasion. (Walton, 2017) A presumption can be regarded as a rationalizing process of relying on a fact or obeying a rule to accept a proposition, by which an inference is made to persuade the reader. Usually, the notion of presumption includes three subcategories, namely, hearsay, argument and guess. (Halliday & Matthiessen, 2004) Moreover, the propositional comment from the aspect of the presumption is signed by due linguistic resources. For example:

(77) On Tuesday, as Mr. Bush's security men flew him around the country, he **reportedly** insisted that he wanted to go "home"—to Washington. (Text 7)

(78) America's NATO allies have also been briefed on the evidence, and some of them would **presumably** communicate their doubts if Mr. Blair were overstating the case. (Text 75)

Example (77) uses the modal adverb "reportedly", which identifies the presumption done with the hearsay proposition. Example (78) shows that the writer guesses "some of America's NATO allies would communicate their doubts" in certain situation provided by the conditional clause "if Mr. Blair were overstating the case".

Correspondingly, the guessing presumption is marked out clearly by the modal adverb "presumably". Then the writer identifies his presence covertly in the discourse by choosing this kind of modal adverbs.

The statistical results show that none of the argument occurs in SAEC. The argument is often drawn on as a kind of reasoning used for some purpose of persuading the reader to accept the designated ultimate probandum. As we all know, English editorials are mainly to motivate and persuade the reader to consider ideas or to give opinions that oppose or support the information provided in those editorials as well as to express strong opinions in order to stimulate some reactions from readers. (Tongsibsong, 2012) Therefore, reasonable explanation and solid facts speak much louder than personally eloquent argument. Obviously, it is a strategy and intelligent choice that no argument is used in SAEC.

6.2.3 Persuasive Rationalization with Respect to Speech Functional Comments

6.2.3.1 Rationalization Marked in Unqualified Speech Functional Comments

Within SFL, the speech role cutting across the nature of the commodity which is exchanged determines four primary speech functions: offer, command, statement and question. These primary speech functions are matched by a set of desired responses. (Halliday & Matthiessen, 2004) The writer usually hints his desirability by means of proper operation.

Speech functional comments express the writer's attitude to the particular speech function, by which the writer realizes certain interpersonal function. The unqualified type includes persuasive and factual subtypes. Traditionally, persuasion is defined as "human communication designed to influence the autonomous judgements and actions of others" (Simons, 2001), which actually acts as interactive information technology designed for changing users' attitudes or behavior (Fogg, 2003). It is often wielded by the writer as the discourse strategy, by which he effectively indicates to the reader the assurance or admission of the proposition. In SAEC, 16 variants are used as signs of assurance and 33 variants as signs of admission. (see Figure 4.6) For example:

(79) Decades of equivocation and Hobbesian calculations have left American

relations with Saudi Arabia in an untenable and unreliable state. The deformities must be **honestly** addressed before they do further damage to both nations. (Text 79)

(80) Zubaydah, a 31-year-old Palestinian with close ties to Osama bin Laden, is the first man under American interrogation ... he almost **certainly** played a key role in the Sept. 11 attacks and in numerous other plots. (Text 45)

In Example (79), the writer uses the modal adverb "honestly" to imply his assurance of the modulized proposal to persuade the reader to do it. It is interpreted contextually as "I assure you that both America and Saudi Arabia must address the deformities from doing further damage to them". However, in Example (80), according to Zubaydah's background information mentioned in above text, the writer makes his judgement in the concession that he grants the reader conservatively that Zubaydah plays a key role in the Sept. 11 attacks and in numerous other plots. Correspondingly, the writer's modal judgement is marked by the modal adverb "certainly". Basically, a persuasion is a process of analyzing information which emphasizes the role of comprehension and attention of contextual information (McGuire, 1973). Since persuasion is to influence the attitudes and behavior of others, whatever strategies the writer uses, admission or concession, he mainly tries to convince the reader of something. That is to say, persuasion relies primarily on symbolic strategies that demonstrate the logical process of information and trigger the emotions, which appeals to the readers' reason and intelligence so as to convince them. (Miller, 2002) Therefore, the uses of speech functional comments are to stick out this procedure of processing information as well as to catch the reader's attention to this persuasion process.

Besides, speech functional unqualified type includes factual subtype, which can also be realized by due modal adjuncts. In SAEC, 48 cases are used as claiming of veracity in terms of factual aspects. (see Figure 4. 6) In fact, factual subtype is used to prove that the proposition is highly warrantable. By using the expressions of factual subtype, the writer gives expression to explicit authorial interventions or interpolations in the text to set against or rule out alternative positions. Therefore, the factual subtype is regarded as the way that the writer pronounces his presence, and it constitutes an overt intervention into the text of the authorial presence to assert or insist on the value or warrantability of the proposition. (Martin & White, 2005)

For example:

(81) The Bush administration has framed the dispute as being over the separation of powers and the right of the executive branch to oversee the waging of war. The courts have, **in fact**, given the political branches considerable leeway where wars are concerned. (Text 63)

In Example (81), the modal adjunct "in fact" is used to lead the reader's interests into the thing that happens in practice. In return, what actually takes place will then support the writer's judgement. In this study, factual intervention is identified as one effective strategy that the writer takes advantage of to reinforce his opinion.

6.2.3.2 Rationalization Marked in Qualified Speech Functional Comments

Compared with unqualified speech functional comments, the qualified type mainly consists of two subtypes: validity and personal engagement. (Halliday & Matthiessen, 2004) The subtype of validity indicates to what degree the writer is warrantable of the judgement of the proposition. The subtype of personal engagement concerns in which way the writer shares his assessment with the reader. No matter whether the degree or the manner is evaluated, both are expressed in the declarative clause. Characteristically, the qualified type can be realized in the projecting clause with the subjective-explicit orientation.

The word "valid" is derived from the Latin "validus", meaning strong. Validity is the degree to which a concept, conclusion or measurement is judged as well-founded and corresponds to the real world. (Brains et al., 2011) Thus, the writer can employ various linguistic resources of validity to express his judgements towards the valid degree of a proposition. In this way, he can make his evaluation sound more acceptable in order to invite the reader to agree with him effectively. As shown in Figure 4.6, 19 variants of the validity are used in SAEC. For example:

(82) **Collectively**, the stories that are emerging of these lives do not perfectly represent the demographics of America. (Text 6)

(83) But it will be the new authority's job to steer Mr. Silverstein in the right direction, **aesthetically speaking**, and to make sure that whatever he does fits the city's larger needs and is linked to the surrounding neighborhoods of Battery Park, Chinatown, Little Italy and Soho. (Text 23)

In Example (82), the modal adverb "collectively" is used to sign the writer's comment. As "collectively" means "as a group", the modal judgement made here seemingly represents a tendency or determination of a group. The writer dresses the proposition up as if it is upheld by a group so that it will be accepted easily. Example (83) uses extensive modal adjuncts "aesthetically speaking", which means that this assessment is fairly true in the domain of aesthetics. Then, the judgement of this kind is of much more approval. As far as SAEC is concerned, 13 of these 19 variants of validity are of the high degree, which tells that the writer usually expresses his assessment of validity seemingly as one approved by a group of people. Thus, such judgement is accepted by more people.

On the contrary, the personal engagement of the qualified is concerned with the ways in which the writer presents himself in the discourse with respect to the value position being advanced. In many respects, engagement is comparable to evidentiality, which refers to the means for the authorial voice to construct in the current communicative context. (Martin & White, 2005) Although this personal engagement type contains 5 subtypes, all of them only occur 8 times, with subtypes of honesty, individuality and hesitancy appearing only once, accuracy 5 times and secrecy zero. Generally speaking, as the editorial writer is to convince the reader of his opinion by means of stating facts and resorting to logical reasoning, he rarely gives expression to his ideas directly, not to mention to deliver them secretly. That is the reason why the type of personal engagement is seldom used. For example:

(84) We were **frankly** less certain that he would show equal sympathy in Washington, when the time came to make a commitment to support the enormous task of beginning restoration of lower Manhattan. (Text 7)

(85) But Tom Ridge, President Bush's chief of homeland security, must **personally** ensure that deployment of the bomb-screening devices is a top priority. (Text 35)

(86) **Wisely**, Afghanistan's new provisional leader, Hamid Karzai, has dropped talk of a possible amnesty for Mullah Omar. (Text 27)

(87) As Mr. Cheney **accurately** noted, Saddam Hussein has twice attacked his neighbors. (Text 66)

Examples (84), (85) and (86) are corresponding to the subtypes of honesty, individuality, and hesitancy respectively. Example (87) is recited here as an example of the subtype of accuracy. Clearly, "frankly", "personally" and "accurately" are modal adverbs, but "provisional" is a modal adjective used as an epithet in the nominal group. Anyhow, all of them are linguistic markers that indicate in which way the writer engages his evidential ideas covertly in the discourse to convince the reader of his value position.

6.3 Construction of Persuasiveness in Terms of Judgement

Judgement is one of the basic types of APPRAISAL (Martin & White, 2005), which is the resources for enacting judgements in terms of some parameter of people, typically their behaviour. It is regarded as institutionalised feelings in accordance with shared community values, by which judgement reconstructs feelings in the realm of proposals about behaviour.

6.3.1 Affective Effect of Institutionalized Judgement

Judgement as one type of APPRAISAL relates directly to propositional comments (Eggins & Slade, 1997; Halliday & Matthiessen, 2004; Martin & Rose, 2003; Martin & White, 2005). Linguistic resources that express the writer's judgement are considered as patulous propositional comments which are used to extend the writer's judgements strategically. Language resources of realizing judgement with respect to certain parameters are negotiable in discourse. Theoretically, linguistic resources that the writer chooses to express tropism of judgements will then construe his assessment in the course of producing discourse.

The system of JUDGEMENT is concerned with evaluation coming into being in the process of making a discourse, in which the writer introduces various kinds of attitudes and enables them to be negotiated so as to achieve the communicating goal. It is the whole discourse instead of any part of it that constructs different tendencies of judgements. Although judgement is realized in the course of producing discourse, it is practically presented by due linguistic tokens which explain the phenomena that some ideational meanings can be invoked to express judgement meanings in certain context. (Li, 2004) Therefore, the context sensitivity underlines the importance of determining judgement at discourse level; then, it is important to take the context into account, instead of analyzing items one by one. (Martin & Rose, 2003) The realization of judgements should not be discussed only at the lexical level, but it can take advantage of all kinds of language resources consisting of lexical items, grammatical structures, and even discourse structures. (Hu, 2001; Thompson & Hunston, 2009) It is sure that all kinds of linguistic resources will be involved in this process, ranging from lexical elements to discourse structures. In this study, linguistic resources of judgement are concerned only with resources from lexical level to clausal level. For example:

(88) If New York is going to get the help it needs, its leaders are going to have to be both restrained and politically **canny** in what they ask for. (Text 85)

(89) In its greatest hour of need, the city must be grateful that he **rose to the occasion**, and demonstrated that he is president of the entire country. (Text 7)

(90) **The administration takes the spread of nuclear, chemical and biological weapons dangers extremely seriously**. (Text 57)

Examples (88), (89) and (90) show that lexcio-grammatical forms ranging from the lexical item to the clause can be drawn on directly to realize judgements. However, judgement can be realized indirectly. Concretely, some linguistic forms and linguistic devices are consciously adopted to invoke meanings of judgement in discourse that writer wants to convey to the reader. For example:

(91) Helping New York survive Sept. 11 was a mission that actually occupied only a few months of Mr. Giuliani's eight years in office, but it seemed as if he had been in training for it all along. He always ran the city **like a warrior king**. (Text 32)

(92) The Bush administration has sharply **ratcheted up the pressure** on Pakistan this week, as well it should, and Pakistan indicated yesterday that it may cooperate. (Text 4)

Examples (91) and (92) show indirect realizations of judgement. In Example (91), the form—like a warrior king—occurs in lexical metaphor form, which implicates a judgement of a person's action in this way. Then, it functions superficially to express ideational meaning, but in fact it provokes an attitudinal response in the reader. In Example (92), the verbal group "ratchet up" means "to increase by a fixed amount or degree, and unlikely to decrease again", which infuses with manner connote attitude and means "increasing gradually and effectively". Contextually, this verbal group can be interpreted as the way that the writer connotatively flags his attitude of praising the Bush administration's capacity of effective actions. Evidentially, indirect realizations of judgement are much more sensitive to context and construing position for interpretation than lexical metaphor and direct inscriptions.

There is a range of other mechanisms which can similarly be used to evoke attitudes, and which likewise fall between affording an attitude and provoking it. (Martin & White, 2005) Another typical character of judgements refers to the phenomenon that they can be scaled in accordance with graduation. Graduation of judgements can be intensified from two aspects: force and focus. "Force" deals with the degree of gradable items. In other words, the writer can amplify "volume" of attitudes operated by up-scaling or down-scaling gradable items through intensification of quality, e. g. "far more formidable" (Text 24), or process, e. g. "successfully prosecute" (Text 28), or by means of quantification of number, mass or extent, e. g. "the most generous" (Text 71). However, focus refers to the phenomenon that non-gradable items can be amplified by softening or sharpening. For the non-gradable item "risk", it can be sharpened as "a real risk" (Text 24).

Above all, the system of JUDGEMENT is to realize the interpersonal meaning, which is to some extent regarded as "the interpersonal tool" that the writer can resort to to influence the reader. (Li, 2004) Therefore, it is very important to study how this interpersonal tool is constructed in editorials.

6.3.2 Expression of Modalization/Modulization with Respect to Judgement

The notion of moral judgement is very popular in the age of Aristotle: his idea of phronēsis is a familiar one. Some modern scholars also concern the importance of judgement in terms of virtues. Hursthouse (1999: 12) claims that "each of the virtues involves getting things right, for each involves phronēsis, or practical wisdom, which is the ability to reason correctly about practical matters". And,

Aristotle's idea of phronēsis can be interpreted as "practical wisdom" or "moral wisdom" (Hursthouse, 1999: 59), which is the form of judgement that allows us to recognize due courses of action (Provis, 2013: 49). The idea of phronēsis is closely related to the idea of "intuition" when it is understood as decision making. In this sense, the idea of intuition is to some extent the basis of ethical judgement.

The concept of basing ethical judgements on intuition has been gradually proven, in fact, by recent studies in modern cognitive science which has absorbed ideas from psychology, biology, computing etc. to advance our understanding of decision making. (Clark, 2000) Theoretically, intuition is defined as a process of thinking, to which the input is mostly offered by knowledge stored in the long-term memory primarily acquired via associative learning. The input is processed automatically and without conscious awareness. Opposite to the input, the output of the process is a feeling that can serve as a basis for judgement and decisions. (Betsch, 2008: 4) With judgement, we step into the region of meaning which construes attitudes to people and the way that they measure up. Then, the system of JUDGEMENT is concerned with resources for assessing behavior according to various normative principles, by which the writer expresses his attitudes of admiration or criticism, praise or condemn.

Editorials are argumentative and persuasive in nature. (Farrokhi & Nazemi, 2015) In editorials, the writer gives expression of verdicts and opinions on the actual events. And, they can recommend ways of making an alternative solution or possible choices of events to occur, aiming to suggest what should be done actually. Correspondingly, the writer will indicate argumentative and persuasive intentions by means of delivering judgements on characters or behaviors related to the people involved in discourse. Halliday's work on the system of modality and the interpersonal metaphor provides the bridge between interpersonal grammar and the system of JUDGEMENT, which underpins these connections (Halliday, 1994; Martin, 1992, 1995). Ways of expressing judgement correspond to grammatical distinctions reflected in the course of realizing modalization and modulization. As Table 4. 5 shows, in terms of frequency, modulization is much higher than modalization. The former occurs 1008 (94. 57%) times while modulization appears only 58 (5. 43%) times.

As the editorial is essentially argumentative and persuasive, it regularly includes a key evaluation, interpretation and presentation of significant issues with an intention to inform, educate, entertain and influence the reader. (Ate, 2008) The writer will then make the best use of language potential to fulfill this goal because the way that the editorial writer chooses linguistic forms to create favorable or unfavorable bias in the arguments is the most significant aspect for editorials. (Bhatia, 1993) In SAEC, the writer prefers to choose modulization so as to stimulate the reader to take proper actions in face of the catastrophic attack and its terrible aftermath, after making a detailed analysis of behaviors that we praise and that we condemn from three aspects: how capable, how dependable and how far beyond reproach. When we are associated with the secondary finding that expressions of modulization and modalization occur frequently in positive, both of them are of much more explanatory power. The editorial writer encourages the reader to make a full understanding of this kind of catastrophic attacks and its aftermath influences before dealing with them, i. e. to have the ability to meet the disastrous events, and to be confident of the willpower to live through them and at the same time to reveal the dirty tricks behind them and express reproaches. In a word, the writer preps the readers up to cope with this kind of complex situations actively while making them fully evaluate how confused they are.

6.4 Support of Persuasiveness in Terms of Perspectivization

In editorials, the writers always indicate the point of view from which they have their own opinions expressed. As people usually talk about events in which they are participants, the point of view is usually that of the writer. (Chafe, 1994) The point of view can also shift from the writer to another character. All the meanings expressed in the text must be attributed to their purported personal sources. (Palacas, 1993) Subjectivity is created by presupposing the presence of a character's active consciousness to which the mental state is attributed. (Sanders & Redeker, 1996) Thus, subjectivity can be expressed in two ways: as a connection to the speaker, which we call subjectification, or as a connection to concrete or abstract characters other than the writer, which we call perspectivization.

6.4.1 Persuasiveness Expressed in Terms of Subject Perspective

6.4.1.1 Subject Perspective and Conceptual Sources

As Benveniste (1958) points out, subjectivity is an essential property of language, and it is determined by the linguistic status of the speaker who is capable of positing himself as "subject". In other words, it is the personal form that constitutes the indicator of subjectivity. Fundamentally, "this manifestation of subjectivity does not stand out except in the first person" (Benveniste, 1958: 178).

In the domain of the modality system, modality is defined as "the speaker's judgement, or request of the judgement of the listener, on the status of what is being said" (Halliday & Matthiessen, 2004: 141). Speaking from the angle of the subject "I", the writer can play the subjective role as conceptual sources, and he has "an interest in an event either occurring or not occurring" (Heine, 1995: 29), and he can flexibly indicate his attitude to the statement he is making, existing internally or externally as the modal subject. As a consequence of subjectification, the modal operator gradually and crucially involves the writer's intentional forces or the authoritative which affects choices. (Sweetser, 1990; Traugott & Dasher, 2002) Subjectivity is infused as an essential property into the modal operator (Lyons, 1977; Coate, 1983), by which the writer can express his judgement on the proposition or a potential future event separately in epistemic modality or deontic modality (Palmer, 2001). Thus, the writer's attitude is also internally infused into the modal operator. Within the realm of SFL, the speaker acting as the conceptual source determines the variable of the orientation. If the speaker acting as the conceptual source internally works in the scope of modality, the speaker takes the subjective orientation. Furthermore, if the speaker likes to give prominence to his own point of view and then to dress it up as if it is the one that constitutes the assertion, e.g. "I think...", he makes the subjective orientation explicit. For example:

(93) The initial surge of national sympathy for New York City and the victims of the terrorist attack may have subsided, but **we believe** most Americans, including members of Congress, still want to help heal the wounds of Sept. 11. (Text 29)

Of course, the speaker, as one member of the plural "we", exactly conveys his attitude of certainty as to the assertion that "most Americans, including members of Congress, still want to help heal the wounds of Sept. 11". In SAEC, only 42 (2.58%) variants of modal assessments occur in the explicitly subjective orientation, which indicates that the writers are careful to make their opinions expressed subjectively and explicitly. When the writers adopt modal operators to express attitudes towards the assertion, they just employ the implicitly subjective orientations. For example:

(94) Seven weeks after the disaster, the level of coordination among the 180 charitable groups involved in the relief effort is not what it **ought to** be. (Text 87)

In view of the contextual information, the quasi-modal "ought to" used here expresses exactly the writer's requirement that the 180 charitable groups should strengthen their coordination at a higher level. Therefore, by the use of "ought to", the writer intentionally conveys both an epistemic inferential meaning and a deontic moral meaning in one utterance. In general, 1195 variants of modal operators are used in SAEC, and the percentage is 73.49%, which proves that the modal operators are preferred in editorials.

However, when the speaker as the conceptual source functions externally beyond the scope of modality, the speaker takes the objective orientation. Then, if the speaker finds it was not his point of view at all, he takes the objective explicit orientation, e.g. "it's likely that...". For example:

(95) But if the Afghans are to stop fighting with each other and start building their own nation, **it is likely** they will need some form of sustained American aid, diplomacy and military presence. (Text 33)

We explain the function of "it is likely..." especially from the angle of its subject "it". In terms of its function in the pronominal paradigm, the subject "it" is formally the third person that refers to an object not in the domain of direct address, and it exists and is characterized only by the speaker's uttering it. (Benvéniste, 1958:178) The subject "it" semantically stands for the assertion expressed by the projected clause, which seems objectively to be ratiocinated out of the context and appears merely as the factual proposition. Thus, the subject "it" exists formally and meaningfully with no relation to the speaker. To our surprise, merely 20 variants of this kind of structures scatter in SAEC, with a ratio of 1.35% among four orientations, which is determined by the wordings in editorials. However, if the speaker uses modal adjuncts to express his attitudes towards the assertion, he encodes the objective orientation implicitly. For example:

(96) We are just now getting to know these people, the missing and the dead. ... Some had been through the 1993 bombing and **probably** thought about it every day. (Text 6)

The modal adjunct "probably" occurs in the clause with the generic pronoun "some" as the subject. Contextually, this "some" naturally refers to a group of persons living far from the speaker anchored by the pronoun "we" in the above context. In this study, 367 variants of this sort, 22.57% of the general use of modal expressions are used in SAEC, which is second to but much fewer than that of the subjective implicit ones, which also reflects the wording features of editorials.

6.4.1.2 Subject Perspective Realized in Personal Relations

As subjectivity reflects the capacity of the speaker to posit himself as ego subject, "language is accordingly the possibility of subjectivity because it always contains the linguistic forms appropriate to the expression of subjectivity, and discourse provokes the emergence of subjectivity because it consists of discrete instances" (Benveniste, 1958: 227). As a matter of fact, the process of the speaker positing himself as "subject" is to some extent reflected in the course of the writer self-consciously choosing proper forms as the clause subjects when he constructs editorials.

Within the system of MODALITY in SFL, by existing as the subject "I" the writer can of course strengthen his capacity to present his existence overtly, or operate covertly behind the scene to take advantages of other linguistic resources to indicate attitudes. In other words, the speaker can overtly appear as the subject of the modal expressions, making the subjective orientation of the modality explicitly. And, the speaker also can consciously work covertly in the underground by choosing other forms as the subject of the modal expressions. These intentionally chosen subjects can surely influence the way that attitudes are expressed. As to this linguistic phenomenon, Halliday (1994a) claims that the key to a functional interpretation of grammatical structure is a general principle: linguistic items are multifunctional. Then, this principle is used to explain the functions that the subject fulfills in the actual context.

As Benveniste (1958: 226) states, language is so organized that it permits each speaker to appropriate to himself an entire language by designating himself as "I". Accordingly, language provides due linguistic resources defined by depending on the subject "I" in the discourse, such as the pronouns, the indicator of deixis, the demonstratives, adverbs, and adjectives, etc., which in turn can be drawn on to construct the subject "I" in discourse. The personal system supplied in the first step brings up subjectivity in language. By means of person deixis, the role of participants in the discourse is encoded around the subject "I" as the referent. The connotation of the pronoun system is thus derived: the category of the first person is the grammaticalization of the speaker's reference to himself, and the second person refers to the encoding of the writer's reference opposite to the addressees, and the third person is the encoding of reference to persons and entities which are neither the speaker nor the addressees of the utterance in question. (Levinson, 1983: 62)

As shown by this kind of realizations occurring in SAEC, the writer makes his presentation with the pronoun "we" as the subjects, which indicate the appearance of the subject indicator "I". The subject can also be established by using its cognate variant "our" in prepositional phrases, but only two of which occur, namely, "in our mind" (Text 32), "to our modern way of thinking" (Text 81) in SAEC. In this way, the writer encodes himself overtly as the subject who expresses his attitudes explicitly. By the way, the question "what the uses of 'we/our' mean to the instantiation of the subject 'I'" is to be dealt with immediately. As to the second person, "you" just occurs as the subject four times in SAEC, including one that appears in the direct speech, as is shown in Example (97):

(97) Some had already printed fliers asking, "Have **you** seen this person?" (Text 6)

Here, "you" in the direct speech is used in a gestural style, which must be interpreted with reference to an audio-visual-tactile. (Levinson, 1983) Therefore, this usage of "you" is actually not the instance of referring to the writer of this editorial, but to the reader in this context who is signified by the indefinite pronoun "some". The other three "you" are the cases of referring to the writer of the editorial as the referent. For example:

(98) Some had never gotten over the view from the twin towers, and some no longer saw it at all. **You** could have found people living in nearly every neighborhood in New York and much of northern New Jersey. (Text 10)

Obviously, the writer of the editorial regards the potential addressees as the conceived partners that are spoken of.

However, as the third person encodes the reference to persons and entities existing distinctively outside of the discourse, the category of the third person is usually realized by the third person deixis, such as the common noun, the proper noun, the appellation noun, the determiner and adjectives expressing some generic concept. (Halliday & Matthiessen, 2004) As far as SAEC is concerned, the cases of using the third person as the subjects are complex. Compared with the usages of the first and the second person, more various forms of the third person are adopted in editorials. No matter how complicated the third persons appear, they are clearly designated around the indicator "I/we" of the ego-subject in the course of producing discourse. The designation of the third person referring to the first person is correspondingly exploited effectively when the Theme (T)-Rheme (R) model is studied. (Halliday, 1994a; Halliday & Matthiessen, 2004) Then, one piece of the passage is chosen at random from SAEC in order to explain in detail how all these forms realizing the third person are encoded systematically by taking the Theme-Rheme model into consideration.

(99) As America searches for Osama bin Laden in the mountainous wilderness of eastern Afghanistan, we (T1) are learning that even in victory, finding the end point can be frustratingly elusive (R1).

President Bush (T2) has been clear-headed about this possibility (R2). Since Sept. 11 he (T3) has often said that the fight against terrorism will be difficult and prolonged (R3). Yet **no amount of presidential speechmaking** (T4) can really prepare Americans for the possibility that the fate of Osama bin Laden may remain unclear for some time (R4). **The uncertainty** (T5) seems especially maddening just days after everyone saw the videotape of **the terrorist leader** chuckling over the collapse of the World Trade Center towers(R5).

He (T6) could turn up, dead or alive, at any time—or not at all (R6). **He** (T7) may be hiding in the inhospitable, snow-capped high country above Tora, the last redoubt of the Qaeda network in Afghanistan (R7). **He** (T8) could be entombed in one of the area's many caverns, if an American bomb happened to hit the right cave during the heavy bombardment of recent days (R8). Or **he** (T9) may have slipped away days ago and melted into the desolate region along the Pakistani border (R9). (Text 18)

Accordingly, the T-R mode of the information flowing can be abstracted as:

(T1 = T2 = T3)—R1—R2—R3 (T4)—R4 (T5)—R5 (R6, R7, R8, R9)—(T6 = T7 = T8 = T9).

In Example (99), the writer sets up the position of the ego subject by using the pronoun "we" which means "we-inclusive-of-others" (Benveniste, 1958). According to the context, the appellation noun "President Bush (T2)" is connotatively inclusive in "we-inclusive-of-others" and surely signified by this "*we*". Similarly, as the text information flows on, other forms of the third person are chained together. Therefore, the elements of the subject functioning as theme embodies the writer's consciousness of choosing them.

6.4.1.3 Subject Perspective Realized in Plural Form

Modality takes the speaker's angle, either on the validity of the assertion or on the rights and wrongs of the proposal. Under most circumstances, the writer likes to give prominence to his own point of view in the most effective way of doing this explicitly by using this sort of expressions, e.g. "I think...". However, the plural form "we" is used to meet this need, as the materials in SAEC show.

Language is possible only because each speaker sets himself up as a subject by referring to himself as "I" in his discourse. (Benveniste, 1958: 225) To be precise, the foundation of subjectivity as the property of language is that the ego-subject is saying "ego" in words. Therefore, the first person "I" as the indicator "ego" always has a position of transcendence with respect to the second and the third person. Although the plural "we" is traditionally regarded as the plural form of the first person "I", it entails two meanings "we-inclusive-of-addressee" and "we-inclusive-of-others" according to the situation. (Benveniste, 1958; Halliday, 1994a; Halliday & Matthiessen, 2004; Levinson, 1983.) That is, "we" is not conceived of as a multiplication of identical objects but a junction between the writer "I" and the "non-I", no matter what the content of this "non-I" may be. This junction form "we" is of a new totality and its components are not equivalent because the indicator "I" always dominates the "non-I" element due to its transcendent quality. Therefore, the form alike "we think..." is essentially a variant that still expresses the subjective orientation explicitly. That is exactly the reason why we judge some forms as the explicitly subjective orientation. For example:

(100) As America searches for Osama bin Laden in the mountainous wilderness of eastern Afghanistan, **we are learning** that even in victory, finding the end point can be frustratingly elusive. (Text 21)

(101) The only acceptable risks, **to our modern way of thinking**, were the ones we deliberately courted ourselves. (Text 81)

(102) **In our minds** he will always be standing at ground zero, his back to the towering shards and smoke from the World Trade Center. (Text 32)

Examples (100), (101) and (102) show obviously that the speaker works out the explicitly subjective orientation. While Example (100) encodes the speaker's cognitive acknowledgement clearly as a projecting clause, Examples (101) and (102) take advantage of the prepositional phrases to fulfill the same function.

As the connotative meaning of "we" is situation-specific, it must be understood on the basis of the context in which it is appearing. Searching thoroughly through SAEC, the writers uniquely make the best use of the plural "we" when they encode the subjective orientation explicitly. What's more, judging from the context, all these plural "we" forms are of the distinct "we-inclusive-of-reader", which tells that the writer pays special attention to assigning the reader in the same line. This is a discourse strategy that the writer draws on to persuade the reader to share and follow his opinions. The motivations related to expressing the subjective attitudes explicitly in this way can be explained in association with the persuasive feature of the editorial genre.

6.4.2 Construction of Persuasiveness with Respect to Perspectivization

6.4.2.1 Information Engaged in Terms of Perspectivization

Facts and evidence must be introduced into the discourse in due forms. Halliday (1994a) points out that reports, ideas and facts can be projected into the discourse as representations of linguistic resources. The projections that the writer operates in the course of producing the discourse are quotes, reports, and facts which enter into structural relationships in the grammar. Furthermore, it is important to stress that quotes, reports and facts are categories of language: anything that can be expressed in language can have the status of a fact; and the referents of ideas and locutions are linguistic phenomena with an idea representing a semantic phenomenon and a locution representing a lexico-grammatical one. (Halliday, 1994a: 272)

Then, they must be related to some responsible sources, no matter whether they exist inside or outside the discourse. Usually, there are four ways that these sources are attributed: as projecting clauses, as names for speech acts, as projecting within clauses, and as scare quotes. (Martin & Rose, 2003: 52) These information sources may be subdivided into primary sources, secondary sources, and tertiary sources. As subjectivity is a fundamental property of language which is responsible for it in all its parts, it is thus embodied in the process of communication in language. Ego is he who says it—that is where the foundation of subjectivity is determined by the linguistic status of "person" (Benveniste, 1971: 224). In this way, the opposition of persons, by which the speaker sets himself up as a subject by indexing himself as "I" and refers to the address as "you", is established in the fundamental condition of language. Therefore, the status of person belongs only to the polarity "I" versus "you" and is lacking in the case of "he". (Benveniste, 1971)

Clearly, the system of the third person, in fact, represents the unmarked member of the correlation of people in the discourse and escapes the condition of a person in spite of his individual nature, so it fundamentally doesn't refer to itself but to an objective situation. (Benveniste, 1971) Thus, in the system of pronouns, the third person is, with their function and their nature, entirely different from the first person represented by "I" and the second person by "you". Correspondingly, in the context of communication, while "I" and "you" get the language status of speech roles, the third person, say, "he", "she", "it", "they", can replace one or another of the material elements in the discourse instead of functioning speech roles. (Halliday, 1994) As the essential character of subjectivity is the speaker's capacity to posit or construe himself as "subject", the first person designating ego obtains a status of transcendence which enables "I" to ask the third person for evidence to persuade "you". Thus, the third person can function as the information source that would bring facts or evidence into the discourse and help express the writer's proposition.

The system of the third person includes common noun, proper noun and (personal) pronoun. Common nouns refer to classes of persons, other living things, collectives, objects and institutions, and are typically accompanied by a deictic and other elements. Proper names are defined as names of particular persons (individually or as a group), institutions of all kinds, and places. In terms of personal pronouns, the referent is defined interpersonally in accordance with the linguistic situation. Usually, personal pronouns and proper names are used without any other elements of the nominal group. In SAEC, personal pronouns, common nouns and proper names that appear in proper forms as information sources lead various propositions into the discourse. Those forms of information sources are classified into six types: the third person single form, pronoun, organization name, institutional name, non-known person and collective.

The six types of information sources represent different ways of importing the third party's proposition into the discourse. The third person single form refers to the proper name of a particular person, who often occurs singly, e. g. "Robert Pear", or with greeting honorific, e. g. "Mr.", or professional honorific, e. g. "President", as epithet, or with the professional status, e. g. "the director of central intelligence", or the modifier clause, as qualifier. Pronouns include personal pronouns with variants of forms, e. g. "they", "he", "it", or demonstratives, e. g. "this", "those", which function to identify people by accurately presuming them in the context. Organizations involve particularly functional departments of the government, such as the Secret Service, The Port Authority of New York and New Jersey, the Justice Department etc. Institutional names deal with names which metonymically can replace the whole unit and appear as the products of a certain institution, e. g. the regulations, or refer to certain social post, e. g. the attorney general, or represent metonymically certain institutions, e. g. Beijing. Non-known persons mainly refer to using indefinite pronouns, e. g. "many", "anyone", to present new persons in the discourse. In linguistics, a collective noun is used to define a group of people, animals, emotions, inanimate things, concepts, or other things. Here, collective nouns occur in the form of nominal groups with the head in plural form with epithet, e. g. many trial lawyers, or in compound form, e. g. the United States and its allies, or as the collective noun, e. g. people, the public, or as the indefinite pronouns with qualifier, e. g. anyone who has watched the president over the last year.

By looking through the SAEC, we can see that the information source appears generally in these cases. Firstly, the source acts as the subject of the independent clause, or in the circumstantial clause, or even in the qualifier clause. For example:

(103) **Most Americans** will find that the language of thanks has an unaccustomed eloquence this year. (Text 22)

(104) When **people** say they want something splendid in Lower Manhattan—and they say that repeatedly—they mean more than just the memorial itself. (Text 52)

(105) This is a troubling pattern, especially now that **President Bush** has said he will base his decisions about Iraq on the latest intelligence reports. Intelligence findings should guide presidential policy. (Text 64)

Secondly, the source occurs in the prepositional phrase and as the object of the preposition, which can exist at the beginning, or in the middle part of the clause. For example:

(106) **Among New York's senior political figures**, there is an emerging consensus that a special commission or authority should be created to oversee the reconstruction. (Text 13)

(107) Warnings **by federal officials** that terrorists may strike again in this country have ratcheted up concerns about everything from suicide bombers to explosions in apartment buildings or at prominent landmarks. (Text 50)

Sometimes, the source comes in the possessive form as a part of the nominal group with the nominalization of the reporting verb as its head. This combination can act as the subject of the clause, or as the complementary element to the verb or to the preposition. For example:

(108) **President Bush's plan** to use secret military tribunals to try terrorists is a dangerous idea, made even worse by the fact that it is so superficially attractive. (Text 20)

(109) Americans are wondering how to respond to **Attorney General John Ashcroft's warning** that terrorists are planning new attacks against the United States in the near future. (Text 14)

The information source discovers directly the source of information and is responsible for the proposition brought into the discourse, which usually collocates with the variants of reporting verbs or cognitive verbs, as our study shows. There is no doubt that we can change the logical relationship between the source and the proposition. However, we can choose different sources to lead the proposition along with its source existing or omitted into the discourse according to our expectation. And, the form in which the source is presented, and the place where it is put are also under operation of the writer. The process of bringing in the proposition is inevitably full of prints left by the writer.

6.4.2.2 Construction of Persuasiveness with Respect to Engaged Information

It has been proven that the proposition is frequently brought into the discourse by means of reporting verbs or cognitive verbs. (Martin & White, 2005) It is inevitable to discuss the relation between the sources and the verbs, which import propositions inside.

As we have studied how facts and evidence are introduced into the discourse, we have worked out three categories that the writer uses to express his opinions in the discourse, and they are revised here as: entertainment and pronouncement concern the writer's expressing himself covertly; endorsement and acknowledgement deal with the writer's supporting his position with that of the third party indirectly; contrastively, distance deals with the evidence that the writer adopts to go against the opposite positions, by which the writer distances himself from the responsibility.

And, in the Section 4.2.2, we have studied the six types of sources that can draw the propositions into the discourse. In this section, we mainly focus on how the writer introduces the propositions into the discourse by studying the collocation between the strategies leading into the proposition and the sources taking care of the proposition.

The writer expresses himself overtly or covertly by means of entertainment and pronouncement. Traditionally, entertainment is covered under the headings of "epistemic modality" (Palmer, 1986) and "evidentiality" (Chafe & Nichols, 1986). Within SFL, it is discussed under the heading of "reality phase", "modals of probability" and "interpersonal metaphor". (Halliday, 1994) It consists of linguistic resources realizing likelihood through modal auxiliaries, modal attributes, modal adjuncts, certain mental verbs or attribute projections, or circumstances of the "in my view" type. (Martin & White, 2005) Pronouncement contains various forms interpolating explicitly authorial interventions into the discourse to emphasize his maximal investment in the present proposition. Fundamentally, both entertainment and pronouncement concern how the writer expresses his modal assessment. Therefore, there is no surprise that there are seldom such cases here only with one case of entertainment or pronouncement.

Strategically, the writer always detours to indicate his communicative intention by using the opinion of the third party as evidence, which is discussed under the heading of acknowledgement, endorsement and distance. Acknowledgement and endorsement belong to the same category, and the writer supports his position with importing the third party's opinion indirectly by using them. However, distance is the strategy that the writer adopts to fend off the opposite position without taking any responsibilities. Acknowledgement and endorsement are used 247 times, 206 times of acknowledgement and 41 times of endorsement, almost involving all kinds of sources. As statistical results tell, the strategies of acknowledgement and endorsement reveal the tendency that the writer likes to draw on the speeches or citations delivered by authoritative powers, which are imported inside as the direct speech or the indirect speech with respect to the context. For example:

(110) These included public and private warnings from **George Tenet, the director of central intelligence**, that Al Qaeda could strike at any time. (Text 48)

Example (110) shows that the indirect speech made by the authoritative power is cited as the warning of Al Qaeda's strike at any time. In this way, the proposition is clearly acknowledged to the authoritative influence whose powerful identity is classified in Qualifier as the director of central intelligence. Likewise, reports, decisions, statistic data, and experiment results made by the official branch, the credible institution, or the authority etc. are tactically quoted to support the writer's opinion. Contextually, all these entities can be replaced by pronouns, which help presume them in the following passage. Or in other words, pronouns are adopted to identify the traces of the source. This, to some extent, can explain why sources related to pronouns are used most in the discourse.

Distance is adopted 83 times in SAEC, collocating with all these sources. Essentially, an editorial is an opinion piece with an issue of news. It is necessary for the writer to quote relevant speeches, opinions etc. directly or indirectly, no matter whether their sources are special persons, governmental branches, or organizations and so on, which can presumed by pronouns to mention again. For example:

(111) Officials already made one such mistake when **they tried to sell the** story that the president had avoided returning to Washington on Sept. 11 because there was a credible threat of a terrorist plot against Air Force One. (Text 14)

In Example (111), the proposition is led in as embedded clause of the nominal group "the story". And the pronoun "they" acts as the source which refers back to the plural noun "officials" at the beginning of the clause. Sometimes, the critical description and analysis around the issue and relevant speeches are provided, which then are tracked by demonstratives. Strikingly, the cases of non-source that appear in this category are up to 17 times out of the total 23 cases in SAEC, which can be roughly classified into three groups. Firstly, there is really no source, for the proposition is conceptualized by the writer to analyze the roundabout factors relevant to the issue. For example:

(112) **It is a reasonable presumption** that the terrorists who attacked New York and Washington aimed not just to kill American civilians but also to draw the United States into an indiscriminate and brutish military response that might attract Muslims around the world to their cause. (Text 11)

Clearly, the proposition has no practical source at all because it is exactly presumed as the result of the writer's conceiving of all related factors, which is just what the nominal group "a reasonable presumption" suggests. Secondly, the writer invokes the widespread views pertaining to the issue, which is hard to track its exact source. For example:

(113) The horrific attacks of Sept. 11 give credence to **the notion** that these foreign terrorists are uniquely malevolent outlaws, undeserving of American constitutional protections. (Text 20)

In Example (113), the proposition expressed by the clause—these foreign terrorists are uniquely malevolent outlaws, undeserving of American constitutional protections—is popular in certain social community, so the writer summarizes it as the notion without real source.

Thirdly, a given speech is commonly known, because it is cited without referring to its sources here but it can be easily tracked contextually. For example, "enemy combatant" is always regarded as "common knowledge", because it comes from Mr. Bush announcement as everyone knows.

Evidentially, strategies of acknowledgement and endorsement are used much more frequently than that of distance, which tells that the writer prefers to turn to the third party's proposition to prop up his position rather than object to the opposite proposition. Contrary to the general trend, the cases of non-source used in the strategy of distance are by far higher than those in acknowledgement and endorsement, which shows that the writer tends to repel the opposite opinion with the aid of propositions without clearly-mentioned sources.

6.5 Summary

In SFL, a genre is demarcated as a staged, goal-orientated social process. (Martin & White, 2003) The discourse is the instantiation of a genre. Clearly, it is true that the course of producing a discourse is fundamentally a process that the writer implements a certain social action. Therefore, this social action is goal-orientated, which must be enslaved to the writer's individual bias; and the writer usually makes the best use of linguistic resources to construct such individual opinion to reach the communicating intention, which aims to give goods, services, and information to the reader. Although we use the term "subjective opinion" here, it doesn't refer to the stubborn, stupid, foolish idea with paranoid bias. However, it refers to an insightful opinion upheld by the individual person or institution. To explain editorial opinions, van Dijk (1995: 3) states clearly that "opinions... are associated with individuals, deemed to be subjective in the sense that they are what someone thinks to be true, but which others know or believe to be false or at least not justified". Fundamentally, these opinions refer to the evaluations and judgements given in editorials resulting from "a mental judgement"—what the writer believes to be right or wrong; (Elyazale, 2014) and they can be judged and justified to be acceptable in accordance with the socio-cultural norms of a specific community (van Dijk, 1995).

Besides, the writer certainly bears the goal of enacting certain actions in mind the moment he plans to write the discourse, for which the writer would be aware of the whole producing process: making the design, collecting the materials, organizing them etc. As far as the editorials are concerned, they function as opinion articles, and aim to persuade and convince the reader by expressing the legitimacy and validity of ideas. The editorial "plays a definitive role in the formation and altering of public opinion, promotes social interaction among journalists, readers, and influences social debate, decision making and other forms of social actions" (Belmonte, 2008: 2). To achieve this aim, the writer chooses to express SA by means of forms of modality, attitudinal adjectives, stance adverbials, intensifiers, rhetorical questions etc., and operates to justify his subjective opinion by depending on linguistic devices, say, quotes, numbers, grammar metaphor, and so on, all of which are exploited and statistically illuminated by Elyazale's (2014) study.

Chapter 7
Conclusion

This study has revealed that various expressions are used to realize subjectivity in editorials, which function to construct argumentativity and persuasiveness and aim to enact the persuasion. This chapter starts with a summary of major findings in the present study. Then, it particularly discusses the limitations pertaining to the data and methodology of this study. Finally, it gives some suggestions for further study.

7.1 Major Findings

The present enterprise is a subjectivity-theoretical study of various realizations of the modal assessment in editorials around hard news within the realm of SFL. Honestly, it is a germinant attempt to carry out the study on subjectivity in the field of SFL. Therefore, the theoretical frame based on SFL is designed, not only referring to the three arenas of studying subjectivity and subjectivisation proposed by E. Finegan, but also absorbing the researching findings achieved in fields of cognitive linguistics and pragmatics. The present study guided by such a frame is identical to SFL's basic principle that the writer carries out the social action in the process of creating the discourse. Accordingly, the term subjectivity is revised to cover various realizations of modal assessments which connotatively fuse the joint meanings of subjectivity into a whole: the subjective opinion oriented to certain communicative intention is realized in the process of producing the discourse consciously by choosing subjectivized forms and by operating with self-participating prints left. In this way, the theoretical frame and the researching objects are clearly defined. The data are editorials around the hard news of the terrorist attack of September 11, 2001 in America, which come from *The New York Times*. With those editorials, the self-construction database SAEC is made. Based on the research goal, corresponding methodology is designed properly. The annotating file is worked out in accordance with this frame, and the software brat is used to carry out the annotation to materials and do statistical work. Then, the theoretical frame and methodology are harmoniously combined in the study. Consequently, quantitative and qualitative analysis are implemented in this study to give support to the findings.

7.1.1 Major Findings Concerning the Patterns of Realizing Subjectivity in Terms of Modal Assessment

According to SFL, expressions of modal assessment are language resources applied to realize subjectivity. This study mainly involves the network system of MODALITY, the system of ENGAGEMENT and the system of JUDGEMENT in appraisal, and sets up the following research categories: modality, propositional comments, speech-functional comments, judging appraisals and engaging opinions.

In the system of MODALITY, realizations of subjectivity take on the following characteristics. In terms of modality type, the writer prefers to express subjectivity by using modalized propositions rather than address modulized proposals. As to orientation, the writer tends to choose modal operators or modal adjuncts to realize subjectivity implicitly instead of expressing subjectivity explicitly. For the variable of value, the writer realizes subjectivity in medium value when expressing subjectivity in modalized propositions or modulized inclinations, but strikingly emphasizes to take high values when construing subjectivity in modulized obligatory.

Moreover, propositional comments and speech functional comments are valid resources to realize subjectivity. Propositional comments include making assessment on subject in terms of wisdom or morality properties, or on the whole proposition with respect to asseverative or qualificative attributes, which involve seven aspects that can be subdivided into 14 varieties. 63 cases of properties of wisdom and morality are about the subject's capacity and property respectively, all of which appear in the objective orientation. 75 variants of asseverative comments express subjectivity from natural, obvious and sure aspects, which index statements of conviction and truth, dispersing in the discourse to show the credibility of propositions. 450 qualificative comments are used to express subjectivity, and can be subcategorized into three aspects: prediction, presumption, and desirability; they indicate that the proportion is correctly relevant to the context in logical ratiocination. Speech functional comments include qualified and unqualified types. 97 variants of the unqualified take the implicitly objective orientation, which hints the writer's desirability of persuasive inclination with warrantable proposition. 27 variants of the unqualified type are adopted to indicate the validity of propositions from the writer's perspective.

As for expressions of JUDGEMENT, it has the following features. The frequencies of capacity and property are much higher than those of the rest three types; and the positive is preferred in normality, capacity, tenacity and veracity, with type of capacity being of the highest frequency; however, the negative is adopted most in property. According to further analysis from the angel of social esteem and social sanction, it is clear that judgements of esteem are much more preferred than judgements of sanction in editorials; expressions of negative sanction are much more preferred than those in positive as to the status of social sanction. As far as modalization and modulization are concerned, two typical features appear: realizations of modulization are much more than those of modalization; and both modulization and modalization occurring in positive are much more than those in negative.

The system of ENGAGEMENT is defined here to deal with cases of expressing subjectivity with the help of importing facts and evidences sourced to the third party, which is regarded as strategic devices to support intended opinions or challenge the opposite opinions. The importing ways include entertain, pronounce, endorse, acknowledge and distance. In this study, the strategies of acknowledge and endorse are used most in SAEC, which reveals that subjectivity is preferred to be realized indirectly by resorting to speeches or citations made by authoritative powers inside. The strategy of distance is adopted secondly involving all sources, which is realized subjectively and indirectly by departing the writers from any responsibilities. Therefore, the strategies of entertain and pronounce concern that subjectivity is expressed covertly by the writer here in figures of speech, e. g. rhetoric questions. Characteristically, subjectivity is realized indirectly by introducing the third party's proposition to support intended proposition or fend off the opposite opinion.

7.1.2 Major Findings Concerning How Subjectivity Works to Fulfill Persuasive Function in Terms of Argumentativity and Persuasiveness

Being argumentative and persuasive, editorials are credited as argumentative texts written mainly to influence the opinions of the reader with the aim to persuade them. Argumentativity and persuasiveness are its fundamental properties, which reflect the writer's capacity of choosing modal assessment consciously to express his subjective stance in the process of producing editorials. Both of them work interactively in editorials to have the persuasive function fulfilled successfully.

Firstly, the editorial is treated as a communicative process of enacting persuasive function, which has social, aesthetic, psychological or moral aspects. Modal assessments advocate a given system of values, encourage a particular attitude and evaluation, and function as persuasive instruments to support a specific conclusion. In SFL, modal assessments are involved in the system of MODALITY, the system of APPRAISAL, and the system of ENGAGEMENT, and are chosen to scatter in discourse to realize the subjective stance. The choices of modal assessments reflect the process in which the writer expresses his subjectivity that demonstrates the writer's self-consciousness and capacity of taking advantages of language potential to construct argumentativity and persuasiveness in editorials with the aim to fulfill the persuasive function.

Secondly, as an essential feature of editorials, argumentativity is constructed in the process of reasoning elaboration, which characterizes the writer's self-consciousness of choosing due linguistic forms to have his subjective stance argued with the aim to convince the reader. Argumentativity plays a critical role in convincing the reader, and it works from two perspectives: argumentative direction and argumentative strength, which are explored with respect to modal orientation, modal value, judging appraisals and engaging opinions in this study. To be concrete, the writer chooses modal adjuncts and modal operators to realize subjectivity in implicitly subjective and implicitly objective orientations so as to spare some space to have the reader involved to negotiate with. As for the variable of value, the writer realizes subjectivity in medium value in propositions or inclinations, but takes high values in obligatory, which shows that the writer expresses subjective judgement on the proposition referring to the textual information and interacts politely with the reader, but that he unflinchingly delivers the desirability that the reader is obliged to accept the suggested proposals. Argumentative strength is expressed on the basis of evaluation according to social esteem and social sanction, by which the writer expresses his condemnation on the terrorism attack, reflects on the misconducts around the terrorism attack, and highlights the capacity of the relevant people in dealing with the negative effects caused by these attacks. To transmit directly the argumentative strength, the writer constructs the expectancy mainly by acknowledging and endorsing supporting opinions, but he indicates his counter-expectancy by distancing opposite opinions to weaken the strength, which work as the textual strategies to express the subjective expectation in order to prop up the subjective stance advance in discourse.

Thirdly, persuasiveness of editorials emphasizes the power constituted through the persuasive technology to change the reader's attitudes and behaviour. The general principle of persuasiveness is to have the reader enlightened with reason and move in emotional words. Persuasive technology here is an intangible phenomenon involving both explicit choices of meaning and implicit choices to express the authorial stance to the reader, and deals with the strategies of modality, affective judgement and perspectivation. In SFL, the system of MODALITY realizes subjective assessments on propositions and proposals, and the system of JUDGEMENT concerns the assessments on the characters and behaviors of the relevant person. Both of them involve modalization and modulization, with the former occurring much more than the later, which shows that the writer gives his recommendation after making full argument and analysis of relevant information. Moreover, propositional comments and speech functional comments scatter in discourse, acting as cues to guide the reader's construement of the stance. The writer makes the best use of qualificative propositional comments, especially prediction, presumption, and desirability, by which he explains the persuasive power of the proportion by referring to the context with logical ratiocination. Furthermore, speech functional comments are chosen to indicate the validity of propositions from the writer's perspective, and they function as linguistic signs to lead the reader to follow rationalizing procedure. The writer takes the strategy of perspectivation so as to adopt the speeches or citations made by the authoritative powers, and then persuasiveness is intensified by the supporting opinions sourced to the third party.

7.2 Implications

The present study combines both cognitive and functional approaches to study the realizations and the persuasive functions of subjectivity in editorials, and the findings contribute to researches on subjectivity at the discourse level and shed light on discourse analysis.

Theoretically, this study proposes a relatively comprehensive and integrated analytical framework in SFL for studying the realizations and the persuasive functions of subjectivity in editorials. Based on Finegan's established framework on the study of subjectivity, the theoretical framework of this study is tentatively constructed within the field of SFL. Following the viewpoint that a discourse is the dynamic process of performing a certain social action, the study explores the realizations of subjectivity by turning to the linguistic resources of modal assessment, which involve three arenas: the system of MODALITY, the system of JUDGEMENT and the system of ENGAGEMENT. Moreover, by focusing on the ways of realizations of subjectivity in the process of producing editorials, the study goes further on the way that argumentativity and persuasiveness are constructed in modal assessment with the aim to fulfill the persuasive function. This study extends the researches on subjectivity from the lexical and grammatical levels to the discourse level. It provides a systemic account for the persuasive function of editorials from the perspective of subjectivity. Although it is not a new practice to make discourse study of editorials, to explore the persuasive function in the conscious process of constructing subjectivity is exactly a new trial.

Methodologically, this study adopts a systemic-functional approach to study subjectivity, which is another attempt to show that the principles of SFL can function to study subjectivity at discourse level. Besides, a new corpus tool "brat" is introduced to make annotations and do statistics, and it does help in the field of linguistic research.

Practically, this research analyzes the realizations and the persuasive functions of subjectivity in editorials, which is of great significance both for the editorial writer and the reader. The analytical model is also helpful for English learners to have a better understanding of the persuasive power of editorials from the authorial perspective.

7.3 Limitations of the Present Study

Although this study has answered all research questions raised in Chapter 1, there are unavoidably some limitations.

Firstly, a major advantage of this framework created here is that it puts the study within the realm of SFL and helps to carry out a comprehensive study on how subjectivity is realized in editorials with the aim to perform the persuasive function. However, as for the scope of this frame, it seems a bit narrow because it doesn't cover modal adjuncts related to temporarity and intensity. If these two parts are included, more comprehensive studies on subjectivity will inevitably be made. Besides, because the frame involves too many variables, it seems to be too delicate when it is applied to the corpus-based analysis which requires to "focus on fewer variables across a corpus of texts" (Martin & White, 2005: 260). In the future research, therefore, a better balance needs to be held between the delicacy of the frame and the orientation of the study.

Secondly, a major weakness pertaining to this study is the lack of strong empirical support to some of the interpretations of data. Although we have tried our best to make annotations according to the criteria explained in SFL, sometimes it is hard to divide them into due categories. Therefore, it is of much possibility to make determinations just out of individual judgements. It is then easier to raise disputes due to different interpretations and cultural divergences. In face of this dilemma, we make the final decision through three processes: making initial judgement strictly based on the criteria; distinguishing subtle construements according to the context; asking native speakers for help if there is still not a decision made after the first two steps. In this way, we do our best to make proper annotations according to the materials in SAEC.

Thirdly, although we have practically analyzed realizations and the persuasive functions of subjectivity based on editorials' communicative intention which is closely related to the genre characteristics of editorials, we just refer to achievements of the former studies of editorials in terms of genre without doing practical analysis on the editorials collected in this study. Achievements resulting from the former studies can surely give beneficial guidance to this study, but if we make analysis of realizations of subjectivity based on the comprehensive study of genre features of the editorials in SAEC, it would give more useful enlightenments to this study.

7.4 Suggestions for Further Study

This book has attempted to study how the writer expresses subjectivity with the aim to enact the persuasive function in editorials. Although it is a completely new attempt of studying subjectivity within SFL, what have done and achieved in the study will surely shed light on the further study in similar field.

A newly-created theoretical frame has been testified to be workable in the process of studying the way that subjectivity is realized. Meanwhile, the present study shows that various perspectives can be adopted to carry out the study on subjectivity; in other words, the three areas of this model can be regarded as different angles of exploring subjectivity. That is to say, we can study subjectivity realized in the system of MODALITY with modal adjuncts of temporarity and intensity included; study subjectivity with respect to the system of APPRAISAL; study subjectivity in accordance with the system of ENGAGEMENT. Those three systems can combine together to contribute to much more comprehensive study on subjectivity. Thus, the study within SFL is clearly sketched at the discourse level.

As to the individual interposition when doing annotations, the strategies of keeping annotations as identifiable as possible have been mentioned with three steps. In the process of using the corpus tool brat to make annotations and do statistics, its great power is really figured out in the field of linguistic research. Particularly, as its designing file shows, it can demarcate four categories: [entities], [events], [relations] and [attributes], which can be used to demonstrate the theoretical principles put forth in the domain of SFL with a little redefinition. In return, brat can push ahead the study of subjectivity in the domain of SFL.

According to Martin & White (2005), a genre is a staged, goal-oriented social process. The genre features of editorials reveal how editorials implement social actions. The editorial writer expresses subjectivity justified with facts and evidence in order to motivate the reader to accept proposed opinion and take actions, which can be exploited under the heading of the concept of the subjective stance. Fundamentally, stance is considered as a larger activity which is relatively sustained in terms of its topical coherence and goal-driven course of action, which is to some extent based on affect dispositions, other interpersonal attitudes and strategic intentions and is strongly dependent on the contributions of other communicators. Personally, the stance can be regarded as the stance-taking and discourse-producing process, in which the writer can make the best use of various linguistic resources to achieve the goal of enacting a social action.

References

Abney, S. (1991). Parsing by chunks. In R. C. Berwick, S. P. Abney & C. L. Tenny (eds.), *Principle-based Parsing* (pp. 257-258). Dordrecht: Kluwer Academic Publishers.

Aikhenvald, A. Y. (2004). *Evidentiality*. Oxford: Oxford University Press.

Ajzen, I. (1991). Organizational behavior and human decision process. *The Theory of Planned Behavior*, 50.

Alaoui, H. I. (2010). Introduction. In H. I. Alaoui (ed.), *Modern Books*. World: Jordan.

Albright, S. (2006). Sights and sounds of a newspaper's editorial. *Nieman Reports*: 70-71.

Ansari, H. & Babaii, E. (2005). The generic integrity of newspaper editorials: A systemic functional perspective. *RELC Journal*, 36.

Anscombre, J. C. & Ducrot, O. (1989). Argumentativity and informativity. In M. Meyer, (ed.), *From Metaphysics to Rhetoric* (pp. 71-87). Dordrecht: Kluwer.

Arnold, E. J., Wasow, T., Losongco, A. & Ginstrom, R. (2000). Heaviness vs. newness: The effects of structural complexity and discourse status on constituent ordering. *Language*, 76 (1).

Ate, A. A. (2008), Agenda-setting role of the Nigerian press: A case study of third term agenda. *Journal of Arts & Social Sciences*, 1(1).

Athanasiadou, A. (2006). Adjectives and subjectivity. In Athanasiadou, A.,

Canakis, C. & Cornillie, B. (eds.), *Subjectification: Variou Paths to Subjectivity* (pp. 209-239). Berllin/New York: Muton de Gruyter.

Athanasiadou, A. (2007). On the subjectivity of intensifiers. *Language Sciences*, 29(4).

Athanasiadou, A., Canakis, C. & Cornillie, B. (eds.). (2006). *Subjectification: Various Paths to Subjectivity.* Berlin: Mouton de Gruyter.

Baker, P., Hardie, A. & McEnery, T. (2006). *A Glossary of Corpus Linguistics.* Edinburgh: Edinburgh University Press.

Bakhtin, M. M. (1981). *The Dialogic Imagination.* Emerson, C. & Holquist, M. (trans.). Austin: University of Texas Press.

Bamberg, M. (1997). Oral versions of personal experience: Three decades of narrative analysis. *Journal of Narrative and Life History*, 7(1-4).

Banfield, A. (1982). *Unspeakable Sentences : Narration and Representation in the Language of Fiction.* Boston: Routledge & Kegan Paul.

Baumgarten, N., I. Bois, D. & House, J. (2012). *Subjectivity in Language and Discourse.* Amsterdam: Brill.

Bednarek, M. (2008). *Emotion Talk and Corpora.* Houndsmills: Palgrave Macmillan.

Bednarek, M. (2010). Corpus linguistics and systemic functional linguistics: Interpersonal meaning, identity and bonding in popular culture. In M. Bednarek & J. R. Martin (Ed.), *New Discourse on Language: Functional Perspectives on Mutlimodality, Identity, and Affiliation* (pp. 237-266). London/New York: Continuum.

Belmonte, A. I. (2008). Newspaper editorials and comment articles: A cinderella genre? *Volumen Monográfico*, (1).

Benveniste, E. (1958). *Problems in General Linguistics.* M. E. Meek & C. Gablres (trans.). Florida: University of Miami Press.

Bergström, O. & Knights, D. (2006). Organizational discourse and subjectivity: Subjectification during processes of recruitment. *Human Relations*, 59(3).

Besnier, N. (1990). Language and affect. *Annual Review of Anthropology*, 19.

Besnier, N. (1993). Reported Speech and affect on Nukulaelae Atoll. In J. H. Hill & J. T. Irvine (eds.), *Responsibility and Evidence in Oral Discourse* (pp. 161-181). Cambridge: Cambridge University Press.

Betsch, T. (2008). The nature of intuition and its neglect in research on judgement and decision making. In H. Plessner, C. Betsch & T. Betsch, (eds.), *Intuition in Judgement and Decision Making* (pp. 3-22). New York: Psychology Press.

Bhatia, V. K. (1993). *Analysing Genre: Language Use in Professional Settings.* London: Longman.

Biber, D. & Finegan, E. (1988). Adverbial stance types in English. *Discourse Processes*, 11.

Biber, D. & Finegan, E. (1989). Styles of stance in English: Lexical and grammatical marking of evidentiality and affect. *Text*, 9.

Biber, D. (2004). Historical patterns for the grammatical marking of stance: A cross-register comparison. *Journal of Historical Pragmatics*, 5(1).

Biber, D. (2006). Stance in spoken and written university registers. *Journal of English for Academic Purpose*, 5.

Biber, D. et al. (2004). *Representing Language Use in the University: Analysis of the TOEFL 2000 Spoken and Written Academic Language Corpus* (*ETS TOEFL Monograph Series*, MS-25). Princeton: Educational Testing Service.

Biber, D., Johansson, S., Leech, G. Conrad, S. & Finegan, E. (1999). *The Longman Grammar of Spoken and Written English.* London: Longman.

Boa, P. (1978). Valéry's "ego poeta": Towards a biography of the authorial self. *Neophilologus*, 62(1).

Bonyadi, A. (2011). Linguistic manifestations of modality in newspaper editorials. *International Journal of Linguistics*, 3.

Brains, C. L., Willnat, L. Manheim, J. B. & Rich, R. C. (2011). *Empirical Political Analysis.* Boston: Longman.

Brannon, E. M. & Roitman, D. (2003). Nonverbal representations of time and number in animals and human infants. In W. H. Meck (ed.), *Functional and Neural Mechanisms of Interval Timing* (pp. 143-182). Boca Raton: CRC Press.

Brazeal, G. (2009). Against gridlock: The viability of interest-based legislative negotiation. *Harvard Law & Policy Review* (Online), (3).

Bréal, M. (1900). *Semantics: Study in the Science of Meaning.* Cust, H. (trans.). New York: Dover.

Bredan, T. (2006). Grammaticalization and subjectification of the English adjectives of general comparison. In A. Athanasiadou, C. Canakis & B. Cornillie (eds.), *Subjectivity and Subjectification* (pp. 241-278). Berllin: Muton de Gruyter.

Brinton, L. J. (1996). *Pragmatic Markers in English: Grammaticalization and Discourse Functions.* Berlin/New York: Mouton de Gruyter.

Bühler, K. (1990). *Theory of Language: The Representational Function of Language.* D. F. Goodwin (trans.). Amsterdam: John Benjamins.

Butt, D., Fahey, R., Feez, S. and Spinks, S. (2012). *Using Functional Grammar: An Explorer's Guide.* South Yarra: Palgrave Macmillan,

Bybee, J. L., Perkins, D. & Pagliuca, W. (1994). *The Evolution of Grammar: Tense, Aspect, and Modality in the Languages of the World.* Chicago: University of Chicago Press.

Caballero, M. J., Dickinson, A. & Townsend, D. (1984). Aristotle and personal selling. *Journal of Personal Selling and Sales Management*, 4.

Carreras, X. & Marquez, L. (2005). Introduction to the CoNLL-2005 shared task: Semantic role labeling. In *Proceedings of the 9th Conference on Natural Language Learning* (pp. 152-164). Association for Computational Linguistics.

Chafe, W. & Nichols, J. (1986). *Evidentiality. The linguistic coding of epistemology.* Norwood, NJ: Ablex Publishing Corporation.

Chafe, W. (1994). *Discourse, Consciousness, and Time. The Flow and Displacement of Conscious Experience in Speaking and Writing.* Chicago: University of Chicago Press.

Clark, A. (2000). Word and action: Reconciling rules and know-how in moral cognition. In R. Campbell & B. Hunter (eds.), *Moral Epistemology Naturalized* (pp. 267-289). Calgary: University of Calgary Press.

Clark, E. V. (1990). Speaker perspective in language acquisition. *Linguistics*, 28.

Coates, J. (1983). *The Semantics of the Modal Auxiliaries.* London: Croom Helm.

Coates, J. (1995). The expression of root and epistemic possibility in English. In J. Bybee & S. Fleischman (eds.), *Modality in Grammar and Discourse* (pp. 55-66). Amsterdam: John Benjamins.

Company, C. C. (2006). Subjectification of verbs into discourse markers. Semantic-pragmatic change only? In B. Cornillie & N. Delbecque (eds.),

Topics in Subjectification and Modalization (pp. 97-121). Amsterdam/ Philadelphia: John Benjamins.

Crowne, D. P. & Marlowe, D. (1960). A new scale of social desirability independent of psychopathology. *Journal of Consulting Psychology*, 24 (4).

Cunningham, H., Maynard, D., Bontcheva, K., Tablan, V., Aswani, N., Roberts, I., Gorrell, G., Funk, A., Roberts, A., Damljanovic, D., Heitz, T., Greenwood, M. A., Saggion, H., Petrak, J., Li, Y. & Peters, W. (2011). *Text Processing with GATE* (Version 6).

Davidse, K., Vandelanotte, L. & Cuyckens, H. (eds.) (2010). *Subjectification, Intersubjectification and Grammaticalization.* Berlin: Mouton de Gruyter.

Davies, B. & R. Harré. (1990). Positioning: The discursive production of selves. *Journal for the Theory of Social Behavior*, 20(1).

de Smet, H. & Verstraete, J. C. (2006). Coming to terms with subjectivity. *Cognitive Linguistics*, 17.

Defour, T. (2010). The semantic-pragmatic development of well from the viewpoint of (inter) subjectification. In H. Cuyckens, D. Kristin & L. Vandelanotte (eds.), *Subjectification, Intersubjectification and Grammaticalization* (pp. 155-195). Berlin: Mouton de Gruyter.

Denison, D & Alison, C. (2010). Better as a verb. In H. Cuyckens, D. Kristin & L. Vandelanotte (eds.), *Subjectification, Intersubjectification and Grammaticalization* (pp. 349-383). Berlin: Mouton de Gruyter.

Derewianka, B. (1995). *Language Development in the Transition from Childhood to Adolescence: The Role of Grammatical Metaphor.* Ph. D thesis. Macquarie University.

Du Bois, J. W. (2007). The stance triangle. In R. Englebretson (ed.), *Stancetaking in Discourse: Subjectivity, Evaluation, Interaction* (pp. 139-182). Amsterdam: John Benjamins.

Edwards, D. (2006). Discourse, cognition and social practices: The rich surface of language and social interaction. *Discourse Studies*, 8.

Edwards, D. (2008). Intentionality and *mens rea* in police interrogations: The production of actions as crimes. *Intercultural Pragmatics*, 5.

Eggins, S. & Slade, D. (1997). *Analysing Casual Conversation.* London: Cassell.

Elyazale, N. (2014). Characteristics of newspaper editorials: "Chouftchouf" in

Almassae Moroccan newspaper as a case study. *New Media and Mass Communication*, 32.

Englebretson, R. (2007). Stancetaking in discourse: An introduction. In R. Englebretson (ed.), *Stancetaking in Discourse* (pp. 1-26). Amsterdam: John Benjamins.

Entman, R. M. (2004). *Projection of Power.* Chicago: The University of Chicago Press.

Fanego, T. (2010). Paths in the development of elaborative discourse markers. In H. Cuyckens, K. Davidse & L. Vandelanotte (eds.), *Subjectification, Intersubjectification and Grammaticalization* (pp. 197-237). Berlin: Mouton de Gruyter.

Farrokhi, F. & Nazmi, S. (2015). The rhetoric of newspaper editorials. *International Journal on Studies in English Language and Literature*, 3 (2).

Fasold, R. & Connor-Linton, J. (2006). *An Introduction to Language and Linguistics.* Cambridge: Cambridge University Press.

Finegan, E. (1995). Subjectivity and subjectivisation: An introduction. In Stein, D. & S. Wright, (eds.), *Subjectivity and Subjectivisation: Linguistic Perspectives* (pp. 1-15). Cambridge: Cambridge University Press.

Fishbein, M. & Ajzen, I. (1975). *Belief, Attitude, Intention and Behavior: An Introduction to Theory and Research.* Reading, MA: Addison-Wesley.

Fisher, R., Ury, W. & Patton, B. (1984). *Getting to Yes: Negotiating Agreement without Giving in.* New York: Penguin Books.

Fitzmaurice, S. (2004). Subjectivity, intersubjectivity and the historical construction of interlocutor stance: From stance markers to discourse markers. *Discourse Studies*, 6(4).

Fogg, B. J. (2003). *Persuasive Technology: Using Computers to Change What We Think and Do.* San Francisco: Morgan Kaufmann Publishers.

Fowler, R. (1977). *Linguistics and Novel.* London: Methuen.

Fowler, R. (1986). *Linguistic Criticism.* Oxford: Oxford University Press.

Gales, T. (2010). Identifying interpersonal stance in threatening discourse: An appraisal analysis. *Discourse Studies*, 13(1).

Gartner, M. (2005). Gripping about newspaper editorials doesn't change. *Nieman Reports for Journalism*, 59 (3).

Gauthier, G. (2007), La structure et les fondements de l'argumentation editorial. *Les Cahiers du Journalism*, 17.

Ghesquière, L. (2010). On the subjectification and intersubjectification paths followed by the adjectives of completeness. In K. Davidse, L. Vandelanotte & H. Cuyckens (eds.), *Subjectification, Intersubjectification and Grammaticalization* (277-315). Berlin: Muton de Gruyter.

Gildea, D. & Jurafsky, D. (2002). Automatic labeling of semantic roles. *Computational Linguistics*, 28(3).

Golder, C. & Coirier, P. (1994). Argumentative text writing: Developmental trends. *Discourse Processes*, (18)2.

Greenberg, J. (2000), Opinion discourse and Canadian newspapers: The case of the Chinese boat people. *Canadian Journal of Communication Corporation*, 25 (4).

Haddington, P. (2004). Stance taking in news interviews. *SKY Journal of Linguistics*, 17.

Halliday, M. A. K. (1969). Options and functions in the English clause. *Brno Studies in English*, 8.

Halliday, M. A. K. (1975). Talking one's way in: A sociolinguistic perspective on language and learning. In A. Davies (ed.), *Problems of Language and Learning* (pp. 8-26). London: Heinemannl.

Halliday, M. A. K. (1993). The act of meaning. In J. E. Alatis (ed.), *Georgetown University Round Table on Languages and Linguistics* 1992: *Language, Communication and Social Meaning* (pp. 7-21). Washington, D. C.: Georgetown University Press.

Halliday, M. A. K. (1994a). *An Introduction to Systemic Functional Grammar* (2nd edition). London: Arnold.

Halliday, M. A. K. (1994b). Systemic theory. In R. E. Asher (ed.), *The Encyclopedia of Language and Linguistics* (Vol. 8) (pp. 4505-4508). Oxford: Pergamon Press.

Halliday, M. A. K. (1997). Linguistics as metaphor. In A. M. Simon-Vandenbergen, K. Davidse & D. Noel (eds.), *Reconnecting Language: Morphology and Syntax in Functional Perspectives.* Amsterdam: John Benjamins.

Halliday, M. A. K. (1998). Things and relations: Regrammaticizing experience as technical knowledge. In James. R. M. & R. Veel (eds), *Reading Science: Critical and Functional Perspectives on Discourses of Science* (pp. 185-235). London: Routledge.

Halliday, M. A. K. (2002). Modes of meaning and modes of expression: Types of grammatical structure and their determination by different semantic functions. In J. Webster (ed.), *On Grammar* (pp. 196-218). London: Continuum.

Halliday, M. A. K. (2003) On Language and Linguistics. In J. J. Webster (ed.), *The Collected Works of M. A. K. Halliday*. London: Continuum.

Halliday, M. A. K. (2004). *An Introduction to Systemic Functional Grammar* (3rd edition). London: Arnold.

Halliday, M. A. K. & Martin, J. R. (1993). *Writing Science: Literacy and Discursive Power*. London: Falmer.

Halliday, M. A. K. & Matthiessen, C. M. I. M. (2004). *An Introduction to Functional Grammar*. London: Hodder Arnold.

Halliday, M. A. K. & Matthiessen, C. M. I. M. (2006). *Construing Experience: A Language-based Approach to Cognition*. London: Continuum.

Hasan, R., Matthiessen, C. M. I. M. & J. Webster. (2005) *Continuing Discourse on Language* (2 Volumes). London/Oakville: Equinox.

Haugh, M. (2008a). Intention and diverging interpretings of implicature in the "uncovered meat" sermon. *Intercultural Pragmatics*, 5.

Haugh, M. (2008b). The place of intention in the interactional achievement of implicature. In I. Kecskes & J. Mey (eds.), *Intention, Common Ground and the Egocentric Speaker-Hearer* (pp. 45-86). Berlin: Mouton de Gruyter.

Heine, B. (1995). Agent-oriented vs. epistemic modality: Some observations on German modals. In J. Bybee & S. Fleischman (eds.), *Modality in Grammar and Discourse* (pp. 17-53). Amsterdam: John Benjamins.

Heritage, J. & Sorjonen, M. L. (1994). Constituting and maintaining activities across sequences: and-prefacing as a feature of question design. *Language in Society*, 23.

Hinzen, W. & Lambalgen, M. (2008). Explaining intersubjectivity: A comment on Arie Verhagen, construcions of intersubjectivity. *Cognitive Linguistics*, 19 (1).

Hollmann, W. B. (2005). Passivisability of English periphrastic causatives. In S.

Th. Gries & A. Stefanowitsch (eds.), *Corpora in Cognitive Linguistics: Corpus-based Approaches to Syntax and Lexis* (pp. 193-223). Berlin: Mouton de Gruyter.

Holtgraves, T. (2004). Social desirability and self-reports: Testing models of socially desirable responding. *Personality and Social Psychology Bulletin*, 30.

Hopper, P. J. & Traugott, E. (2003). *Grammaticalization* (2nd Edition). Cambridge: Cambridge University Press.

Horn, L. R. (1972). *On the Semantic Properties of Logical Operators in English.* Ph. D dissertation, University of California.

Hunston, S. & Thompson, G. (2000). Evaluation: An introduction. In S. Hunston & G. Thompson (eds.), *Evaluation in Text: Authorial Stance and the Construction of Discourse* (pp. 1-27). New York: Oxford University Press.

Hursthouse, R. (1999). *On Virtue Ethics.* Oxford: Oxford University Press.

Hyland, K. & Tse, P. (2005). Evaluative that constructions signaling stance in research abstracts. *Functions of Language*, 1.

Hyland, K. (1998). *Hedging in Scientific Research Articles.* Amsterdam: John Benjamins.

Hyland, K. (2005). Stance and engagement: A model of interaction in academic discourse. *Discourse Studies*, 2.

Iedema, R., Feez, S. & White, P. (1994). *Media Literacy (Write It Right Literacy in Industry Project: Stage Two).* Sydney: Metropolitan East Region's Disadvantaged Schools Program.

Irvine, J. (1982). Language and affect: Some cross-culture issue. In H. Byrnes (ed.), *Geogetown University Round Table on Language and Linguistics.* Washington, D. C.: Geogetown University Press.

Jaffe, A. (2009). *Stance. Sociolinguistic Perspectives.* New York: Oxford University Press.

Jakobson, R. (1957). Shifters, verbal categories and the Russian verb. Russian Language Project. Department of Slavic Languages and Literature, Harvard University.

Kärkkäinen, E. (2003). *Epistemic Stance in English Conversation: A Description of Its Interactional Functions, with a Focus on I Think.* Amsterdam: John Benjamins.

Katajamäki, H. & Koskela, M. (2006). The rhetorical structure of editorials in English, Swedish and Finnish business newspapers. *Teoksessa Proceedings of the 5th International Aelfe Conference.* Prensas: Universitarias de Zaragoza.

Kauter, M., de Smet, B. & Veronique H. (2015). The good, the bad and the implicit: A comprehensive approach to annotating explicit and implicit sentiment. *Lang Resources & Evaluation*, 49.

Kiefer, F. (1994). Modality. In R. E. Asher (ed.), *The Encyclopedia of Language and Linguistics* (pp. 2515-2520). Oxford: Pergamon Press.

Kilpert, D. (2003). Getting the full picture: A reflection on the work of M. A. K. Halliday. *Language Sciences*, 25.

Kim, Jin-Dong, Ohta, T. & Jun'ichi Tsujii. (2008). Corpus annotation for mining biomedical events from literature. *BMC Bioinformatics*, 9(1).

Langacker, R. W. (1985). Observations and speculations on subjectivity. In J. Haiman (ed.), *Iconicity in Syntax* (pp. 109-150). Amsterdam: John Benjamins.

Langacker, R. W. (1987). *Foundations of Cognitive Grammar: Theoretical Prerequisites* (Vol. 1). Standford: Standford University Press.

Langacker, R. W. (1990). Subjectification. *Cognitive Linguistics*, 1(1).

Langacker, R. W. (1991). *Foundations of Cognitive Grammar, ii. Descriptive Application.* Stanford: Stanford University Press.

Langacker, R. W. (1993a). Reference-point construction. *Cognitive Linguistics*, 1.

Langacker, R. W. (1993b). Universals of construal. In J. S. Guenter, B. A. Kaiser & C. C. Zoll (eds.), *Proceedings of the Nineteenth Annual Meeting of the Berkeley Linguistics Society* (pp. 447-463). Berkeley: Berkeley Linguistics Society.

Langacker, R. W. (1999a). Losing Control: Grammaticalization, Subjectification and Transparency. In A. Blank & P. Koch (eds.), *Historical Semantics and Cognition* (pp. 147-175). Berlin: Mouton de Gruyter.

Langacker, R. W. (1999b). *Grammar and Conceptualization.* Berlin: Mouton de Gruyter.

Langacker, R. W. (2001). Discourse in cognitive grammar. *Cognitive Linguistics*, 12 (2).

Langacker, R. W. (2002). Deixis and subjectivity. In F. Brisard, (ed.), *Grounding: The Epistemic Footing of Deixis and Reference* (pp. 1-28). Berlin: Mouton de Gruyter.

Langacker, R. W. (2006). Subjectification, grammaticization, and conceptual archetypes. In A. Athanasiadou, C. Canakis, & B. Cornillie, (eds.), *Subjectification: Various Paths to Subjectivity* (pp. 17-40). Berlin: Mouton de Gruyter.

Langacker, R. W. (2008). *Cognitive Grammar. A Basic Introduction.* New York: Oxford University Press.

Le, E. (2010). *Editorials and the Power of Media: Interweaving of Socio-cultural Identities.* Amsterdam: John Benjamins.

Leech, G. (2007). New resources, or just better old ones? In M. Hundt, N. Nesselhauf & C. Biewer (eds.), *Corpus Linguistics and the Web* (pp. 134-149). Amsterdam: Rodopi.

Levinson, S. (1983). *Pragmatics.* Cambridge: Cambridge University Press.

Lindqvist, G. J. (2008). *Klassisk retorik för vår tid.* Lund: Studentlitteratur.

Liu, B. (2015). *Sentiment Analysis: Mining Opinions, Sentiments, and Emotions.* Cambridge: Cambridge University Press.

Lucius-Hoene, G. & Deppermann, A. (2002). *Rekonstruktion narrativer Identitat.* Opladen: Leske und Budrich.

Lyons, J. (1977). *Semantics* (Vol. 2). Cambridge: Cambridge University Press.

Lyons, J. (1982). Deixis and subjectivity: Loquor, ergo sum? In R. J. Jarvella & W. Klein, (eds.), *Speech, Place, and Action: Studies in Deixis and Related Topics* (pp. 101-124). New York: John Wiley.

Lyons, J. (1995). *Linguistic Semantics: An Introduction.* Cambridge: Cambridge University Press.

Margerie, H. (2010). On the rise of (inter) subjective meaning in the Grammaticalization. In K. Davidse, L. Vandelanotte & H. Cuyckens (eds.), *Subjectification, Intersubjectification and Grammaticalization* (pp. 315-348). Berlin: Muton de Gruyter. .

Markkanen, R. & Schroder, H. (eds.). (1990). *Hedging and Discourse. Approaches to the Analysis of a Pragmatic Phenomenon in Academic Aexts.* Berlin: Mouton de Gruyter.

Martin J. R. (2004). Sense and sensibility: texturing evaluation. In J. Foley (ed.), *Language, Education and Discourse.* London: Continuum.

Martin, J. R. & Rose, D. (2003). *Working with Discourse: Meaning beyond the Clause.* London and New York: Continuum.

Martin, J. R. & Rose, D. (2007). *Working with Discourse: Meaning beyond the Clause.* London and New York: Continuum.

Martin, J. R. & White, P. R. R. (2005). *The Language of Evaluation: Appraisal in English.* London and New York: Palgrave Macmillan.

Martin, J. R. & White, P. R. R. (2007). *The Language of Evaluation: Appraisal in English.* London and New York: Palgrave Macmillan.

Martin, J. R. & Wodak, R. (2003). Re/reading the past: Critical and functional perspectives on time and value. *Discourse Studies*, 27(2).

Martin, J. R. (1992). *English Text: System and Structure.* Amsterdam: John Benjamins.

Martin, J. R. (1995). Interpersonal meaning, persuasion and public discourse: Packing semiotic punch. *Australian Journal of Linguistics*, 15(1).

Martin, J. R. (2000). Beyond exchange: Appraisal systems in English. In Thompson, G. & Hunston, S. (eds.), *Evaluation in Text: Authorial Stance and the Construction of Discourse* (pp. 87-112). Oxford: Oxford University Press.

Martin, J. R. (2009). Genre and language learning: A social semiotic perspective. *Linguistics and Education*, 20(1).

Matthiessen, C. M. I. M. & Bateman, J. A. (1991). *Systemic Linguistics and Text Generation: Experience from Japanese and English.* London: Frances Pinter.

Matthiessen, C. M. I. M., Teruya, K. & Lam, M. (2010). *Key Terms in Systemic Functional Linguistics.* London: Continuum International Publishing Group Ltd.

Matthiessen, Christian M. I. M. (2007). *The lexico-grammar of emotion and attitude in English.* Published in electronic proceedings based on contributions to the Third International Congress on English Grammar (ICEG 3), Sona College, Salem, Tamil Nadu, India, January 23-27, 2006.

McEnery, T. & Hardie, A. (2012). *Corpus linguistics: Method, theory and practice.* Cambridge: Cambridge University Press.

McGuire, W. J. (1973). Persuasion. In G. A. Miller (ed.), *Communication, Language, and Meaning: Psychological Perspectives.* New York: Basic Books.

Miller, G. (1980). *Persuasion: New Directions in Theory and Research.* Beverly Hills, CA: Sage Publications.

Miller, G. R. (2002). On being persuaded: Some basic distinctions. In P. D. James & M. W. Pfau (eds.), *The Persuasion Handbook: Developments in Theory and Practice.* Beverly Hills, CA: Sage Publications.

Murphy, A. (2005). *A Corpus Based Contrastive Study of Evaluation in English and Italian.* Milano: ISU Università Cattolica.

Narrog, H. (2005). Modality, mood, and change of modal meanings—a new perspective. *Cognitive Linguistics*, 16.

Nivre, J. (2003). *An efficient algorithm for projective dependency parsing.* In *Proceedings of the* 8*th International Workshop on Parsing Technologies* (pp. 149-160).

Nuyts, J. (2001). Subjectivity as an evidential dimension in epistemic model expressions. *Journal of Pragmatics*, 33(3).

Nuyts, J. (2005). Modality: Overview and linguistic issues. In W. Frawley (ed.), *The Expression of Modality*(pp. 1-26). Berlin: Mouton de Gruyter.

Ochs, E. & Schieffelin, B. (1989). Language has a heart. *Text*, 9(1).

Oliver, R. (1974). Expectancy theory predictions of salesmen's performance. *Journal of Marketing Research*, 11.

Owings, D. H. & Morton, E. S. (1998). *Animal Vocal Communication: A New Approach.* Cambridge: Cambridge University Press.

Palacas, A. (1993). Attribution semantics: Linguistic worlds and point of view. *Discourse Processes*, 16.

Palmer, F. (1986). *Mood and Modality.* Cambridge: Cambridge University Press.

Palmer, F. (2001). *Mood and Modality.* Cambridge: Cambridge University Press.

Passante, C. K. (2007). *The Complete Idiot's Guide to Journalism.* New York: Alpha.

Pontiki, M., Galanis, D., Pavlopoulos, J., Papageorgiou, H., Androutsopoulos, I. & Manandhar, S. (2014). SemEval 2014 Task 4: Aspect based sentiment analysis. In *Proceedings of the International Workshop on Semantic Evaluation*,

SemEval'14, Dublin, Ireland.

Powell, M. J. (1992). The systematic development of correlated interpersonal and metalinguistic uses in stance adverbs. *Cognitive Linguistics*, 3.

Provis, C. (2010). Virtuous decision making for business ethics. *Journal of Business Ethics*, 91(1).

Pyysalo, S., Ohta, T., Rak, R., Sullivan, D., Mao, C., Wang, C., Sobral, B., Tsujii, J. & Ananiadou, S. (2012). Overview of the ID, EPI and REL tasks of BioNLP Shared Task 2011. *BMC Bioinformatics*, 13(suppl. 8).

Quirk, R., Greenbaum, S., Leech G. & Svartvik, J. (1985). *A Comprehensive Grammar of the English Language.* London: Longman.

Reardon, K. (1991). *Persuasion in Practice.* Beverly Hills, CA: Sage Publications.

Renkema, J. (2009). *The Texture of Discourse—Towards an Outline of Connectivity Theory.* Amsterdam: John Benjamins.

Richardson, J. E. (2007). *Analyzing Newspapers: An Approach from Critical Discourse Analysis.* New York: PAL Grave MacMillan.

Rohrdantz, C. et al. (2010). Comparative visual analysis of cross-linguistic features. In J. Kohlhammer & D. Keim (eds.), *Proceedings of International Symposium on Visual Analytic Science and Technology* (pp. 1-7). Bordeaux: Eurographics Association.

Rossetti, Y. & Pisella, L. (2002). Several "vision for action" systems: A geode to dissociating and integrating dorsal and ventral functions. In W. Prinz. & B. Hommel (eds.), *Attention & Performance XIX: Common Mechanisms in Perception and Action* (pp. 375-396). London: Oxford University Press.

Sadock, J. M. (1974). *Toward a Linguistic Theory of Speech Acts.* New York/London: Academic Press.

Salgado, D., Krallinger, M., Depaule, M. Drula, M. E. & Tendulkar, A. V. (2010). Myminer system description. In *Proceedings of the Third BioCreative Challenge Evaluation Workshop 2010* (pp. 157-158).

Sanders, J. & Redeker, G. (1996). Perspective and the representation of speech and thought in narrative discourse. In G. Fauconnier & E. Sweetser (eds.), *Spaces, Worlds, and Grammar* (pp. 290-317). Chicago: Chicago University Press.

Scheibman, J. (2001). Local patterns of subjectivity in person and verb type in American English conversation. In J. Bybee & P. Hopper (eds.), *Frequency and the Emergence of Linguistic Structure* (pp. 61-89). Amsterdam: John Benjamins.

Schwenter, A. & Traugott, E. C. (2000). Invoking scalarity: The development of in fact. *Journal of Historical Pragmatics*, 1.

Schwenter, A. & Waltereit, R. (2010). Presupposition accommodation and language change. In H. Cuyckens, K. Davidse & L. Vandelanotte (eds.), *Subjectification, Intersubjectification and Grammaticalization* (pp. 75-102). Berlin: Mouton de Gruyter.

Searle, J. (1983). *Intentionality.* Cambridge: Cambridge University Press.

Searle, J. (1992). *The Rediscovery of Mind.* Cambridge, MA: MIT Press.

Searle, John R. (1969). *Speech Acts: An Essay in the Philosophy of Language.* Cambridge: Cambridge University Press.

Searle, John R. (1976). A classification of illocutionary acts. *Language in Society*, 5.

Searle, John R. (1999). *Mind, Language and Society: Philosophy in the Real World.* New York: Basic Books.

Shaffer, B. (2004). Information ordering and speaker subjectivity: Modality in ASL. *Cognitive Linguistics*, 15(2).

Simons, H. W., Morreale, J. & Gronbeck, B. (2001). *Persuasion in Society.* Thousand Oaks, CA: Sage Publications.

Simpson. (1993). *Language, Ideology and Point of View.* London: Routledge.

Sinha, Chris (1999). Situated selves. In J. Bliss, R. Säljö & P. Light (eds.), *Learning Sites: Social and Technological Resources for Learning.* Oxford: Pergamon.

Smet, D. H. & Verstraete, J. C. (2006). Coming to terms with subjectivity. *Cognitive Linguistics*, 17.

Smith, S. (2003). *Mode of Discourse: The Local Structure of Texts.* Cambridge: Cambridge University Press.

Steele, S. (1975). Is it possible? *Stanford Working Papers in Language Universals*, 18.

Stein, D. & Wright, S. (1995). *Subjectivity and Subjectivisation: Linguistic*

Perspectives. Cambridge: Cambridge University Press.

Stenetorp, P. Pyysalo, S. & Topić, G. (2012). BRAT: A web-based tool for NLP-assisted text annotation. In *Proceedings of the Demonstrations at the 13th Conference of the European Chapter of the Association for Computational Linguistics* (pp. 102-107). Association for Computational Linguistics.

Stenetorp, P. Topic, G., Pyysalo, S., Ohta, T., Kim, Jin-Dong & Tsujii, J. (2011). BioNLP shared task 2011: Supporting resources. In *Proceedings of BioNLP Shared Task 2011 Workshop* (pp. 112-120). Association for Computational Linguistics.

Stubbs, M. (1996). Towards a modal grammar of English: A matter of prolonged fieldwork. In M. Stubbs (ed.), *Text and Corpus Analysis* (pp. 196-229). Oxford: Blackwell.

Sulkunen, P. & Törrönen, J. (1997). The production of values: The concept of modality in textual discourse analysis. *Semiotica*, 113(1/2).

Swales, J. M. (1990). *Genre Analysis: English in Academic and Research Settings.* Cambridge: Cambridge University Press.

Sweetser, E. E. (1990). *From Etymology to Pragmatics: Metaphorical and Cultural Aspects of Semantic Structure.* Cambridge: Cambridge University Press.

Temperley, D. (2003). Ambiguity avoidance in English relative clauses. *Language*, 79 (3).

Thelwall, M., Buckley, K. & Paltoglou, G. (2011). Sentiment in Twitter events. *Journal of the American Society for Information Science and Technology*, 62 (2).

Thelwall, M., Buckley, K., Paltoglou, G., Cai, D. & Kappas, A. (2010). Sentiment strength detection in short informal text. *Journal of the American Society for Information Science and Technology*, 61(12).

Thompson, G. & Hunston, S. (2001). *Evaluation in Text Authorial Stance and the Construction of Discourse.* Oxford: Oxford University Press.

Thompson, G. (1996). *Introducing Functional Grammar.* London: Arnold.

Thompson, S. A. & Hopper, P. J. (2001). Transitivity, clause structure, and argument structure: Evidence from conversation. In Bybee & Hopper (eds.), *Frequency and the Emergence of Linguistic Structure* (pp. 27-60). Amsterdam: John Benjamins.

Tomasello, M. (1999). *The Cultural Origins of Human Cognition.* Cambridge,

MA: Harvard University Press.

Toulmin, S. E. (2003). *The Uses of Argument.* London: Cambridge University Press.

Traugott, E. C. & Dasher, R. B. (2002). *Regularity in Semantic Change.* Cambridge: Cambridge University Press.

Traugott, E. C. & König, E. (1991). The semantics-pragmatics of grammaticalization revisited. In Traugott, E. C. & B. Heine (eds.), Approaches to *Grammaticalization* (Vol. I) (pp. 189-218). Amsterdam: John Benjamins.

Traugott, E. C. (1985). On conditionals. In John Haiman (ed.), *Iconicity in Syntax* (pp. 289-307). Amsterdam: John Benjamins.

Traugott, E. C. (1989). On the rise of epistemic meaning in English: An example of subjectification in semantic change. *Language*, 65(1).

Traugott, E. C. (1995a). Subjectification in grammaticalisation. In D. Stein & S. Wright (eds.), *Subjectivity and Subjecivisation: Linguistic Perspective* (pp. 31-54). Cambridge: Cambridge University Press.

Traugott, E. C. (1995b). The role of discourse markers in a theory of grammaticalization. Paper presented at the 12th International Conference on Historical Linguistics, Manchester, August 1995.

Traugott, E. C. (1998). Pragmatic Strengthening and Grammaticalization. In *Proceedings of the Annual Meeting of the Berkeley Linguistic Society* (pp. 406-416). Berkeley Linguistics Society.

Traugott, E. C. (1999). The rhetoric of counter-expectation in semantic change: A study in subjectification. In A. Blank & P. Koch (eds.), *Historical Semantics and Cognition* (pp. 61-89). Berlin: Mouton de Gruyter.

Traugott, E. C. (2003). From subjectification to intersubjectification. In R. Hickey (ed.), *Motives for Language Change* (pp. 124-139). Cambridge: Cambridge University Press.

Traugott, E. C. (2006). Where subjectification, intersubjectification, and grammaticalisation meet. Speech on September 1, 2006 in Language Institute of the Chinese Academy of Social Science.

Traugott, E. C. (2010). *Regularity in Semantic Change.* Cambridge: Cambridge University Press.

Ungerer, F. (2000). *English Media Texts Past and Present: Language and Textual Structure.* Amsterdam: John Benjamins.

Valery, Paul. (1973). *Cahiers, T. I. -XXIX.* 1957-1961. Paris: C. N. R. S.

van Dijk, T. A. (1988a). *News and Discourse.* Hillsdale, NJ: Erlbaum.

van Dijk, T. A. (1988b). *News Analysis: Case Studies of International and National News in the Press.* Hillsdale, NJ: Erlbaum.

van Dijk, T. A. (1993). *Elite discourse and racism.* Thousand Oaks, CA: Sage Publications.

van Dijk, T. A. (1995a). Discourse, opinions and ideologies. *Current Issues in Language and Society*, 2(2).

van Dijk, T. A. (1995b). Power and the news media. In D. Paletz (ed.), *Political Communication and Action* (pp. 9-36). Cresskill, NJ: Hampton Press.

van Dijk, T. A. (1995c). *Ideological Discourse Analysis.* New Courant, Helsinki: University of Helsinki Press.

van Dijk, T. A. (1995d). Discourse analysis as ideology analysis. In C. Schäffner & A. Wenden (eds.), *Language and Peace* (pp. 17-33). Aldershot: Dartmouth.

van Dijk, T. A. (1996). Opinion and ideologies in editorials. Paper for the Fourth Annual International Symposium of Critical Discourse Analysis, December 14-16, Athens.

Vandelanotte, Lieven. (2004). From representational to scopal "distancing indirect speech or thought": A cline of subjectification. *Text*, 24.

Verhagen, A. (1995). Subjectification, syntax, and communication. In D. Stein & S. Wright (eds.), *Subjectivity and Subjectivisation: Linguistic Perspectives* (pp. 103-128). Cambridge: Cambridge University Press.

Verhagen, A. (2005). *Constructions of Intersubjectivity: Discourse, Syntax, and Cognition.* Oxford: Oxford University Press.

Verhagen, A. (2008). Intersubjectivity and explanation in linguistics: A reply to Hinzen and van Lambalgen. *Cognitive Linguistics*, 19(1).

Verstraete, J. S. (2006). Coming to terms with subjectivity. *Cognitive Linguistics*, 17 (3).

Virtanen, T. (2005). Polls and surveys show: Public opinion as a persuasive device in editorial discourse. In H. Halmari & T. Virtanen (eds.), *Persuasion across Genres: A Linguistic Approach* (pp. 153-180). Amsterdam: John Benjamins.

Voloshinov, V. N. (1995). Marxism and the philosophy of language. In S. Dentith, L. Matejka & I. R. Titunik (eds.), *Bakhtinian Thought: An Introductory Reader*. London: Routledge.

Walton, D. (2001). Persuasive definitions and public policy arguments. *Argumentation and Advocacy*, 37(3).

Wang Junhui. (2015). Studies of subjectivity in language. *Studies in Literature and Language*, 10(3).

Wekesa, N. B. (2012). Assessing argumentative normativity in the English medium Kenyan newspaper editorials from a linguistic-pragmatic approach. *International Journal of Humanities and Social Science*, 2(21).

Widdowson, H. G. (1975). *Stylistics and the Teaching of Literature*. London: Longman.

Wiebe, J. (1994). Tracking point of view in narrative. *Computational Linguistics*, 20(2).

Wiebe, J., T. Wilson, R. Bruce, M. Bell & M. Martin. (2004). Learning subjective language. *Computational Linguistics*, 30(3).

Wiebe, J., Wilson, T. & Cardie, C. (2005). Annotating expressions of opinions and emotions. *Language Resources and Evaluation*, 39(2-3).

Wu, R. R. (2004). *Stance in Talk: A Conversation Analysis of Mandarin Final Particles*. Amsterdam: John Benjamins.

Yaguello, M. (ed.). (1994). *Subjecthood and Subjectivity: The Status of the Subject in Linguistic Theory*. Paris: Ophrys.

Zimbardo, P. & Leippe, M. (1991). *The Psychology of Attitude Change and Social Influence*. New York: McGraw-Hill.

陈鸿瑶:《副词“也”主观性的认知解释》,载《东北师大学报》(哲学社会科学版)2012 年第 2 期。

陈前瑞:《汉语体貌系统研究》,华中师范大学博士学位论文,2003 年。

陈小荷:《主观量问题初探—兼谈副词“就”“才”“都”》,载《世界汉语教学》1994 年第 4 期。

陈征:《基于主观性和交互主观性连续统的语篇言据性分析——以辩论性语篇

为例》,上海外国语大学博士学位论文,2014 年。

邓英树、黄谷:《论“不 A 不 B”的否定意义及其制约因素》,载《汉语学习》2002 年第 4 期。

段开成:《舍尔的意向性理论》,载《西安外国语学院学报》2004 年第 3 期。

房红梅、马玉蕾:《言据性 · 主观性 · 主观化》,载《外语学刊》2008 年第 4 期。

冯光武:《语言的主观性及其相关研究》,载《山东外语教学》2006 年第 5 期。

高莉、文旭:《“看”“想”“说”主观性标记功能差异的成因》,载《外语学刊》2014 年第 4 期。

郭圣林:《“NP + 我”与“我 + NP”的语用考察》,载《南京师大学报》2007 年第 4 期。

胡建刚:《主观量度和“才”“都”“了”的句法匹配模式分析》,载《世界汉语教学》2007 年第 1 期。

胡壮麟:《语篇的评价研究》,载《外语教学》2009 年第 1 期。

李德超、王克非:《新型双语旅游语料库的研制和应用》,载《现代外语》2010 年第 1 期。

李凌燕:《新闻叙事的主观性研究》,复旦大学博士学位论文,2010 年。

李青:《现代汉语把字句主观性研究》, 吉林大学博士学位论文,2011 年。

李善熙:《汉语主观量的表达研究》,中国社会科学院研究生院博士学位论文,2003 年。

李战子:《评价理论:在话语分析中的应用和问题》,载《外语研究》2004 年第 5 期。

林忠:《口语句式的主观性表达——以“天气那叫一个冷”为例》,载《外语学刊》2015 年第 3 期。

刘瑾:《汉语主观视角的表达研究》,首都师范大学博士学位论文,2009 年。

刘瑾:《语言主观性的概念探析》,载《西安外国语大学学报》2009 年第 3 期。

刘瑾:《语言主观性的哲学考察》,载《外语学刊》2009 年第 3 期。

刘兴兵:《Langacker 的语言主观性理论仍需解决的问题》,载《外语教学》2015 年第 6 期。

苗兴伟:《否定结构的语篇功能》,载《外语教学与研究》2011 年第 2 期。

苗兴伟:《语言的人文精神观照》,载《外语学刊》2009 年第 5 期。

祁文娟:《现代汉语普通话被动句的主观性分析》,载《山西大学学报(哲学社会科学版)》2013 年第 1 期。

沈家煊:《汉语的主观性和汉语语法教学》,载《汉语学习》2009 年第 1 期。

沈家煊:《如何处置"处置式"? ——论把字句的主观性》,载《中国语文》2002 年第 5 期。
沈家煊:《形容词句法功能的标记模式》,载《中国语文》1997 年第 4 期。
沈家煊:《语言的"主观性"和"主观化"》,载《外语教学与研究》2001 年第 4 期。
石毓智、白解红:《将来时标记向认识情态功能的衍生》,载《解放军外国语学院学报》2007 年第 2 期。
王海峰:《"A 什么 B"结构式初探》,载《四川大学学报》2003 年第 3 期。
王振华:《"硬新闻" 的态度研究》,载《外语教学》2004 年第 5 期。
王振华:《评价系统及其运作》,载《外国语》2001 年第 6 期。
魏在江:《隐喻的主观性与主观化》,载《解放军外国语学院学报》2007 年第 2 期。
文旭、伍倩:《话语主观性在时体范畴中的体现》,载《外语学刊》2007 年第 2 期。
吴福祥:《近年来语法化研究的进展》,载《外语教学与研究》2004 年第 1 期。
吴一安:《空间指示语与语言的主观性》,载《外语教学与研究》2003 年第 6 期。
席留生:《"把"字句的认知研究》, 河南大学博士学位论文,2008 年。
肖燕:《空间描述的主观性与参照框架的选择》,载《外语教学》2012 年第 1 期。
徐晶凝:《情态表达与时体表达的互相渗透—兼谈语气助词的范围确定》,载《汉语学习》2008 年第 1 期。
徐晶凝:《现代汉语话语情态研究》,昆仑出版社 2008 年版。
徐晶凝:《语气助词"吧"的情态解释》,载《北京大学学报(社会科学版)》2003 年第 4 期。
徐晶凝:《语气助词"吧"的情态解释》,载《语言教学与研究》2007 年第 3 期。
徐盛桓、廖巧云:《意向性解释视域下的隐喻》,载《外语教学》2013 年第 1 期。
叶建军:《"被 NP_施 VPNP_受"的生成机制与动因》,载《中国语文》2014 年第 3 期。
张宝胜:《副词"还"的主观性》,载《语言科学》2003 年第 5 期。
张伯江:《施事和受事的语义语用特征及其在句式中的实现》,复旦大学博士学位论文,2007 年。
张德禄:《系统功能语言学》,载《中国外语》2011 年第 3 期。
张旺熹、姚京晶:《汉语人称代词类话语标记系统的主观性差异》,载《汉语学习》2009 年第 3 期。
张现荣、苗兴伟:《主观化与主位信息组织》,载《外国语》2017 年第 5 期。
张现荣:《外来构词词缀主观性的认知识解》,载《语言文字应用》2016 年第

2 期。
张振亚、王彬:《应答语“那是”的语用环境及效果》,载《当代修辞学》2009 年第 3 期。
赵秀凤:《语言的主观性研究概览》,载《外语教学》2010 年第 1 期。
周红:《客体致使句的认知语义分析》,载《语言研究》2006 年第 3 期。
朱永生:《概念意义中的隐性评价》,载《外语教学》2009 年第 4 期。

Appendices

Appendix Ⅰ Information about Data①

List Number	Title	Publishing Date
Text 1	Demands of Leadership	September 13, 2001
Text 2	Allies against Terror	September 13, 2001
Text 3	The Necessary Courage	September 13, 2001
Text 4	Rendezvous with Afghanistan	September 14, 2001
Text 5	War without Illusions	September 15, 2001
Text 6	The Faces Emerge	September 16, 2001
Text 7	President Bush's First Win	September 17, 2001
Text 8	Intelligence and Terrorism	September 17, 2001
Text 9	Wall Street Returns	September 18, 2001
Text 10	Mr. Bush's Most Important Speech	September 21, 2001
Text 11	Calibrating the Use of Force	September 22, 2001
Text 12	The Home Front: Security and Liberty	September 23, 2001
Text 13	Rebuilding Downtown	September 24, 2001

① All the data come from *The New York Times*, which are published in its official website *http://www.nytimes.com/*.

List Number	Title	Publishing Date
Text 14	Nation-Building in Afghanistan	September 27, 2001
Text 15	The Mayor's Dangerous Idea	September 28, 2001
Text 16	An Outpouring of Dollars	October 1, 2001
Text 17	The Next Mayor's Job	October 4, 2001
Text 18	Terrorism and Immigration	October 5, 2001
Text 19	The Case against bin Laden	October 6, 2001
Text 20	Fears of Anthrax and Smallpox	October 7, 2002
Text 21	The American Offensive Begins	October 8, 2001
Text 22	Mr. Bush's New Gravitas	October 12, 2001
Text 23	Reconsidering Saudi Arabia	October 14, 2001
Text 24	Collaborative Charity	October 15, 2001
Text 25	Coping with Bioterrorism: Beyond Safety	October 18, 2001
Text 26	Detention and Accountability	October 19, 2001
Text 27	The Ground War Begins	October 20, 2001
Text 28	When Terrorists Log on	October 21, 2001
Text 29	A Pragmatic Aid Plan	October 26, 2001
Text 30	The War Has Just Begun	October 27, 2001
Text 31	Charity and Red Tape	October 30, 2001
Text 32	Life in a Time of Terror	October 31, 2001
Text 33	The Spy Puzzle	November 4, 2001
Text 34	Mayor-Elect Michael Bloomberg	November 7, 2001
Text 35	A Homeland Pep Talk	November 9, 2001
Text 36	Disappearing in America	November 10, 2001
Text 37	The Pilgrimage to Lower Manhattan	November 14, 2001
Text 38	A Travesty of Justice	November 16, 2001
Text 39	The Deepest Thanks	November 22, 2001
Text 40	The Revival of Lower Manhattan	November 24, 2001
Text 41	The Wrong Time to Fight Iraq	November 26, 2001
Text 42	The Victims' New Referee	December 1, 2001

List Number	Title	Publishing Date
Text 43	John Ashcroft Misses the Point	December 7, 2001
Text 44	The Taliban Exits	December 8, 2001
Text 45	Terrorism and Justice	December 13, 2001
Text 46	Vital Help for New York	December 15, 2001
Text 47	The Hunt for Osama bin Laden	December 18, 2001
Text 48	A Turbulent First Year	December 28, 2001
Text 49	How to Try a Terrorist	December 29, 2001
Text 50	Mayor Giuliani Bows out	December 30, 2001
Text 51	The Challenge in Afghanistan	January 5, 2002
Text 52	Terrorism's Other Battlefields	January 9, 2002
Text 53	Back on the Homeland Front	January 18, 2002
Text 54	Putting a Value on Lives	January 24, 2002
Text 55	The Limits of Power	January 31, 2002
Text 56	Starting at Ground Zero	February 2, 2002
Text 57	The Pentagon Spending Spree	February 6, 2002
Text 58	Revisiting Homeland Security	February 7, 2002
Text 59	Ending the Oil Addiction	February 18, 2002
Text 60	Unfinished War in Afghanistan	March 5, 2002
Text 61	Six Months Later	March 11, 2002
Text 62	Rebuilding Downtown	April 3, 2002
Text 63	A Master Terrorist Is Nabbed	April 6, 2002
Text 64	Afghanistan's Marshall Plan	April 19, 2002
Text 65	How the Towers Collapsed	May 7, 2002
Text 66	The Blame Game	May 17, 2002
Text 67	Distractions and Diversions	May 21, 2002
Text 68	Heading Off Nuclear Terrorism	May 25, 2002
Text 69	Reimagining the FBI	May 30, 2002
Text 70	Turning to Renewal	May 31, 2002
Text 71	Warily Circling the Sept. 11 Fund	June 5, 2002

List Number	Title	Publishing Date
Text 72	Back to the Drawing Board	June 7, 2002
Text 73	Dirty Bombs and Civil Rights	June 12, 2002
Text 74	Waiting for Ground Zero Proposals	July 1, 2002
Text 75	America Aloof	July 12, 2002
Text 76	The Downtown We Don't Want	July 17, 2002
Text 77	Coherent Homeland Security	July 19, 2002
Text 78	No Way to Fight a War	July 25, 2002
Text 79	Filling in the Blanks on Iraq	July 30, 2002
Text 80	Ending Secret Detentions	August 6, 2002
Text 81	Unlimited Presidential Powers	August 8, 2002
Text 82	Sharing the Evidence on Iraq	August 21, 2002
Text 83	Examining How the Towers Collapsed	August 23, 2002
Text 84	Summons to War	August 28, 2002
Text 85	Congress Returns to New York	September 6, 2002
Text 86	The War on Civil Liberties	September 10, 2002
Text 87	America Enduring	September 11, 2002

Appendix Ⅱ Data Sample

Disappearing in America

Publishing date: November 10, 2001

Thousands of detainees being held in secret by the government; wiretaps on prisoners' conversations with their lawyers; public debate about the advisability of using torture to make suspects talk. Two months into the war against terrorism, the nation is sliding toward the trap that we entered this conflict vowing to avoid. Civil liberties are eroding, and there is no evidence that the reason is anything more profound than fear and frustration.

We trust the Bush administration is not seriously considering torture—an idea that seems more interesting to radio talk shows and columnists than to government officials. But Attorney General John Ashcroft has been careless with the Constitution when it comes to the treatment of people arrested in the wake of Sept. 11, raising fears he will be similarly careless when it comes to using the broad new investigative powers recently granted him by Congress. A new rule just imposed by Mr. Ashcroft allows the government to listen in on conversations and intercept mail between prison inmates and their lawyers—in effect suspending the Sixth Amendment right to effective counsel. He has also refused to provide basic information about the 11,000-plus people who have been arrested and detained in the course of the government's terrorism investigation.

Even the White House seems uninformed. Questioned about the mass detentions early last week, the president's spokesman, Ari Fleischer, responded that "the lion's share" had been released after questioning. He was forced to backtrack and concede that he did not know any exact numbers when the Justice Department gingerly noted that a majority of all detainees remained in custody.

To justify these extreme measures, the administration has been floating theories about what detainees might have done or known, which turn out upon further investigation to be unfounded. The Justice Department has backed away from Mr. Ashcroft's recent suggestion that three Arab men in custody in Michigan had advance knowledge of the Sept. 11 hijackings. Although the men were suspected of having links to Al Qaeda at the time of their arrest, law enforcement officials have said that no hard evidence to that effect has since emerged.

The limited need for secrecy while investigating domestic terrorism hardly justifies blanket stonewalling. Mr. Ashcroft says that his strategy of "aggressive detention of lawbreakers and material witnesses" has been vital in preventing new horrors. That assertion has to be taken on blind faith, and it would be easier to accept if the attorney general had shown more overall restraint. But his definition of the Bill of Rights includes eavesdropping on lawyer-client conversations and withholding from the public such key facts as the identities of those still in custody, the reason for their continued detention—including any charges filed—and the facilities where they are being held. The secrecy even extends to refusing to explain the resort to secrecy. Meanwhile, reports suggest that some detainees cleared of any connection with terrorism have been held under harsh conditions for prolonged periods, and denied a chance to notify relatives of their whereabouts.

It is time the White House stepped in. Just as President Bush advises Americans to learn to lead their normal lives while being ever watchful for terrorism, the Justice Department can investigate domestic attacks while respecting the basic rights that we are in this war to preserve.

Appendix Ⅲ Annotating File

[entities]

InformationSource

- Writer3
- Org
- Pron
- PojorativeName
- NonKnownPerson
- Collective

SourceExpression

- attribute
    - acknowledge
    - distance
- porclaim
    - pronounce
    - endorse
- entertain

Attitude

- Judgement
    - normality
    - capaticy
    - tenacity
    - veracity
    - propriety

ModalModulation

- ModPos
- ModUsu
- ModObl

ModInc

Doplus

Modassessment

propositional

wisdom

morality

naturality

obviousness

sureness

prediction

hearsay

argument

guess

luck

reaction

composition

valuation

security

satisfaction

hope

speech-functional

assurance

concession

factuality

validity

honesty

secrey

individuality

accuracy

hesitancy

[relations]

Source Arg1: Person | Org | Pron | Writer1 | Writer2 | Writer3 | PojorativeName | NonKnownPerson | Collective, Arg2: acknowledge | distance | pronounce | endorse | entertain

[attributes]

ValueScale Arg: < ENTITY >, Value: High | Medium | Low | Total
Orientation Arg: < ENTITY >, Value: Subjexpl | Subjimpl | Objexpl | Objimpl
ValueOrientation Arg: < ENTITY >, Value: Positive | Negative
SourceMotivation Arg: < ENTITY >, Value: nonsource | contextsource

Acknowledgments

The journey of completing this book is definitely arduous to me, but in retrospection, it has indeed strengthened my patience, persistence and tenacity. When struggling in those years to cope with life and research, I found myself lucky enough to get into interactions with those great people without whose support, guidance and mentorship this book would not have been accomplished. I would like to extend my sincere gratitude to those people who have provided me with invaluable support and assistance.

My deepest gratitude goes first and foremost to Professor Miao Xingwei, my supervisor, for his illuminating suggestions, constant encouragement and professional guidance in my academic studies. In the formulation of the idea and writing process of this book, he offered me his insightful advice, expert comments and valuable research experience. Moreover, his rigorous scholarship, profound knowledge and spirit of diligence have greatly inspired me and set up an example for my future work. Meanwhile, I want to show my sincere respects to Professor Zhang Keding from He'nan University, and Professor Qin Hongwu from Qufu Normal University, for both of them have always inspired me with helpful suggestions.

I would like to express my heartfelt gratitude to professors in School of Foreign Languages and Literature, Shandong University (Jinan). My sincere thanks go to Professor Wang Junju, Professor Zhang Delu, Professor Liu Zhenqian, Professor Wang Xiangyun, Professor Ma Wen, Professor Wang Ying, Professor Shen Fuying, Professor Liu Shizhu, Professor Lu Min. Their devoted teaching, enlightening lectures and serious attitudes toward academic work have deeply impressed me and

I've benefited a lot from their constructive guidance, valuable suggestions, and insightful criticisms.

I am also greatly indebted to my dear doctoral fellows for their timely assistance, genuine caring and sincere encouragements on me. Whenever I was in anxiety or frustration about the study, they were always there ready to offer immediate help, encouragement and academic support. The strong bond of friendship and trust developed and consolidated during the study is what I value most.

I also owe my sincere gratitude to my close friends who offer their help and time to me always in time. When I was deeply immersed in the study and spared no time for trivial matters in life, they kindly offered their help and encouragement without which the study would not have become a reality.

I owe countless thanks to my family. Although they have been neglected during the study, they have always been there providing caring and encouragement. Without their love, support, understanding and tolerance, I could not have completed this study.

Last but not least, my heartfelt gratitude goes to my mother, whose persistence, tenacity, and patience have been greatly inspiring me and encouraging me to forge ahead. Her love and tenderness gave me power when I felt unable to hold on. It is to my dear mother that I dedicate this book.